STUDIES IN ASIAN AMERICANS
RECONCEPTUALIZING CULTURE, HISTORY, AND POLITICS

I0591684

Edited by
Franklin Ng
California State University, Fresno

A ROUTLEDGE SERIES

STUDIES IN ASIAN AMERICANS: RECONCEPTUALIZING CULTURE, HISTORY, AND POLITICS

FRANKLIN NG, *General Editor*

DYNAMICS OF ETHNIC IDENTITY
Three Asian American Communities in Philadelphia
Jae-Hyup Lee

IMAGINING THE FILIPINO AMERICAN DIASPORA
Transnational Relations, Identities, and Communities
Jonathan Y. Okamura

MOTHERING, EDUCATION, AND ETHNICITY
The Transformation of Japanese American Culture
Susan Matoba Adler

THE HMONG REFUGEE EXPERIENCE IN THE UNITED STATES
Crossing the River
Ines M. Miyares

BEYOND KE'EAUMOKU
Koreans, Nationalism, and Local Cultures in Hawai'i
Brenda L. Kwon

ASIAN AMERICAN CULTURE ON STAGE
The History of the East West Players
Yuko Kurahashi

DOING THE DESI THING
Performing Indianness in New York City
Sunita S. Mukhi

ASIAN AMERICANS AND THE MASS MEDIA
A Content Analysis of Twenty United States Newspapers and A Survey of Asian American Journalists
Virginia Mansfield-Richardson

HOMETOWN CHINATOWN
The History of Oakland's Chinese Community
L. Eve Armentrout Ma

CHINESE AMERICAN MASCULINITIES
From Fu Manchu to Bruce Lee
Jachinson Chan

PRESS IMAGES, NATIONAL IDENTITY, AND FOREIGN POLICY
A Case Study of U.S.–Japan Relations from 1955–1995
Catherine A. Luther

STRANGERS IN THE CITY
The Atlanta Chinese, Their Community, and Stories of Their Lives
Jianli Zhao

BETWEEN THE HOMELAND AND THE DIASPORA
The Politics of Theorizing Filipino and Filipino American Identities
S. Lily Mendoza

HMONG AMERICAN CONCEPTS OF HEALTH, HEALING, AND CONVENTIONAL MEDICINE
Dia Cha

CONSUMPTION AND IDENTITY IN ASIAN AMERICAN COMING-OF-AGE NOVELS
Jennifer Ann Ho

CULTURAL IDENTITY IN KINDERGARTEN
A Study of Asian Indian Children in New Jersey
Susan Laird Mody

TAIWANESE AMERICAN TRANSNATIONAL FAMILIES
Women and Kin Work
Maria W. L. Chee

MODELING MINORITY WOMEN
Heroines in African and Asian American Fiction
Reshmi J. Hebbar

MODELING MINORITY WOMEN
HEROINES IN AFRICAN AND ASIAN AMERICAN FICTION

Reshmi J. Hebbar

Routledge
New York & London

Published in 2005 by
Routledge
Taylor & Francis Group
270 Madison Avenue
New York, NY 10016

Published in Great Britain by
Routledge
Taylor & Francis Group
2 Park Square
Milton Park, Abingdon
Oxon OX14 4RN

Transferred to Digital Printing 2010

International Standard Book Number-10: 0-415-97232-9 (Hardcover)
International Standard Book Number-13: 978-0-415-97232-1(Hardcover)
Library of Congress Card Number 2004025325

Library of Congress Cataloging-In-Publication Data

Hebbar, Reshmi J.
    Modeling minority women : heroines in African and Asian American fiction / Reshmi J. Hebbar.
        p. cm. -- (Studies in Asian Americans)
    Includes bibliographical references and index.
    ISBN 0-415-97232-9
    1. American fiction--Asian American authors--History and criticism. 2. American fiction--African American authors--History and criticism. 3. American fiction--Women authors--History and criticism. 4. Minority women--United States--Intellectual life. 5. African American women--Intellectual life. 6. Asian American women--Intellectual life. 7. Women and literature--United States. 8. African American women in literature. 9. Asian American women in literature. 10. Minority women in literature. 11. Heroines in literature. 12. Women in literature. I. Title. II. Series: Asian Americans.

PS153.A84H43 2005
813.009'9287'08693--dc22   2004025325

ISBN10: 0-415-97232-9 (hbk)
ISBN10: 0-415-88243-5 (pbk)

ISBN13: 978-0-415-97232-1 (hbk)
ISBN13: 978-0-415-88243-9 (pbk)

Taylor & Francis Group
is the Academic Division of T&F Informa plc.

Visit the Taylor & Francis Web site at
http://www.taylorandfrancis.com

and the Routledge Web site at
http://www.routledge-ny.com

For my husband, Shvetal Shah

Contents

Acknowledgments   ix

Introduction   xi

Chapter One   1
Someday My Prince Will Come: Ambivalent Romance
and Ethnicity in the Fiction of the Eaton Sisters

Chapter Two   31
The Fairest of Them All: Ethnicity, Heroines, and
the Objectifying Lens

Chapter Three   57
Cinderella's Understudies: Marginality, Ethnicity,
and the Negotiated Spaces of Heroine Desire

Chapter Four   93
Little Princesses: A New Generation of Ethnic,
Adolescent Heroines

Epilogue   125

Notes   133

Bibliography   143

Index   149

Acknowledgments

I am primarily indebted to my family, particularly my parents, Mohan and Poornima Hebbar, for always, without question, encouraging my passion for literature. Also, to my grandfather, N.V. Ballal, who is a renowned Kannada novelist in India, go my respect and thanks for falling in love with fiction generations ago.

For their expertise, encouragement, and professionalism, and for their willingness to take on such an unconventional project, I thank Professors Catherine Nickerson, Michael Elliott, and Martine Brownley at Emory University, who guided me through this project when I was conceiving it as a dissertation. My graduate coursework at Emory provided me with much of the inspiration for this study, and I thank Professor Deepika Bahri for first introducing me to postcolonial theory and urging me to look for ways to bridge this discourse to ethnic American literature.

I would also like to thank Rebecca Mitchell and Jennifer Watts for editing portions of this book.

Introduction

FEMINISM, ETHNIC STUDIES, AND *PRIDE AND PREJUDICE*

At the core of my inquiry into African American and Asian American heroine construction are specific questions that go beyond any of the individual texts I discuss in this project: What are some structural differences between a "woman's text" and an "ethnic woman's text?" Which elements of canonical women's fiction can also be identified in contemporary ethnic women's fiction? How is ethnicity defined, produced and performed by a text, and how might readers consume and understand these effects? How do different concepts of ethnicity influence African American and Asian American women's fiction? Do separate and distinct patterns of cultural poetics emerge within the traditions of African and Asian American women's fiction? In women's fictional texts, which are, in many ways, "minority" works, what are the relationships between feminine identity and ethnic identity? One larger, unanswered inquiry hovers between the lines of these pages, though the potential for insight into this question fuels my project. To what extent is subjective identity comprised of dynamic relationships between self and other, and to what extent is it a product of an individual's cohesive, experiential essence? Moving through these and other questions regarding the complex and often inscrutable relationship between "race" and "ethnicity" in twentieth-century discourse, this project will focus on relationships between anglo, Asian American, and African American heroines in order to point to the ways in which literary narrative helps to shape and define these different concepts of identity.[1] My analysis spans the twentieth century and ranges from an examination of turn-of-the-century sentimental heroines in the fiction of Onoto Wantanna and Emma D. Kelley-Hawkins to the contemporary heroine of Gish Jen's *Mona in the Promised Land*(1996).

The practice of reading feminine characterization in contemporary American novels with an eye towards race, nation, and class has gained much credence in recent ethnic studies scholarship as a means of expanding the practice of critiquing cultural domination; yet, though current theoretical treatments of the female subject choose to explore these terms and concepts within separated academic fields comprised of ethnic subgroups (African American, Asian American, Arab American), these examples of scholarship share the project of challenging the politics of representation in several discursive forms. As Lisa Lowe explains in *Immigrant Acts* (1996), seemingly innocuous concepts like nationality and citizenship are informed by racist and gendered civic codes that not only participate in cultural hegemony operating less obviously in anglocentric narratives but actually capitalize on the promise of equality while promoting exclusion and social hierarchy. Noting the "index of the historical and persistent racial, class, and gender contradictions of American society," Lowe contextualizes Asian American literary subjectivity as a "decolonizing" critique of several forms of imperialist narrative forces, including "the realist aesthetic as a regime for the production of history" (ix, 104). Her critique represents an ongoing challenge to the politics of white or anglo Western narrative structures, and is a theoretical practice that exemplifies and enacts the potent exchange between the fields of race theory, feminist criticism, postcolonial theory and ethnic studies. *Immigrant Acts* establishes Asian American poetics as an alternative to putatively civilizing, nation-building narrative structural elements like subjectivity, autobiography, romance, and resolution.[2]

Intriguingly, the text whose transcultural popularity and resonance Lowe chooses to deconstruct by casting it as a colonizing novel of manners is Jane Austen's 1813 *Pride and Prejudice*, the same novel critiqued by Ann duCille's 1993 study of marriage plots in African American women's fiction, *The Coupling Convention*. Both scholars devalue Austen's complex narrative form, which weaves free-indirect discourse with social and economic satire, discussing her novel as "the reconciliation of bourgeois individualism and the social order through the marriage contract" and as the ultimate signifier of white feminine frivolity "preoccupied with matrimony and affairs of the heart and pocketbook" (Lowe 99; duCille 1). From their vantage points, Austen's novel is apolitical as it fluctuates between entertainment in its "simple" exploration of "differences in station, parental disapproval, false pride, or silly prejudice" and moral instruction, while it candy-coats its gendered narrative of anglocentric virtue and vice (duCille 39).[3]

Lowe and duCille's shared targeting of a nineteenth-century British woman's text inspires my examination of transcultural heroine construction.[4] By choosing to critique *Pride and Prejudice*, these two practitioners of American ethnic studies underscore the permeability of ideas of nation and race; inadvertently, they demonstrate the ways in which the idea of British femininity impacts the articulation of the various subgroups of American ethnic identity.[5] This instance of singling out the same text also suggests that the seemingly divergent fields of African American and Asian American studies, separated by the experiential differences between social displacement through immigration and the legacy of slavery and institutional racism, configure similar strategies of ethnic feminist articulation. Although Alice Walker celebrates a textual heritage of contemporary black women writers and considers Zora Neale Hurston to be a foremother of the female African American novel, the study of textual traditions is too often restricted in academia to categories of race and nation (Walker 401). Second-wave feminist texts like Gilbert and Gubar's *The Madwoman in the Attic* (1979) and Elaine Showalter's *A Literature of their Own* (1977), espouse text-based models of transhistorical female literary traditions, but these studies emphasize only anglo traditions. While anglo feminism has slowly incorporated ethnic texts into its purview [examples include Elizabeth Abel et al.'s *The Voyage In* (1983), Lee Edwards's *Psyche as Hero* (1984), Suzanne Juhasz's *Reading From the Heart* (1994), and Helena Michie's *Sororophobia* (1992)], ethnic studies feminists seem unwilling to reciprocate this critical attention.

One might explain this pattern by unproductively and erroneously presuming that anglo feminism now participates in a forced integration with minority writers, fueled by a sense of intellectual guilt for past exclusionary habits, while ethnic studies scholars are free to pursue their own culturally-informed projects. Another problematic conclusion one might draw from these trends is that anglo and ethnic women writers have not and do not read each other's works. Thus, we are reluctant to identify and discuss the anglo literary foremothers of black fiction, or for that matter, the black foremothers of Asian American fiction. Should we then interpret the fact that Paule Marshall recalls having been a fan of Austen's fiction (as she did at a 2001 reading at Spelman College) and her consumption of "writers of the purple sage" as solely indicative of exclusionary power dynamics influencing a young black immigrant woman's reading habits? When Maxine Hong Kingston tells us that Louisa May Alcott's portrait of a "Chinaman" in her fiction alienated Kingston as a young reader, in lieu of the politics of "talking back," must we assume that Kingston's fiction necessarily holds nothing in common with Alcott's novels, or with anglo fiction in general?[6] And as we read Jamaica Kincaid's *Lucy,* and the heroine's aloof remembrance of reading Austen and Brontë's fiction as a girl in Antigua, are we to interpret this memory only as a critique of colonialist literature? Such explanations are inadequate interpretations today, and these explanations problematically deploy the dominant view that any exchange between ethnic and anglo texts is that of colonialist racism. Perhaps these trends in literary analysis prevail because we do not have viable alternative models, models of inclusion and interpretive schemas emphasizing the forces that drive reader consumption. We do not have enough models for exploring our investments in common, gendered narrative structures that transcend concepts of race, nation, and class.

Challenging conventional assumptions and conceptualizations of "ethnicity," Werner Sollors uses a rhetorical strategy similar to Ralph Ellison's in his "The World and the Jug" and bemusedly observes some contradictions and problematic elements of contemporary ideas of literary tradition: "Is Zora Neale Hurston only Alice Walker's foremother? In general, is the question of influence, of who came first, more interesting than the investigation of the constellation in which ideas, styles, themes, and forms travel?" ("A Critique" 257). Sollors's work on ethnicity prescribes the development of scholarship that mediates the "constellation" of "polyethnic" American art without resorting to "cultural pluralism," or a practice resulting in an emphasis on impossible categorizations striving to document an experiential "pure" racial, national, or cultural essence" (256, 279). "Ethnicity," he argues, "is not merely a matter of cultural (let alone biological) survival," but is "constantly recreated as people . . . set up new distinctions, make new boundaries, and form new groups" ("Nine Suggestions" 95). In his edited anthology *Theories of Ethnicity* (1996), Sollors outlines a history of cultural debates between the concepts of "race" and "ethnicity," wherein the specific contextual uses of these terms involve unsatisfactory, unstable assumptions about individual and collective identity. Pointing to the relationships between religious, biological, and cultural categorizations that overlap in even the most rigorous systems of identification, Sollors finally concludes that the "refusal to find any relationship" between the two concepts of race and ethnicity "does not seem promising as a program of scholarship" (*Theories* xxxv). The complex questions inspired by the critical practices of "multicultural recanonization" lead to forms of cultural essentialism, and more importantly "prevent the formation of radical transnational models of American literary studies" (Huang 142).

CULTURAL POLITICS AND THE POETICS OF HEROINE CONSTRUCTION

Two noteworthy studies in particular, Lee Edwards's *Psyche as Hero* (1984) and Pin-chia Feng's *The Female Bildungsroman by Toni Morrison and Maxine Hong Kingston* (1998), simultaneously discuss African and Asian American women's literature as narrative alternatives to and evolutions of anglo female plot structures. Feng, however, immediately begins her analysis by positing these women as "ethnic" writers offering a "new twist" to "the literary identity of American literature" (1–2). In furthering an emphasis on the poetics of ethnic female identity, I assert that a preoccupation with political commentary, "cultural politics," and political themes in current academic practices results in a lack of interaction between ethnic studies feminist scholarship and anglo feminism, and more importantly, it exposes a lack of willingness to explore non-political models in studying minority texts. These divisions in scholarly enterprise inspire my project's challenge to the ethnic studies precept that ethnic texts must necessarily be read as political texts. My study compounds this issue by focusing on women's fiction and also responding, directly and indirectly, to anglo-feminist concerns, including the politics of representation, patriarchal discourse, and the divergent ways of reading marriage plots and domestic fiction. I acknowledge that my project is entering onto a stage upon which the clearest articulation and realization of individuated female, and other forms of minority identity, is the prize most vigorously, and often desperately sought. Academic politics drive scholars to stake out new critical positions that will be regarded as more progressive than the previous ones. For these reasons, current academic paradigms assume that ethnic American narratives, like postcolonial fiction, must always "manifest stories about racial politics" (Tate, *Psychoanalysis* 5).

Asian American-novelist Frank Chin's 1991 *Donald Duk* provides us with a useful model for complicating our contemporary understanding of authorship, narrative subjectivity, and the minority politics. For Mr. Duk, the keeper of ancient Chinese culture, artistic expression always involves a quasi-belligerent self-assertiveness and a warlike dedication to the discipline necessary to master a craft, even and most especially (in Chin's case) for male artists.[7] Reading Chin's description of Chinese culture in tandem with feminist and ethnic studies arguments about narrative suddenly complicates our contemporary assumptions that only women and minorities write with ideologically and politically charged ink. As Chin offers us a glimpse at an ancient Chinese (not Chinese American) view of artistic endeavor in which all art is political and necessarily polemic, those simplified schemas that associate white male Western literary production with a traditional aesthetic practice and minority writing with political reactionism come unhinged. "Writing as war" here is a concept derived from an ancient tradition, according to Chin, that is removed from the colonial encounter and all other associations of contemporary cultural politics. My concern with much of the pedagogical force fueling many examples of ethnic studies scholarship lies in the assumption that anglo fiction offers confident and totalized visions of selfhood in relation to society and the world, whereas ethnic narratives offer fragmented and thereby more "serious" ideas of political reformation.[8]

These analytical trends suggest that reading ethnic literature requires paying attention to depictions of "real" lived experience and imply that examinations of poetics should be reserved for anglo, "master," or canonical fiction. My project challenges this theoretical double-standard while viewing ethnic American women writers' practices of heroine construction as the result of transcultural and transnational narrative influences that shape concepts of ethnicity. I treat the fictional text as a canvas of figurative rhetoric that contributes to more than just a reconstruction and a mimesis of the essentialized experiences of political subject positions. My goal is to show how cultural meanings and specificities are as much created in fiction's frames as they are supposedly represented there. Having said this, I should point out that my attempt to concentrate on poetics and form versus political themes is not a novel project; in fact, some recent examples of Asian American literary scholarship move away from the "reductive view" that positions "a text's ideological effect as equivalent to its literary effect" (Ling, Jinqui 145).[9] However, I will challenge a current model of analysis that focuses on the poetics of minority fiction only in order to highlight systems of cultural politics, which are configured as unique challenges to cultural domination. Consider, for example, Ann duCille's *The Coupling Convention*, a study of African American women's fiction I have already mentioned. Ducille explicates the work of Jessie Fauset and Nella Larsen in a chapter entitled "The Bourgeois, Wedding-Bell Blues." She devotes this chapter's energies to refuting the charge of elitism and frivolity accorded to Larsen and Fauset by those scholars who claim that these writers do not participate in an acceptable politics of racial critique but instead narrate in whiteface. Significantly, in her astute reconsideration of these writers, duCille excavates the language of a subversive sexuality that she then incorporates into her larger theme of marriage as a political sign. Thus, duCille's work, like many of those studies that work to counter exclusionary, generalizing scholarly practices, ultimately finds a larger pattern of counter, or "cultural," politics within which to subsume her arguments.

My study offers an alternative to the model of ethnic studies criticism described above by placing emphasis on transcultural structural patterns, or poetics, in heroine construction. "Poetics," in my project refers to structural form, and I use the term not only to highlight formal instead of thematic concerns, I also use it to delimit those features of a text that do not articulate minority cultural politics in the conventional sense. Additionally, my study of poetics inscribes and responds to a narrative transhistorical and intertextual tradition of heroine construction. That is, my project foregrounds the ways in which women are represented and ideas of femininity are produced instead of what these representations signify about specific social or historic periods. By commenting on the role of forces of narrative tension such as authorial anxiety, ambivalence, desire, and subjective longing that drive female characters' movement towards self-actualization, self-consequence, and identity-affirmation in anglo, African, and Asian American women's novels, I will discuss these texts' interactions with some overarching discursive elements of fictional female development. These include the language of romance and marriage plots, the language of heroine objectification, the symbolism of space, and the narration of female adolescent coming-of-age.

THEORETICAL CONTEXT AND METHOD

Viewing fiction as the narrative ordering of the psychological forces mentioned above is, of course, a practice of psychoanalytic criticism, and to that end there are some examples of this type of scholarship relevant to this project. In his 1984 *Reading for Plot*, Peter Brooks uses psychoanalysis to schematize narrative form as "an anatomy of human desire," describing a fictional protagonist's ability to "construct meanings in ever-larger wholes, to totalize . . . experience of human existence in time" as a way to placate the anxiety of a final and incomprehensible death (Brooks 39, 40). Suzanne Juhasz's 1994 *Reading From the Heart* supplements Brook's predominantly male study with object-relations psychology in attempting to articulate women readers' attraction to typically female plots. Claudia Tate's more recent *Psychoanalysis and Black Novels* (1998) usefully bridges psychological models to the less political, less studied narratives of personal desire in black fiction. In this project, I intend to further a narrative-based approach in tune with the studies listed above. But instead of employing the language of psychoanalysis, my methods will concentrate on the poetics of heroine construction in light of transcultural articulations of marriage plots, the language of heroine objectification, the search for place and position, and the narration of adolescent coming-of-age, in an effort to show that the self-assertive cultural politics of ethnic fiction have definite—if ambivalent—relationships with canonical anglo narratives. Lowe and duCille assert that ethnic texts displace conventional narrative modes like romance and resolution by emphasizing fragmented identities and material realities that lie beyond fiction's more tidy frames. My goal is to seek out and expose ethnic women writers' use of conventional elements, in a process one might see as analogous to unveiling the unwittingly faithful members within a congregation made up of agnostics.

Asian American and African American scholarship justifiably point to a politics of fragmentation, diversification, and destabilization in ethnic women's texts and my analysis will work in tune with these veins of criticism. However, I will at the same time look at what remains whole(some) and attempt to excavate a residual and cohesive transcultural tradition. This project will, on occasion, engage with assignations of positive and negative female developmental scope, and I will refer to narrative tone, mode, and resolution. As any consideration of ethnicity must necessarily consider the tension of publicly political concerns versus more private, personal affairs, my observations challenge the subjective bleakness associated with the politics of ethnic fiction. My discussion of structural relationships between anglo, African, and Asian American women's novels veers more towards an affirmation of the poetics of female identity construction rather than the politics of deconstruction. I hope to reveal the powers of narrative language as it not only aids in representing the voice of the repressed ethnic female subject but also as its common structures ensure that anglo and ethnic concepts of female development are more similar than we might think. These structures provide familiar templates within which heroines signify their differentiated identities in relation to each other, across time, and across boundaries of race, nation, or class.

For example, in chapter 4 of this study, I examine contemporary ethnic narratives of adolescence that configure conventional feminine virtues of beauty, inner strength, and wit, which are textually standardized as necessary female attributes by late eighteenth-and early nineteenth-century anglo heroine production. As I emphasize the relationships between transcultural texts, I will use the term "relational" in all of the four chapters of this study as a modifier for the intersubjective processes occurring within articulations and performances of individual identity. Anglo and ethnic women protagonists develop in relation to dominant cultural mores prescribing feminine behavior as well as in relation to popular constructions of narrative femininity in the literary marketplace.

In attempting a narrative-based exposition of female ethnicity in twentieth-century American fiction, my project inscribes and responds to several renowned articulations and definitions of the poetics of socially-displaced persons. Gayatri Spivak, in her now fifteen- year-old essay "Three Women's Texts and a Critique of Imperialism," remarks that even those narratives lauded and reread as hallmarks of feminism such as *Jane Eyre* and *Frankenstein,* participate in an anglocentric performance of individualized female subjectivity as they perpetuate "incidental imperialist sentiment" (Spivak 273). Abdul JanMohamed uses Franz Fanon's concept of the "representational economy" of the "simple machinery of the manichean allegory" to provide a useful taxonomy of nineteenth-century "colonialist literature" by differentiating between levels of structural imperialism in the work of novelists like Forster and Conrad (JanMohamed 83). His study asserts that the literature of the nineteenth century, and indeed anything written after the colonial encounter, always inscribes imperialist rhetoric. Such analyses lay the groundwork of a postcolonial critique of master narratives, which attempt to highlight the more refined or "cultural" envoys of domination best explicated by Edward Said's 1993 *Culture and Imperialism*. These studies work to destabilize lingering networks of exclusion by exposing them at every narrative level. Literary examinations of race and nation consequently look both for other examples of similarly reprehensible cultural concepts and for moments of resistance to such hierarchical schemas through recovery efforts and the contextualization of cultural politics in narratives written by marginalized subjects. Thus, Lisa Lowe's 1996 *Immigrant Acts* marks a specific moment in ethnic studies scholarship during which considerations of race and nation reveal subversive politics and anti-assimilationist agendas of texts, which cohere around a specific cultural or racial signifier. Her study might be grouped with the scholarship of King-kok Cheung; Cheung's *Articulate Silences* (1993) also makes an eloquent case for culture-specific readings of immigrant texts.[10] Both texts are clear examples of ethnic studies scholarship that, while understanding and working to demonstrate the performativity of concepts like nationality and race, consciously position their readings of ethnic literature as alternatives to Western intellectual ideologies. Such scholarship is often reluctant to consider the possibility that works of ethnic fiction may be less separatist than is commonly envisioned.

These theoretical investigations into the relationship of literature and alterity have been vital for encouraging a politics of inclusion and tolerance necessary to a "postmodern deconstruction of cultural and social hegemony" (Feng 14). A politics of decentered reading and rereading helps us diversify our perspectives, a necessary skill if we are to learn from the past, be more enlightened about the decisions we make individually and socially, and claim more responsibility for how we script the way we think the world operates. Much of the current multiculturalist scholarship does participate in a responsible politics of cultural sensitivity. These types of studies may be informed by the demands of an intellectual market that fosters the furiously conscientious, yet often skeptical, politics of destabilization, which are performed by challenging tradition in its many manifestations from cultural ideals to literary forms. Muffled by the roar of this critical motor are those voices of anxiety and subjective longing in ethnic American fiction, which are ordered into narratives (and anti-narratives) that we read as political characterizations of marginalized identities who impart stringent social commentary. I will explore the force of subjective longing as it orders narrative tensions into a performance of individual identity; this longing manipulates structural form to resolve anxieties of production, cultural expectations, and the weight of tradition.

Some useful examples of recent feminist criticism pursue a line of analysis that considers the dynamic, rather than static, elements of character and identity, allowing a much-needed examination of the tensions, pressures and anxieties underlying social relationships. One such recent study, *Sororophobia: Differences Among Women in Literature and Culture* (1992), counters a critical assumption shared by first and second-wave feminist criticism that sisterhood and cooperation are intrinsically female qualities and strengths. In it, Helena Michie examines the fear of sameness and the fear of difference in anglo novels like George Eliot's *Middlemarch* and Thomas Hardy's *Tess of the d'Urbervilles* as well in ethnic American fiction like Nella Larsen's *Quicksand* and *Passing*. Michie looks at an evolving pattern of encoding feminine character in relational terms of sameness and difference across lines of nationality, race, and sexual orientation.

Like Michie's *Sororophobia,* my project configures subjective pressure and competition as important catalysts of identity formation and development within literary texts. My purpose in doing so is to point to the more harmonious relationships between women's texts across time, despite modern and postmodern responses to the networks of colonialism, neocolonialism, and institutionalization, which have influenced the politics of contemporary canon formation as well as the discursive conceptualization of various national and racial identities. My pairing of African and Asian American female subjectivity allows me to challenge conceptualizations and stereotypes that assign a "model minority" status to Asian American subjectivity in relation to a lower-class, ghettoized image of African American subjectivity.[11] Certain textual relationships also inform my decision to examine these two ethnic textual traditions simultaneously. Consider, for example, the shared biblical reference "I have sold my birthright for a mess of potage," found in both James Weldon Johnson's *The Autobiography of an Ex-Colored Man* (1912) and *Me* (1915), Onoto Watanna's autobiography, both published anonymously. This shared rhetorical strategy of religious allusion exemplifies the fact that in the early twentieth century, before African and Asian American literary traditions were as established as they are today, thematic moments conveying ideas of political responsibility were often articulated in similar ways, regardless of the specific cultural backgrounds of writers. In addition, Onoto Watanna's turn-of-the-century romantic fiction employs the mode of sentimentalism in ways similar to the late nineteenth-century African American novelist Pauline Hopkins. Finally, of course, Ann duCille's and Lisa Lowe's shared critique of *Pride and Prejudice* demands an investigation into similar practices of self-articulation against an anglo norm. My point in this pairing of ethnic subjectivities is that although historic differences exist between American racism and the legacy of slavery and the exclusionary policies of immigration legislation and social prejudice towards immigrants, the narratives of female development within these textual traditions maintain significant structural similarities that demand that we re-examine our definitions and categorizations of ethnicity.

By pointing to a common ground of heroine construction shared transculturally, I suggest the potential for even more exchange between anglo and ethnic fictional and scholarly enterprises. While I indicate that certain narrative templates of feminine development exist on both sides, I do not mean to imply that anglo-feminism and anglo-feminist fiction provide the earliest and thereby best solutions for mitigating social domination. In fact, my analysis of textual moments in *Jane Eyre, Villette, Little Women,* and *The House of Mirth,* to mention a few examples, underscores the power of class dynamics which give meaning to singular acts of "feminist individualism" (Spivak, "Three Women's Texts" 263). Thus, this project takes as a given the overdetermined, intersectional forces of materialist, feminist, and postcolonialist discourse that have often shaped literary production and our expanding practices of critical reading. Although I focus in this project on ethnic female subjectivity and its relational acts of articulation, I assert that intertextual dynamics within anglo fiction provide all heroines with influential narrative models. I consider these transcultural relationships as elements configuring the evolution of the narrative of the socially-displaced woman. This assertion does not necessitate my privileging one type of feminism over another but implies instead that much work remains to be done in determining the reasons for, and challenging the need for, the divisions between anglo and ethnic feminism since transcultural women's texts themselves do not evince quite the same degree of exclusiveness. I consider all of the works of fiction discussed at length in this study to be feminist novels in that they present female protagonists whose stories of development challenge sexist cultural mores and critique social hierarchies of race, nation, and class. Many of the ethnic narratives named in this study have also been the objects of anglo feminist literary criticism.

Structural similarities between nineteenth-century anglo narratives and twentieth-century African and Asian American women's fiction point to underlying questions of heroine construction which are being worked out text by text, reader by reader, as each new emergent voice represents what I see as a metaphoric expansion of the narrative of the socially-displaced out-classed/outcast Other. I will ground this study in a commitment to explore the meaning of the term "ethnicity," hoping to expose its metaphoric quali-ties; I view ethnicity in these works of fiction as the narrative compounding of social exclusion and alienation existent in transatlantic nineteenth-century and early twentieth-century novels like Charlotte Brontë's *Jane Eyre* (1847) and *Villette* (1853) or Theodore Dreiser's *Sister Carrie* (1900), which critique class hierarchies. Ethnicity functions like social prospect (or lack thereof) in the twentieth-century fiction discussed in this project as heroines are created with an eye towards marriageability and marketability. Articulations of ethnicity can ultimately influence and be influenced by mar-ket forces, both marriage and publishing markets. Simply put, for several of the heroines discussed in this study, racial or national background and cul-ture is at some level a personal quality, just like beauty, brains, or wealth, and these qualities must be developed in certain ways to configure the prom-ise of romantic fulfillment. Jessie Fauset's *Plum Bun* (1928), for example, features a young black heroine whose development Fauset narrates in terms of going "to market." The narrator formulates Angela Murray's self-actualization and marital prospects by highlighting the heroine's dual per-formances of whiteness and blackness; in both cases, men find her desirable, but it is not until Angela can wholeheartedly embrace her black heritage, and a lineage less glamorous than the one she creates for herself, that she is rewarded with true love as well as artistic success. The force of markets thus pervades these novels not only as obvious critiques of socioeconomic in-equities that configure class and racial hierarchies, they also influence the characterization of heroines within the intersection of publishing trends and audience consumption. The works of fiction discussed in this study thus in-scribe Cinderella stories in more ways than we might imagine.

Having made the above clarifications, I should also discuss the limita-tions of the project at hand. While I occasionally and sporadically hypothesize about market forces and their influence on heroine production, and while I make the claim in chapters 2 and 3 that narratives of class-mobility inscribe ethnicity as an element of class, this is not a materialist analysis. My objective is to examine the ways in which ethnicity, as a concept, is articulated in a vari-ety of dynamic ways, and that it is in fact a component of narrative. The cen-tral purpose of all of these chapters is to explicate a series of relationships that evince transcultural dynamics, which problematize our categorical, essentialized, canon-based conceptualizations of subjective narrative. Thus, this project will explore the poetics of ethnic identity as a way of countering the scholarly trend of emphasizing the political themes of minority narratives.

This concentration on structure and poetics of ethnic heroine construction, however, does not fall within one large theoretical model, like psychoanalysis, object-relations theory, postcolonialism, or New Historicism. Although in different moments of this study I refer to relationships between writer, reader, and heroine, my approach here is more suggestive than declarative. While reader-oriented studies like Janice Radway's *Reading the Romance* (1984) and Suzanne Juhasz's *Reading from the Heart* inform some of the analytic movements in my project, I do not pretend to conduct a reader-response analysis in these pages. The openness of my critical approach performs an alternative to the schisms of subject position I see hindering the possibility of a more productive exchange between anglo feminism and ethnic studies. Nevertheless, I understand that my open-ended strategy here prohibits me from fully exploring certain critical avenues within the space of this book.

TERMINOLOGY AND LANGUAGE

The assertion that "ethnic" equals non-white is both oversimplified and incorrect, and ethnicity in popular and civic discourse operates in a more inclusive register, "Caucasian" being an ethnic category as much as "African American." However, in most literary studies, ethnicity connotes non-white, non-anglo subjective identity, and, accordingly, I follow that pattern in this project. As my aim is to provide a line of analysis in which these categories begin to blur, my language must be necessarily (perhaps paradoxically) exacting. To provide a clearer semantic map of my movements through these categories, my use of labels performs a pairing between "ethnic" and "anglo," both in the lowercase, because these concepts are less defined and more theoretical than the established racial and ethnic subheadings of "African American" and "Asian American," both of which I will capitalize. The term "anglo" is a derivation of Lowe and duCille's use of the label "Anglo-American." I will thus use the term "anglo" continuously to represent those transatlantic white canonical texts that are held apart from ethnic American texts within academic scholarship. This system risks distancing the terms "ethnic" and "anglo" from the nuances of identification and cultural histories invoked by these concepts, but I see this cost as necessary in articulating alternative models of subject formation supported by the poetics of female identity in the texts at hand.

The titles of my project's chapters allude to fairy tales such as "Cinderella," "Snow White and the Seven Dwarves," and "Sleeping

Beauty," and I explore the ways in which the supposedly more politically-vigilant camp of ethnic fiction evokes modes of romance and resolution. Chapters 1 and 2 most directly address ethnic texts' interactions with marriage plots, while Chapter 3, "Cinderella's Understudies: Marginality, Ethnicity, and the Negotiated Spaces of Heroine Desire," examines transcultural redirections of marriage-plot energies as heroines search for a sense of place, or belonging, in society as opposed to pursuing marriage. The idea of the castle of one's dreams, however, lingers in the spatial dynamics of ethnic and anglo fiction as the significance of personal estates, entitlement, or other measures of self-consequence drives the search for female self-actualization. "Modeling Minority Women," the title of this study, thus refers to the ways in which works of ethnic as well as anglo fiction engage with similar narrative models of feminine development, including conventional fairy-tale-like marriage plots. The title invokes not only the cultural stereotype of Asian Americans as "model minorities," "modeling" emphasizes the active processes and the narrative dynamism of ethnic and feminine identity-construction. Finally, my pairing of "minority" and "women" performs a sort of conscious critical redundancy that references the evolving purview of the minority subject position within academic discourse.

TRANSCULTURAL HEROINE CONSTRUCTION: AN OUTLINE

Each of the four chapters represents an essential component of conventional literary heroine construction: the role of romance, the language of heroine objectification, the search for place, and the stage of adolescence. I have selected these elements because they exemplify four main (though not exclusive) transhistorical factors shaping the narratives of young female protagonists. My concept of a heroine is a young, usually unmarried woman whom the writer introduces to the reader at an early part of the heroine's development. This development culminates with the heroine's realization of self, a state usually arrived at through marriage or through another form of personal "success," highlighting artistic enterprise or other socially-affirmed acts of individual expression. As mentioned above, chapters 1 and 2 discuss transcultural heroine construction in light of marriage market dynamics, while chapters 3 and 4 address contemporary authors' efforts to veer away from the limits of the marital paradigm. I will, however, note repeatedly that although writers redirect energies away from conventional heterosexual marriage plots, contemporary texts often use these energies to convey narrative effects similar to those earlier texts in which the pursuit of marriage is more obviously at the center of the plot.

Chapter 1 concentrates on a pair of sister writers, the earliest known writers of Asian American fiction, Edith and Winnifred Eaton (or Sui Sin Far and Onoto Watanna). Working to challenge academic biases in favor of "political" fiction, I discuss the different receptions both writers' works have received in contemporary scholarship, which are due to each sister's individuated, although textually ambivalent, choice about the role of romance in her writings. By focusing on the divergent careers of the Eaton sisters, this chapter inaugurates a larger project of problematizing easy distinctions between "traditional" and "ethnic," while examining the configuration of class, race, nation, and gender in the thematics and poetics of social displacement in the production of heroines and their late nineteenth- and early twentieth-century stories. In chapter 2, I discuss "heroine objectification," a term I define as the language of two-dimensionally appraising women in relation to each other within the scale of conventional standards of female beauty, propriety and moral fortitude—a literary system paralleling the sexual objectification of women in mass media. I trace structural connections between Louisa May Alcott's *Little Women* (1868) and Emma D. Kelley-Hawkins's *Four Girls at Cottage City* (1898) and between Edith Wharton's *The House of Mirth* (1905) and Jessie Fauset's *Plum Bun* (1928) by demonstrating their similar investments in the language of heroine objectification. This chapter concludes with a brief investigation of the dynamics of heroine objectification in the mid-twentieth-century fiction of Asian American writer Hisaye Yamomoto as I begin to contextualize contemporary Asian American female characterization's reluctance to employ heroine objectification in ways similar to the texts discussed in the beginning of the chapter. This conclusion provides a transition from the mechanics of the marriage plot to alternative scenarios of independence and female self-actualization discussed in the second half of this study.

Chapter 3 considers the language and symbolism of space in ethnic heroine construction as a shared narrative reordering of marriage plot conventions begun in anglo novels like Charlotte Brontë's *Villette*. I examine the preoccupation with space in Jade Snow Wong's *Fifth Chinese Daughter* (1950), Jamaica Kincaid's *Lucy* (1991), and Paule Marshall's *Brown Girl, Brownstones* (1959) as indicative of a heroine's search for a self-affirming place or position in society. Ultimately, this search involves structural relationships between anglo and ethnic fiction as these writers, like their heroines, move towards the "safe" space of conventional structure. This chapter challenges the emphasis of a feminist model of claustrophobia made famous by Gilbert and Gubar's *The Madwoman in the Attic* (1979) and discusses the power of a subjective and figurative agoraphobia in driving these heroine's quests for place and position in manifestations of cultural agoraphobia. While detailing the symbolism of physical space (houses, closets, rooms) and the significance of positional spaces (vocations, social roles) as manifestations of cauterized, relational selves, I will view the narrative performance of ethnic identity as the ambivalent, spatial manipulation of developmental scope outlined in transatlantic canonical anglo fiction.

Finally, chapter 4 concludes my analysis of transcultural heroine construction by revealing the articulation and cultivation of conventionally feminine virtues and attributes like beauty, inner strength, and wit in contemporary coming-of-age novels or adolescent narratives—characteristics that challenge the critical assumption that contemporary politics have shaped heroines in uniquely empowering, non-traditional molds. At the beginning this chapter, I consider the publishing market's recent investments in popular fiction of female adolescent ethnicity and the increased production and consumption of female adolescence—a trend that is simultaneous to the development of American pre-pubescent spending power. I introduce the question of the co-optation of female ethnic identity within juvenile fiction and other mass media markets in order to contextualize adult or literary ethnic fiction's supposed emphasis on political topics. My subsequent exploration of the configuration of conventional female virtues thus expands the model of emphasizing transcultural feminist poetics begun in the first three chapters. Moving from a discussion of Toni Morrison's *The Bluest Eye* (1970) to Lois-Ann Yamanaka's *Wild Meat and the Bully Burgers* (1996), the chapter's identification of conventional female virtues culminates in an examination of the power of wit in Gish Jen's *Mona in the Promised Land* (1996). As in the other three chapters, this analysis views structural relationships between anglo and ethnic fiction as emblematic of a relational struggle for self-articulation.

By concluding with a fourth chapter that discusses the most current trends in transcultural contemporary heroine construction, my goal is to highlight linguistic responsiveness as the true bearer of tradition in ethnic subjective cultivation. *The Good Negress* (1995) by A. J. Verdelle, a novel depicting a young African American woman's coming-of-age in the 1960s, for example, contains passages that seem at times to echo the rhetoric of juvenile literature in the early twentieth century. Its final message of redemption in the face of social and economic constriction is encoded in rhetorical figures that resonate familiarly to us as readers who are aware of a set of narrative trajectories—both anglo and ethnic—having to do with female adolescence. My point in conducting this type of comparison is to promote the influence of narrative language over any specific cultural experiences as more powerful than we might like to admit in the shaping of tradition. Verdelle's teen-aged heroine, Denise Palms, eloquently acknowledges the subjective power of creativity and narration in a youthful though surprisingly wise admission: "I decide that I have to write myself to a future" (175). As is the case for Denise and for the other twentieth-century ethnic heroines discussed in the pages that follow, the degree of developmental success and fulfillment they achieve depends upon the stories they internalize and learn to apply to their own futures.

Chapter One
Someday My Prince Will Come:
Ambivalent Romance and Ethnicity in the Fiction of the Eaton Sisters

While marriage market dynamics and marriage plots have been subjects of discussion and objects of critique in feminist criticism for decades, the analysis of women's romance narratives remains marginalized from scholarship—the unsophisticated "Other" to socially and politically significant literary criticism. Because ethnic studies feminism positions itself as a corrective to the limitations of anglo feminism, much of this scholarship similarly resists conducting non-political modes of literary criticism and shies away from engaging with literary works that ostensibly adhere to conventional structures.[1] Studies like King-kok Cheung's *Articulate Silences* (1993) and Lisa Lowe's *Immigrant Acts* (1996) usefully provide an Asian American collective subject position with a counter narrative within which to conceptualize its suppressed beginnings and current trajectories of cultural activism. However, ethnic women writers whose works resonate in a less than liberated register—writers of romance or "traditional" narratives more often than not lose the opportunity for consideration in contemporary criticism.[2] In this chapter, I will attempt to bridge this critical divide through a discussion of two of the earliest women writers of Chinese descent published in North America—the Eaton sisters—who now experience dichotomous literary reputations arguably as a result of political biases within academia.

The Eaton sisters are quintessential transnational literary figures. Their English father and Chinese mother moved the family to parts of England, the United States, and Canada before both Edith (Sui Sin Far) and Winnifred (Onoto Watanna) traveled to and lived in different parts of the United States on their own to pursue literary careers (White-Parks, *Sui Sin Far* 14–19). Both sisters wrote within, against, and in engagement with various turn-of-the-century ideas of national, cultural, and racial identity. I choose their works to begin this project on transcultural heroine construction because both writers published at least a half century before the debut of American ethnic-identity politics and also before women's fiction achieved the critical popularity it has since. Their works and lives provide a context transitioning between nineteenth-century ideas about female authorial production and twentieth-century conceptualizations of ethnic identity. They also enable discussions bridging genre-based feminist scholarship on domestic and sentimental fiction to the politics of ethnic studies.

The critical popularity and forerunner status enjoyed by Edith Eaton's (or Sui Sin Far's) short stories and essays today overshadow Winnifred Eaton's (or Onoto Watanna's) own impressive literary accomplishments.[3] The Eaton sisters wrote the earliest examples of Asian American fiction, but Winnifred Eaton hid her Chinese heritage and assumed instead a Japanese-American identity (using the pseudonym of Onoto Watanna), choosing to self-identify with a culture that faced less intolerance and racial discrimination in turn-of-the-century America.[4] Despite her commercial success in the early twentieth century and the fact that she authored the first American novel known to be published by a writer of Asian heritage, *Miss Numè of Japan* (1899), Watanna's work is rarely studied and discussed today in scholarship on Asian American literature; most acknowledgements of her literary career tactfully devalue her efforts while expounding on the merits of her sister's work and political activism.[5] Xiao-huang Yin, for instance, discusses the "courage and integrity" of Sui Sin Far while making cursory mention of Watanna, noting her as a "best-selling writer" who "traded her birthright for recognition and popularity" (89).

Most scholars of Asian American literature choose to study Sui Sin Far's life and work. Annette White-Parks and Amy Ling have both written extensively about Sui Sin Far's career, explicating the thematics of her Eurasian "identity ambivalence" and highlighting those qualities of her fiction which are "far ahead of her time," working from the stance that "integrity in the question of her ethnicity . . . took precedence over everything else in life" (White-Parks, *Sui Sin Far* 3; Ling, *Between Worlds* 30). Although in recent years some pioneering scholars of transnationalism have begun to re-examine Watanna's works—most notably Dominika Ferens in her recent book-length study on both Eaton sisters, entitled *Edith and Winnifred Eaton: Chinatown Missions and Japanese Romances* (2002), and Watanna's granddaughter Diana Birchall, who published a 2001 biography of Watanna—mainstream Asian American literary scholarship has yet to embrace Watanna's work and to read her novels with serious attention to her craft. In her introduction to a 1999 edition of *Miss Numé of Japan,* Eve Oishi explains that the lack of scholarship existing on Watanna's novels is a problem of genre; Watanna crafted romance novels set in Japan, using sentimental language to depict fantastically transnational, beautiful, and strong-willed heroines. Sui Sin Far never published a novel, and she devoted much of her time to writing smaller pieces, which critiqued American prejudice towards Chinese immigrants. Thus, Watanna's literary accomplishments and credibility seem spurious not only because of her decision to hide her Chinese identity, a decision that is flagrantly against the contemporary politics of multiculturalist self-assertion, but also because she chose to write romantic fiction, a mode viewed as unrelated to or in direct conflict with ethnic studies projects of combating cultural hegemony. Those scholars who acknowledge the function of romance in the Eatons' writings do so in order to highlight cultural politics that are in keeping with the collective, decolonizing purview of contemporary ethnic studies discourse. Patricia Chu, in *Assimilating Asians,* for example, lauds Sui Sin Far's "uncompromising moral character" and asserts that, though she wrote her own versions of "immigrant romance," Sui Sin Far's stories serve more political agendas by allowing her to Americanize, and thereby humanize, Asian characters in a stringently anti-Chinese turn-of-the-century social climate (Chu 90–141).

In an attempt to break this pattern and to resist the labels and categories limiting critical approaches to ethnic American writing, this project will actively seek out those features of ethnic texts that are ignored and excluded in much of ethnic studies scholarship in the name of contemporary cultural politics and culture-specific analysis. This chapter will trace the ambivalent language of romance within the Eaton sisters' writings—a language detailing idealized heterosexual matches and unions—as emblematic of their negotiations of marital and publishing anxieties in complex, conflicted narrative articulations of female ethnicity, which problematize our culture-specific and political conceptualizations of ethnic identity. I will begin with a discussion of Onoto Watanna's first novel *(Miss Numè of Japan)* and her autobiography *(Me: A Book of Remembrance),* then examine Sui Sin Far's frequently anthologized as well as lesser-known stories, before turning back to Watanna's *The Heart of Hyacinth,* moving in a direction of criticism that will provide "a better understanding of the complex and manifold connections between racial categories, popular culture, historical context, and personal identity" (Oishi xviii).

ONOTO WATANNA'S *MISS NUMÈ OF JAPAN*

Miss Numè of Japan (1899) is not exactly a recovered novel. Like Watanna's other novels, it was published and highly successful in its time. Eve Oishi

notes that Watanna's later novel, *A Japanese Nightingale* (1901), was translated into multiple languages and adapted as a Broadway play and as a film
(xii). Amy Ling points out that W. D. Howells wrote favorably of *A Japanese
Nightingale* in *The North American Review,* praising the "pretty novelette"
and its artistic quality, "which is like no other art except in the simplicity
which is native to the best art everywhere" (quoted in "Ethnic Chameleon"
9). Although *Miss Numè of Japan* adheres to the structure of courtship and
romance novels, it contains significant moments of cultural sensitivity towards ideas of nationality and ethnic identity. But it remains virtually un-
read today and ignored by ethnic studies scholarship except for a few
references to its author as the sister of the critically-acclaimed Sui Sin Far. If
she encounters the novel at all, today's reader experiences it with the pleasure of surprise and guilt. In hindsight, *Miss Numè's* structurally incongruous
relationship with examples of muted, cynically spirited, and materially suffering heroines of contemporary Asian American fiction provides some
telling insights about the protean, relational processes driving conceptualizations of ethnicity. In this section, I view Onoto Watanna's descriptions of
ethnicity as ambivalent, and even anxious, performances of feminine subjectivity in relation to the dominant discursive elements of romantic and sentimental anglo heroine construction of her era. The novel incorporates the
sisterly friendships and figurative doubles characteristic of domestic fiction
while deploying social commentary on gender roles and minority rights in
twist-of-fate sentimental episodes of the era. Some recognizably domestic
and sentimental elements within Watanna's novel include its over-drawn and
formulaic characterizations, which are driven by conventional courtship-to-
marriage plots and moments of identifiable subversive gender politics within
the softened mode of romance.[6]

Watanna's novel carefully mediates reader expectations for conventional romance and reconfigures these elements by presenting an ethnic (or
transnational) heroine in an unconventional setting that necessitates new
twists on older plots. The novel performs these tasks by not limiting itself to
a simple duplication of a plot involving mismatched couples and the associated melodramatic formulas. *Miss Numè* balances its characterizations of
the four lovers through a counterpoint of ironic distance and intimate detail.
Orito (the Japanese hero) is at once elegant and disconcertingly serious;
Numè (the Japanese heroine) speaks with an English that lacks polish (com-
ically at times), yet her courage to speak her mind to foreigners is rendered
as admirable. And the quality of love in the triangle between Sinclair (the
white American hero), Orito, and Cleo (the white American heroine)—its
ambivalence and entanglement with power dynamics and conventional

mores—is performed structurally through characterization, subtle commentary, and free-indirect discourse as well as through more simple romantic themes. While the love triangle is central (Orito loves Cleo who is engaged to Sinclair who loves Numè), the novel revives and refashions generic conventionalities. Structural details are at the service of Watanna's specifically drawn characters who are all involved in enacting counter-conventional themes and effects rather than being at the mercy of the generic constraints. In contradistinction to the double wedding promised by the plight of the mismatched couples, the novel presses forward at its confident, balanced pace, revealing more and more about Cleo's cowardly spirit, making it seem impossible that the narrative would justify any marriage between the white American Cleo and the Japanese Orito. Also, while readers of sentimental fiction are familiar with female suicide as a fitting end to a complicated love triangle or moral transgression, Watanna makes suicide a part of Orito's narrative scope, an action unlikely to be performed by the confident and spunky Numè. Orito's character, stoic yet constant, represents a specifically upper-class Japanese masculinity (a force which attracts the archetype of white femininity, Cleo) that challenges stereotypes of emasculated male Asian characters that were popular during this time period.[7] Watanna's version of Japanese masculinity emphasizes honor, respect, and integrity.

The romantic plot structure of *Miss Numè of Japan* deserves our unwavering critical attention today especially because, as scholars looking for cultural sensitivity and political critiques, we are at a loss to determine how exactly to read and classify such novels. Rather than assume that Watanna's text lacks the integrity or courage to critique political, national, and racial domination, we might think instead of what special effects this novel's tone and structure achieve that other later Asian American texts are either unwilling or unable to incorporate. The novel's emphasis on romance involves tonal, thematic, and plot details that diverge from our contemporary expectations for Asian American literature. Watanna announces her novel's romantic proclivities by attaching a subtitle that aptly labels the tale a "Japanese-American Romance." Its use of the hyphenated modifier, however, suggests a context different from ethnic American identity labels used today. Readers in 1899 would have expected a cross-cultural romance—between American and Japanese people—as opposed to a romance between Japanese Americans. It is easy for us to imagine the appeal of this subgenre of cross-racial romance in a time that not only disallowed miscegenation but in a publishing market that was dominated by a white male ethos. It is also unlikely that the American public would have been interested in romantic intrigue between a Japanese man and Japanese woman at this time. Like the tea parties and exhibitions

which enthusiastically co-opted Japanese art and style by creating a vogue of
the "exotic," this novel's admiring objectifying gaze lingering over a unique
Japanese heroine is possible only so long as it is relational and supplemental
to a dominant narrative tradition, and Watanna achieves cultural familiarity through her characterization of the brooding critical perspective of
Sinclair and the power enjoyed by the trumping femme fatale, Cleo Ballard.[8]

Perhaps it is this ultimate pairing between the two couples and the implications of self-loathing inscribed by both Japanese characters desiring
white marriage partners that are unpalatable, even offensive, to contemporary practitioners of Asian American studies.[9] On one level, we can read a
colonialist narrative in the fact that the match between the two Japanese
children, decreed in a fairy-tale register at the beginning of the novel, is
destabilized by a usurping foreign imperial presence in the figures of an
American coquette and an official of the American Vice-Consul. Also, the
novel deploys some ethnocentric stings deployed in the speeches of many of
the novel's American characters like Mrs. Ballard, Fanny Morton, and Rose
Cranston (100). However, much of this early text's thematic and structural
credibility lies in its overriding refusal to participate in the ethnocentric perspective of nineteenth-century America.[10] Watanna successfully embeds her
romance in a structure of cultural sensitivity by casting much of the anti-
Asian sentiment in the minds of insecure, narrow-minded women who share
Cleo Ballard's class and circumstances; Watanna then diffuses this sentiment
by characterizing Cleo's frivolity, lack of discretion, and her insecurity in relation to Numè's self-confidence. Additionally, social critiques aimed at
nineteenth-century Japanese favoritism towards male children operate
within the narrator's distanced description of the two old fathers who love
Orito more than Numè. Another chapter begins by detailing one of
Sinclair's legal cases involving an unscrupulous missionary, and Watanna
supplements this more overt indictment of organized Western/Christian efforts at domination with several references to Buddhist temples and wor-
shipping practices. Contemporary critics might also be pleased by the
narrative politics deployed in this novel by which a lower-class geisha girl
named Koto (upon whom Mrs. Davis and all other American women look
down in suspicion) intervenes in the triangle to bring about the novel's cli-
max. In quintessential Austenian closure, Koto and her new husband are
Numè and Sinclair's "most frequent visitors," as the narrator situates the
marriage in community approval and friendly warmth in words reminiscent
of the conclusion of *Emma:* "the predictions of a small band of true friends
. . . were fully answered in the perfect happiness of the union" (Watanna
220; Austen 813).

Despite these and many other structural features of cultural sensitivity, features that demonstrate Watanna's confidence in bending cultural stereotypes while attempting to reformulate generic standards, readers sense in the descriptions of her heroines an authorial frustration in her hyper-conscious adherence to convention. We can read Watanna's heroine as a culmination of innocent, beautiful, and virtuous sentimental heroines, which were revised by the new strong-willed and resourceful American female protagonists of the mid-to-later nineteenth century.[11] As we read, we feel that we have encountered both Numè and Cleo before. Repeated formulas were part of this period in women's fiction that ushered in increased levels of literacy and the rampant creation of new publications.[12] In this publishing climate, variations in genre withstand subtle modulations in subject matter through the characterization of reassuringly similar heroines who personify the necessary feminine virtues and personality traits that are most likely to win reader sympathy and book sales (Papashvily 110-133). Numè Watanabe enacts a narrative performance of ethnic identity as her character blends discursive elements of nineteenth-century domestic femininity with some stereotypes and cultural mores associated with Asian women. As Eve Oishi notes, Watanna's heroines "match, in many ways, the popular stereotypes of Asian femininity—childlike, naïve, and charmingly exotic" (xix).

Numè represents the revisionary feminine template ushered in by American domestic fiction of the late nineteenth-century that provided a substitute for the dully virtuous and pious heroine of sentimental fiction. She is not simply virtuous, but she winces from having to be so conventional while demonstrating her free will and ability to rebel. She is not only beautiful, but passionate, clever, and charming as well. She stands out from a locally envisioned subset of cultural femininity: "Numè was a very peculiar child" the narrator tells us (Watanna 7). In addition, she maintains an already operative tradition in late nineteenth century feminine ethnicity in that the narrator marks her entry into a heterosocial context (or market) by casting her ethnic difference from dominant cultural ideals of beauty in vague terms. Observing her "unstudied grace" in a Western gown, Sinclair only notices that she appears different from other women; he cannot tell that she is Asian, much less that she is Japanese (85).

Emma D. Kelley-Hawkins and Pauline Hopkins, two nineteenth-century African American women writers, also described their heroines in race-free, yet insistently relational, terms within a shared language of sentimentalizing physical beauty. Recent African American feminist scholarship suggests that ethnic women writers' racially ambiguous descriptions of heroines in the nineteenth century are in fact political performances of blackness, which elicit universal reader sympathy by pointing to qualities of beauty that transcend race.[13] Likewise, Sinclair's professed hatred and distrust of Japanese women, coupled with Numè's inability to seem like other Japanese women, and Sinclair's regard for her in spite of his initial prejudice, may be read as problematic or indicative of her as a model minority, less demonstrative of objectionable "Asian" qualities. However, in a maneuver executed repeatedly in the novel, Watanna diffuses Sinclair's anti-Asian sentiment by having Numè tease him openly and good-naturedly about his dislike for Japanese women, an act that results in Sinclair's subsequent bafflement and sheepishness (Watanna 87). Watanna's narrative move here simultaneously allows her heroine a significant amount of agency as well as introducing the prospect of romance between Numè and Sinclair after at first seeming to discredit it.

On the other hand, the white Cleo's reprehensible behavior towards both her lovers causes the reader some confusion within this presumably safe and familiar genre. She is not a loveable and predictably larger than life heroine, but she is drawn instead in the shape of human fallibility; her most significant flaw is her frequent use of her unchecked power as the ideal womanly object. Cleo is a predecessor of Edith Wharton's Lily Bart, fashioned in a time during which readers were becoming familiar with the marketability of an upper-class, white woman's personality and charms. Her characterization demonstrates Watanna's conscious engagement with the craft of writing and creating heroines for mainstream consumption. Our author's need to articulate her white heroine's character in unique narrative terms suggests the pressure of formulaic publishing market and marriage market dynamics on her writing. The reader first learns about Cleo in the remarkably titled chapter "Who Can Analyze a Coquette?," in which the narrator is at a loss for words even while attempting a simple description of Cleo's physical beauty: "Of the rest of her face, you do not need to know, for when one is young and has wonderful eyes, shiny, wavy hair and even features, be sure that one is very beautiful" (16).

This account suppresses and also hints at an anxiety about entering into a mode that even in this nineteenth-century moment seems overdone to the narrator, who understands that the reader must be appeased by some appraisal of the heroine's necessarily superlative beauty. As the sentence enumerates stock attributes of this beauty, the narrator performs an ironic commentary on romance even while asking it to be consumed as a romantic text. The list proves the writer's knowledge of the necessary elements for a romantic heroine, and the distanced ironic tone achieves the merit of discernment by mocking such obvious conventions. This attempt at characterization in the face of generic tradition and convention is one example of the narrator's extreme self-consciousnuess of her readers' and publisher's expectations for heroine construction throughout the novel. Cleo's character demonstrates the powerful weight of tradition in such passages and in the chapter's thematic critique of power, attraction, love, and marketability. Cleo's character achieves a complexity similar to Lily Bart's entanglement with the market context of love and marriage in Wharton's *The House of Mirth* (1905); not content to pursue one man in hopes of achieving her vocation of marriage, Cleo is a relentless, mechanical love object, sure of success where she hopes to win favor.

By comparing Cleo to Lily Bart, I am suggesting that this frustrated and subtly anxious delineation of superlative heroines in the face of generic tradition—a tradition at once cheapened by male dismissal and popular success and marketable in its formulaic incorporation of beauty, virtue, and feminine self-actualization—goes beyond that of an ethnic other attempting to write in the master's language. I am attempting to show here the place of ethnicity within the larger, anxiety-ridden project of heroine construction. Ethnicity, in Watanna's narrative schema, is an exoticized feminine attribute that contributes to the unique quality of an object in the marriage market. Although the politics of this type of ethnic identity may be problematic by contemporary standards, its narrative assimilation into the marriage market plot suggests that ethnic identity can be performed in ways that are referential and relational to dominant cultural mores and is not rigidly fixed within a solid ground of experiential, empirical, and cultural difference. To delve more deeply into the possibilities offered by this model of ethnicity, and to understand Watanna's written voice further as a response to a context of marriage market and publishing market concerns, I will turn briefly to her autobiography, *Me*.

ONOTO WATANNA'S *ME: A BOOK OF REMEMBRANCE*

A curious relationship between the ambition to publish and the desire for heterosexual romantic fulfillment is at the center of Onoto Watanna's 1915 anonymously published autobiography *Me: A Book of Remembrance,* a work that details professional and personal development in the sentimental mode. In the text, Canadian Nora Ascough, a girl of seventeen, leaves her large family in Montreal and travels first to Jamaica and then to the United States to pursue her dream of becoming a writer of popular fiction. From the beginning of the narrative, Nora pairs the idea of romantic fruition and literary market success together:

> I had always believed there were the *strains of genius* somewhere hidden in me; I had always lived in a little dream world of my own, wherein, *beautiful and courted,* I moved among the elect of the earth. Now I had given vivid proof of some *unusual power.* (4; emphasis mine)

Watanna's use of the words "beautiful and courted" evoke the dynamics of a socially and culturally sanctioned marriage typically depicted in sentimental and domestic fiction, a system by which the heroine demonstrates a significant, "unusual power" of attracting male suitors. The phrase "strains of genius," on the other hand, signifies a remarkably productive creative ability—an attribute that rarely, if ever, factors into the conventional evaluative schema of the marriage market within sentimental romantic fiction. Nora's visions for her future thus incorporate a narrative code through the text's invocation of the *kunstlerroman,* or the tale of the artist's development, while also employing a language of fairy-tale potential. Her desire for "unusual power" also announces a modern, syncretic female desire for vocational and interpersonal success—an early example of the cultural idea of a woman's need to "have it all." While Nora acknowledges the force of her "little dream world" in this passage, she prepares her readers for reports of her actual literary success later in the text. This description of "little dream world" serves multiple purposes in Nora's introduction of herself. First, it indicates her emotive, imaginative strength as a heroine and narrator, much in the same way Watanna's sister Sui Sin Far does in "Leaves" as she reflects on her "withdrawn life of thought and musing" and her writing career (Sui Sin Far 290). Watanna's description of her "little" world also introduces readers to the female subject's deepest desire through an ironic lens that almost mockingly takes note of the young Nora's sense of self-consequence. This ego suffers from the mortification of rejection letters from publishers and the disillusionment caused in her adulthood after Nora realizes that her lover is a married man.

In *Me* the narrator conflates romantic fruition with career success at several other points in the text. For example, Nora spends her first evening in Chicago's YWCA in loneliness as she contemplates the idea that all of the other girls there had "positions and friends and beaux," a triumvirate of subjective success she repeats several times in her story (116). As she discusses her early days as a reporter in Jamaica, Nora is always quick to signify the fact that men find her desirable: "I never danced, though lots of men asked me" (47). When her gruff first employer, another elderly father figure for Nora in the text, finally begins to "approve of" her, Nora emphasizes his change of heart towards her by noting that he finally publishes a poem of hers in the paper (43). She notes gleefully, "those same fierce eyes actually beamed upon me." Finally, in announcing her first acceptance letter from a magazine editor, Nora teases the reader by introducing a "glorious day late in the month of November—to be exact, it was November 24," (249). Nora then adds quickly that the day is significant in her life not because her lover, Mr. Hamilton, paid her another visit, but because it marks her first success as a writer (249).

Watanna's autobiography proffers a duality between marriage and publishing-market concerns while suffusing the import of Nora's non-Western heritage, and this quality also distinguishes the text from her bicultural romance novels. As Eve Oishi notes, Watanna chooses not to specify her mother's nationality and race, despite the fact that she repeatedly mentions the fact that her father is an English, Oxford-educated man (Oishi xiii; Watanna 26). In fact, young Nora testifies to her literary education by claiming a familiarity with "Dickens, George Eliot, and Sir Walter Scott" (26). *Me*, thus, is not only a dubious source for details on Asian American cultural politics, its structure also is made up of the narrative gray area between personal and political, fantasy and reality, and fiction and biography. In exploring these tensions, however, one is better able to understand this early Asian American writer's conflicted articulation of ethnic identity. That is, patterns within Watanna's fictional and autobiographic work reveal an undercurrent of ambivalence, which, I argue, is not due solely to the fact that she is a Eurasian writer for a white audience but more due to her ambivalence as a woman writer striving to attain "unusual power" in a literary marketplace dominated by men and accessed by other more fortunate and talented women. Her ethnic identity, in fact, provides her with unique material ("stories I was writing about my mother's land") from which to draw in creating new stories to send to the editors of North American publications (176). However, the specific details of her non-white ancestry are not important in this structurally conventional exploration of romantic and commercial female self-potential. Nora walks the line between romantic fulfillment and the pursuit of vocation in ways similar to anglo female characters like Jo March in *Little Women*, Jane Eyre, and several later heroines to be discussed in this study, including Jessie Fauset's light-skinned, African American Angela Murray in *Plum Bun*.

Scholars skeptical of Watanna's contributions towards developing a poetics or even a politics of ethnic identity might point to her dismissal of her Asian heritage: "I myself was dark and foreign-looking, but the blond type I adored. In all my most fanciful imaginings and dreams I had always been golden-haired and blue-eyed" (41). This statement occurs in the text after Nora's deeply prejudicial treatment of an important black Jamaican citizen, a man who is in love with her but for whom she feels "a sudden panic of almost instinctive fear" (40). Nora's unabashed and candid admissions of racist sentiment strike today's reader as culturally insensitive and certainly problematic because her remarks seem to condone an intra-ethnic hierarchy that places the "dark foreigner" from a "far distant land" as more superior to blackness in a scale favoring white Western ideals. *Me* consists of narrative moments that are politically conflicted as the protagonist reckons with her "vague" sense that "all men were equal as men," and the fact that her "own mother was a foreigner" (40). It also, however, provides an anxious commentary of female potential in an increasingly industrial society dominated by male talent and power, a society in which women must either marry well or develop a signature trade or vocation. The text thus enacts the ambivalence of an identity in the making—an ambivalence stemming from Nora's need both to be accepted and revered by society but also her need to be publicly recognized and affirmed as an individual. In the guise of a text about a "golden-haired" girl with unfulfilled potential, this autobiography of a Eurasian literary foremother eschews the thematic complexities we might expect from a bicultural narrative voice, while it follows instead the pattern of a structurally conventional narrative that we may feel compelled only to read as another anglo subject's development as a woman and writer.

Yet for its time, *Me*'s depiction of feminine independence seems highly unconventional as well. Eve Oishi points out the fact that among all of Watanna's works, her autobiography is her "only book that does not end with the romantic closure of marriage" (Oishi xvi). The text's sense of conventionality is due largely to its emphasis on Nora's sentimental infatuation with Mr. Hamilton, an older, wealthy, married man who offers her literary patronage after only meeting her briefly. These dynamics—the pairing of artistic talent with personal beauty and the search for success in the turn-of-the-century urban setting of Chicago—remind readers of the relationship between Carrie and Mr. Hurstwood in Dreiser's *Sister Carrie* (1900). Watanna rather flatly draws out the potential for romantic scope between the two lovers by coding Hamilton's belief in Nora's literary talent as a sign of his obvious, yet unstated, love for her. Hamilton's anguished reticence and Nora's blind regard for a man she knows little about can only function effectively in the sentimental mode. By detailing Nora's career and social anxieties, Watanna steers her readers towards the understanding that writing and love, two realistically separate concerns, have everything to do with each other in her narrative world. We can thus read Nora's real challenges as a woman and minority writer as romantic struggles. Note the following passage of dialogue between Nora and Mr. Hamilton:

> "Would you take my stories?"
>
> "You better believe I would," he said.

"Why?"

"Well, why do you suppose?"

"Because you think my stories are good or because you like me—which?" (203)

Mr. Hamilton's approval of Nora's stories provides an outlet for the sexual tension between them as Hamilton feigns patronage and fatherly interest in her creative and educational welfare while Nora playfully interprets and re-interprets the layered meanings of his words. The melodrama permeating their interaction with each other becomes the central conflict of the text, as Nora's ultimate decision to move to New York for her literary career occurs only after she finally realizes that Hamilton is married. Although Watanna's *Me* has moments that are more complicated than others, this overall plot structure implies that because she fails at securing the husband of her choice, she must redirect her efforts at her writing career. Thus even in an autobiography of a writer, the narrative focus remains fixed more firmly on romantic intrigue as in domestic or sentimental novels. In this way, *Me*'s structural energies also demonstrate the versatility of literary form as cultural ideas of femininity, ethnicity, and professionalism are distilled into romance. While Onoto Watanna's writings are willing to flirt more obviously with generic conventions of romance and sentimentality that are associated with anglo literary traditions even as they consistently revise certain tropes of romance, her older sister Sui Sin Far writes marital dramas that inscribe themes of greater cultural sensitivity. These themes in no way prove that Sui Sin Far was less conflicted than her sister about articulating ethnic identity to a mainstream audience, yet the political manifestations of that ambivalence have secured her a safer place in the Asian American canon. In the next section, I will challenge the pattern of scholarly favoritism of Sui Sin Far's work by pointing to narrative tensions in her short stories that fall short of political concerns.

SUI SIN FAR'S *MRS. SPRING FRAGRANCE AND OTHER STORIES*

If we study the fiction of both Eaton sisters simultaneously, we glimpse an elusive mechanism by which ideas of love and marriage are linked to authorial concerns about the publishing marketplace. While Winnifred (Onoto Watanna) published over a dozen novels and supported her family with her earnings, her sister Edith (Sui Sin Far) never published a novel, and although she published in reputable magazines, she never enjoyed the financial security of her sister. Sui Sin Far's legacy lingers today as scholars and critics pour over her stories and articles in search of understanding their multivalent layers, while some regard the more commercially successful Onoto Watanna as a sort of traitor to Asian American letters. Scholarly consideration of Sui Sin Far's body of work focuses on her willingness to report the plight of Chinese immigrants who struggled to live as Americans in the midst of strong prejudice, disenfranchisement, material hardship, and the family stress resulting therein. One of Sui Sin Far's most renowned stories is "In the Land of the Free," recently anthologized in *Imagining America* (Amy Ling and Wesley Brown, eds.). The story outlines a worst-case scenario of an immigrating Chinese couple and their infant son, who is seized by American officials and reared by missionaries. Thematically, the narrative exposes the schemes of anonymous arbiters of the exclusionary, exploiting nuances of the American immigration acts. The story's conclusion expresses one of the most powerful fears experienced by the adults in Sui Sin Far's fiction: that a child reared in the land of opportunity will grow to resent the homeland and consider his own parents beneath him. As Lui Kanghi in Sui Sin Far's "Her Chinese Husband" testifies, the smartest and most capable among Western educated Chinese youth lose face in their communities if they do not properly appreciate their Chinese heritage (Sui Sin Far 82).

Along with "In the Land of the Free," those of Sui Sin Far's stories, articles, and essays that overtly articulate social and political critique—including "A White Woman Who Married a Chinese" and "Leaves from a Mental Portfolio"—receive the most critical attention. As Dominika Ferens has asserted in "Tangled Kites," this preoccupation with the surface political themes occludes the richness and variety of her work, ignoring the potential of "other, no less interesting stories . . . that account for a greater range of Sui Sin Far's writings" (Ferens 118). Citing the scholarship of Dorrine Kondo and David Palumbo-Liu on race, genre, and narrative, which insists that "the minority subject" uses "strategies of accommodation and resistance, inserting new elements and modifying former ones," Ferens traces Sui Sin Far's texts through three late nineteenth-early twentieth-century magazines. Each publication calls for a certain degree of narrative navigation between the author's agenda for racial equity and the expectations of an American magazine audience varying from conservative homemakers and their children to liberal free-thinkers. Ferens's descriptions of Sui Sin Far's maneuverings among concerns of genre, her audience's expectations, and her own creative agenda begin to dispel the aura of this foremother of Asian American fiction.[14] In a note at the end of her article, Ferens attempts loosely to name the force responsible for the unclassifiable nature of Sui Sin Far's fiction: "When trying to systematize her views, we repeatedly encounter moments of ambivalence.

For instance, her lasting involvement in Chinatown's missionary societies did not prevent her from repeatedly questioning the movement's ethnocentric assumption" (144). Ferens goes on to add that even though Sui Sin Far worked diligently to foster a writing career, she "considered her predicament anomalous and did not advocate careers for women"(144). By digging into some of the romantic forces at work in Sui Sin Far's fiction, I will use this assumption of ambivalence as a point of entry into those less discussed elements and implications of some of her more familiar, as well as less popular, stories. I will reveal the mechanics of romance operating beneath the surface of Sui Sin Far's seemingly political stories, and contextualize her narrative performance of Asian ethnicity as an ambivalent negotiation of her political agenda, the generic standards of serious political fiction, and the exploration of romantic fantasy in her writing.

The differences between Onoto Watanna's Japanese-American courtship novels and the seemingly more political short stories of her sister Sui Sin Far revolve around strict definitions of genre. However, in the fiction of both sisters, the narrative voice fluctuates between social commentary and sentimental description. Watanna manipulates genre by using conventional thematics while revising the structure of the courtship and domestic novels by including anti-anglocentric moments within the narrative. On the other hand, Sui Sin Far's use of the short story accords her subject matter a sense of political novelty and modern irresolution. Carol Roh-Spaulding has asserted that Sui Sin Far's choice of genre reflects her commitment to presenting a balanced view of ethnic identity and that the medium of the short story allows her to present "a variety of ethnic stances in relation to Chinese American identity, such that no single implied ethnic version of the author predominates" (156). Despite her evasion of the generic standards of the sentimental novel, many critics have pointed to instances of exoticism and orientalism present in Sui Sin Far's stories. Such lapses are read as a cultural ambivalence resulting from her unique position as an insider/outsider minority subject, the demands of a North American publishing market, as well as Sui Sin Far's conflicted feelings of self-loathing in the midst of self-assertion. Some well known theoretical models describing this internal conflict of cultural and racial identity are found in the writings of Franz Fanon and Homi Bhabha whose works provide the field of postcolonial studies with some of its central tenets. Bhabha views ambivalence as a collective feeling, a force operative in the project of "narrating the nation" (Bhabha 2). He explains that the social and political project of creating a sense of national identity involves an ambivalent cultural writing of one unified nationalist perspective through the thrust of modernity that overwrites an uncertain moment of origin and undetermined parameters of a unified community. While the idea of nation-writing as an anxious process bolsters the framework of my analysis here, my observations of ambivalence in Sui Sin Far's writing invoke the challenges and concerns women writers have mediated individually in writing romantic fiction. I will posit a relationship between the marriage market and the publishing market to try and filter out the force of ambivalence in these texts, and I will trace some surprising similarities between the two sisters' writings, similarities which converge around a shared anxiety about love and marriage and writing about love and marriage.

Despite the specificities of personal conflict and anxiety—whether they are marital concerns or anxieties of publishing—latent in the narrative fissures of Sui Sin Far's stories, my analysis points to tensions in her work which suggest influences and motivations that are less political than current scholarship on her work suggests. Roh-Spaulding exposes those narrative tensions that are indicative of Sui Sin Far's ambivalent assertions of her "mixed-race identity," moments which not only challenge the confident championing of Chinese cultural politics ascribed to her stories but that also reveal "the insufficiency and instability of ethnic catergorization" (157, 164). "Contrary to a multiculturalist perspective that regards Sui Sin Far as a turn-of the-century hero for the Chinese," writes Roh-Spaulding, "her stories complicate traditional narratives of assimilation and amalgamation with tales of failed cultural mixing and conflicted identity" (173). The "failed cultural mixing" Roh-Spaulding mentions provides a useful entry point into what I view as Sui Sin Far's suppressed system of idealized unions, a system that I see not so much as highlighting the failure of culturally syncretic identity, but rather as subtly fantasizing about the possibilities for cultural harmony through stories that employ scenarios of romance.

Many of the short stories in the contemporary edition of Sui Sin Far's early twentieth- century writings, *Mrs. Spring Fragrance and Other Stories,* reveal her apprehension about perfect marital matches—ideal pairings between marital partners. In her title story for example, Sui Sin Far goes to some length to detail a symbolic harmony between Chinese and American signifiers of identity, suggesting the import of the reader's evaluation of Mr. and Mrs. Spring's marriage as well as the marital match Mrs. Spring facilitates later in the story. As readers, we are called upon to admire the clever Puck-like ability of this heroine who learns the "American language" and understands the American cultural mindset with such fluency. Noting the "neatly arranged plot, unerring dialogue, satisfying romance, and likeable heroines," Xiao-huang Yin states that the "impact of Jane Austen" on this story is "conspicuous" (Yin 91).

Adding to the story's participation in transcultural exchange is its comparison and contrasting of the nuances of courtship and marriage between two differently conceptualized cultures in the story. Characters participate in cross-cultural discourse as they provide a balance of cultural perspectives. Will Carmen, a young white American man, enters the scene at convenient moments to serve as a contrast to Mr. Spring's more traditionally Chinese point-of-view. Carmen states sensitively: "Oh, yes, I have no doubt that in China it is different" (Sui Sin Far 24). And while Mrs. Spring and her young protége Laura are both engrossed in a discussion, which we read filtered through Tennyson's poetic sentiment—"'Tis better to have loved and lost—," Mr. Spring can make no sense of the meaning of the poetry. These and several other instances suggest the story's structural preoccupation in maintaining a balance of Chinese and American perspectives—a harmonious match—towards which Sui Sin Far's others stories also strive. More importantly, in this idealization of balanced perspectives, we glimpse the creation of ethnicity; in order for Will Carmen's character to represent a breezy, liberated American perspective, Mr. Spring's rhetoric demonstrates that of a conflicted Chinese man.

"Mrs. Spring Fragrance" and its companion story "The Inferior Woman" are the two works which most overtly deal with righting potentially erroneous marital matches, and this plot dynamic provides the background for a stronger rhetorical preoccupation with creating harmony and ideal balance. While we experience Mrs. Spring's skill in ushering in the union of two second-generation Chinese marriage partners against the wishes of their parents, the narrative reveals the match between Laura and her lover as more appropriate for its context than a match between the Americanized Laura and the less culturally-assimilated son of a Chinese government official her parents would prefer her to marry. Sui Sin Far convinces us of the correctness of the match by using signifiers of a balanced Eastern and Western cultural identity. Laura goes by an "American" name and has had a moderately Americanized upbringing; her lover Kai Tzu is as "ruddy and stalwart as any young Westerner," and he plays baseball and sings "Western" songs (Sui Sin Far 17). Similarly, in describing the Springs's marriage, the narrator tells us that they are both "Americanized," although Mrs. Spring is "even more" so. Sui Sin Far creates a sense of poetic legitimacy in their marriage by supportive details such as having them ultimately both quote Tennyson to each other and having Mrs. Spring muse upon the wonderful fact that even though her marriage to Mr. Spring was arranged, she and he both fell in love with each other's pictures before their marriage (25). The gift of a jadestone pendant serves as a symbol for the syncretic blend of

Chinese and American love, and it signifies the closest sense of romantic intrigue between the two Springs. Only after their match is evaluated by Mr. Spring's newfound appreciation for both the American and Chinese qualities in his wife can they participate in this culturally encoded moment of romantic gift-giving.[15]

"The Inferior Woman," a companion story to "Mrs. Spring Fragrance," is seemingly another story about matches and mismatches in the marriage market; however, it provides us perhaps with a better model for the structural manifestations of an anxiety for the perfect match. The mismatched lovers this time are white Americans; Mrs. Spring once again intervenes by matching young Will with the "Inferior Woman" against the initial judgment of Will's mother, who wants her son to marry the educated, articulate, suffragette—the "Superior Woman"—(29–35). Sui Sin Far complicates matters by making the "Inferior Woman" (Alice Winthrop) refuse to marry Will until his mother can welcome her into his family. Thus, the real obstacle in the plot involves the challenge of proving Alice's subjective worth as a young, marriageable woman. Sui Sin Far draws Alice's character in almost impossibly scrupulously ethical terms, reporting her battle with "right and wrong," and offering the reader a study of Alice's well-versed critique of feminism in her letter to the "Superior Woman." This description of Alice demonstrates Sui Sin Far's fixation with narrative balance in characterization, a trend most obvious in the philosophical statements her characters utter. Although Alice and her marital rival are both white women, Sui Sin Far's characterization of both is painstakingly balanced, and her deliberation over female representation is analogous to her preoccupation with cultural blending in other stories involving Chinese characters. We cannot avoid the thematic point in the story, which is presented when the Superior Woman's dialogues with her mother about Alice Winthrop's allegedly morally-compromised rise to independence. At this moment we witness one of the unique characteristics of Sui Sin Far's fiction: the self-abnegation of insightful females who are unwilling to participate or support a marriage market that values superficial qualities in women. While furthering a language of harmonious balance, these women usually offer last-minute advice or reproof to Chinese men who cannot, or do not, understand the value of their Chinese wives' more subtle charms. In "The Wisdom of the New" our Chinese immigrant heroine loses her sanity because she is jealous of her husband's supposed preference for Adah Carlton, a white woman who finally advises Wou Senkwei to cater to the demands of his wife. Another woman named "Adah," in "The Americanizing of Pau Tsu," harshly reprimands Pau's husband Wan Lin Fo for trying to turn his wife into an American woman. This delicate balance between Americaness and Chineseness occurs in the rhetorical blend in Sui Sin Far's description of personality traits, character evaluation from another supporting character's point-of-view, and narrative commentary in the third-person point-of-view.

In preserving a sense of balance, Sui Sin Far objectifies her heroines in accordance with some dominant Asian and American cultural and ethical codes of conduct even as her central aim works to destabilize a patriarchal mode of evaluating women in relation to each other. Sui Sin Far's narrators sincerely admire the selfless sympathy on the part of women in "superior" standing who refuse to concede that they are more desirable or marketable than outcast females or women who are cultural minorities. Mrs. Spring sings the praises of the "Superior Woman's" goodness at the end of the story, wishing her unborn daughter to be like her. The characterization of the "Superior" and "Inferior" women suggests that both women posses an equivalent sense of integrity. Sui Sin Far's inability to vilify either woman is significant for several reasons, most importantly because it confounds our sense of genre as we read. The lack of rivalry between the two women prevents the story from being read as a simple marital melodrama.[16] Compensating for its basic marriage plot, Sui Sin Far intersperses some timely social and political dialogue into her characters' speeches. By characterizing culturally and politically sympathetic women in positions of power, she also adds credibility to her underdog characters. This strategy complicates cultural stereotypes about race and nationality. Alice Winthrop's desire to marry traditionally even when her lover does not require it suggests Sui Sin Far's attempt to diffuse commonly held assumptions about Eastern and Western marriage for her readers. Quite subtly, Sui Sin Far introduces here an idealized notion of having familial approval and culturally sanctioned marriages in white America, as opposed to only in Chinatown. These tensions in the story demonstrate Sui Sin Far's carefully blended vision of balance at the cultural, social, and personal levels. Structural features, like Miss Evebrook's rather unnatural advocacy of Alice Winthrop, serve as the scales of a unique evaluative system created by the stories. Mrs. Spring's character is a narrative mechanism, a respected example cultural balance, by which mismatches are corrected and set right in her community. Sui Sin Far's main point about the value of dynamic perspectives and traditions is unmistakable in her description of each character and its matching principle or point-of-view. Most of her stories strive for this perspective of balance. These "multiple point-of-views," writes Dominika Ferens in "Tangled Kites," "allow for reciprocal criticism by people of different cultural backgrounds instead of privileging the one-way hierarchical gaze" (Ferens 131).

Clearly, such forces in these stories indicate much effort at balancing cultural perspectives and diffusing stereotypes, but they also point to an anxiety about marital dynamics and writing about marriage.

One could argue that the central force of anxiety in many of these stories stems from Sui Sin Far's difficult task of representing marriage-worthy Chinese women and Chinese marital practices to an unsympathetic American audience. However, the plot of "Mrs. Spring Fragrance" and "The Inferior Woman" and their accompanying layers of culturally-sensitive commentary demonstrate not her anxiety but her confidence in cultural representation, and these stories prove her a master of perspective within the genre of the short story. Sui Sin Far's scenarios of idealized marriages amongst immigrants within Mrs. *Spring Fragrance and Other Stories* and the fact that she never published a novel (although she was writing one that she never finished) suggest instead that Eaton's central anxiety had more to do with writing about marriage itself than with the representation of her chosen cultural community.[17]

In her literary biography of Sui Sin Far, Annette White-Parks highlights Sui Sin Far's textual articulation of Eurasian identity as her predominant authorial challenge, one that conveniently places discussions of matrimony to the side. While White-Parks provides an exhaustive history of the writer (considering the relative lack of documentation of her life), she views the fact that Eaton called herself a "serious and sober-minded spinster" as a simple sacrifice the author made to her literary career (White-Parks, *Sui Sin Far* 40). White-Parks briskly summarizes Sui Sin Far's opinions on romance and marriage, treating the author's "decision to not marry" as a political and artistic statement without contextualizing forces in her personal life that would explain such a decision. It may very well be that such information does not exist. White-Parks does speculate that Sui Sin Far found the idea of marriage complicated, especially in light of turn-of-the-century sentiment against interracial marriages (38–39). She provides an account of Sui Sin Far's persistent efforts to have her work published by North American magazines, efforts that necessitated correspondences with the male editors of these magazines in which Sui Sin Far, with her "fragile self-image," positioned herself as a "diminutive" woman needing tutelage (42). While White-Parks points separately to Sui Sin Far's overwhelming ambition to find market success, her fear of entering into an interracial marriage, her modest sense of self, and her decision not to marry, she does not suggest that these forces coalesce and impact Eaton's narrative voice in any significant way. For White-Parks, Sui Sin Far's writings demonstrate the tensions between her political and cultural ambivalence as a passably white Eurasian woman. But even White-Parks's casual description of Sui Sin Far's ideas on love and marriage, in light of her other observations about the author's literary desires and fears of interracial marriage, suggest to me a more turbulent inner self than Sui Sin Far's public image as a committed champion of Chinese rights.

Certainly, both political and personal concerns feed each other in these stories, but Sui Sin Far's marital and authorial apprehensiveness may engage with the structural, rather than the strict thematic, levels of her fiction and thereby demonstrate less resolvable and less political instances of ambivalence. The stories in this collection are remarkably similar and cohesive, and yet there are a few outstanding narratives that distinguish themselves by resisting generic classification. Stories like "Tian Shan's Kindred Spirit," "The Smuggling of Tie-Co," and "The Chinese Lily," I see as indicative of Sui Sin Far's unresolved narrative fantasies, adding to the rest of her more realist stories a less manageable yet short-lived expression of romance. Both "Tian Shan" and "The Smuggling" depict cross-dressing women who courageously enter the male domain of border-crossing intrigue to be with the men they love. "Tian Shan" ends happily and reunites two star-crossed Chinese- American lovers in a jail cell that houses immigrant code violators who are now bound back for China. "The Smuggling of Tie-Co" ends with the rather melodramatic sacrifice of a Chinese woman disguised as a man who jumps into a river to save the hero (a white cowboy type of a man named Jack Fabian), who tries to smuggle her to safety into New York. Almost like Onoto Watanna's bold Miss Numè, Sui Sin Far's Tie-Co awkwardly yet candidly states her feelings of affection for Jack Fabian before killing herself: "I like you" her "boyish voice sounding clear and sweet in the wet woods" (Sui Sin Far 107). Tie-Co then unsexes himself, revealing the fact that his/her smuggling is but a ruse to spend time with Fabian. Both stories obliquely tackle the problematic Chinese Exclusion acts and racist immigration policies by casting heroes who courageously, although not always successfully, combat the system. Eaton also clarifies the fact that Fabian, a white man, smuggles men across the border only to make money. But at the end of the story, the narrators (Fabian's disciples) reveal that he stops and muses over the "mystery" of Tie-Co now and then, a fact that softens the archetype of unscrupulous white opportunism.

The story's political commentary operates, however, in the midst of a curious, quasi-mythical narrative involving a woman dressed as a man, similar to Maxine Hong Kingston's use of the Fa Mu Lan story in *The Woman Warrior* (1976). As the phantasmagoric second chapter in Kingston's contemporary memoir reveals, the narration of reality and romance intermingle in complex and trancultural ways. In Kingston's version of the Chinese story of "Fa Mu Lan," the heroine's accomplishments are deliberately overstated and indicative of wish-fulfillment, and her desires seem to balance cultural ideals of womanly duties and manly strength. She falls in love with her husband, who is chosen for her by her elders, and at this point the language seems lyrically romantic and sentimental. Like the convenience of falling in love with the picture of one's betrothed in the *Mrs. Spring Fragrance* stories, Kingston's matrimonial moment is tinged with a wistful tone. The narrator, "Maxine," remarks that her betrothed is after all her beloved playmate from childhood who has come now to seek her out (Kingston 39). Kingston's contemporary narrative entertains these concerns only momentarily, although the brief instance of romance signifies the role of fantasy in a memoir that has achieved standing as a work of political import since its publication.

Sui Sin Far also enters the marriage-plot mode tangentially, using the frame of post-marital dilemmas to delineate Chinese culture and a sort of Asianess by showing brides raised by their mothers-in-law, conflicts of child-rearing philosophies, and obstacles in the form of cross-cultural and cross-generational disagreement impeding otherwise well-matched unions. Unlike Onoto Watanna, neither Sui Sin Far nor Kingston (nor most of the Asian American writers discussed in this study) involves her heroines in the more typical internal conflict of choosing the right man to marry—an integral feature of the Western courtship and domestic novel. However, narrative moments like the dramatic confession and sacrifice of Tie-Co and, later, Fa Mu Lan's brief lyrical exultation over her fated husband, infuse their stories with a level of fantasy that begs to be translated into a language more synonymous with the romantic longing contained more visibly in the courtship novel. Consider the end of Sui Sin Far's "Tian Shan," in which Fin Fan and Tian Shan are reunited in an idyllic moment in space and time that promises to take them into a friendlier future, as wife and husband in China where neither will have to worry about legal codes or parental approval (Sui Sin Far 125). In this story, as well as in "The Smuggling of Tie-Co," the expression of romantic fantasy and adventure are culturally coded via narrative moments of cross-dressing.

Readers of nineteenth-century domestic fiction know that by gender-bending a heroine proves her subjective worth in a heterosexual patriarchal marriage market, as the act of cross-dressing proves her social compatibility with male marital partners and distinguishes her from nameless other women.[18] More recent Chinese American texts, discussed by Sau-ling Cynthia Wong in her article "Ethnicizing Gender: An Explication of Sexuality as Sign in Chinese Immigrant Literature," outline instances of performed masculinity which play a role in deploying culturally-specific assumptions of ethnicity. For example, the contemporary immigrant stories surveyed by Wong all delineate "Americanized" Chinese women who are masculine in contrast to a textually configured ideal of traditional Chinese femininity. Thus, these texts use "signs" of masculinity (assertive behavior, physical prowess) to connote white American behavior from the perspective of the male Chinese immigrant who is consequently feminized upon arrival and acculturation in the United States. According to Wong, these stories use gender-bending to represent the shifting contexts and codes of cultural power in which a reasonably self-assured Chinese male loses his sense of self as he situates himself into a new dominant culture in which he learns to conceptualize his damaged self-esteem in terms of gender. I refer to Wong's ideas here because of the diligent analysis she conducts of "signs." Through the use of signs, Wong asserts, narratives often have an implicit representational economy, which in different contexts uses a given set of cues (here gender and ethnicity) to elicit desired effects. For my purposes, the instances of adult cross-dressing in Sui Sin Far's writings signify not only transgression of gender roles but also ambivalent crossings into the generic conventions and demands of romance. This type of heroine construction veils fleeting expressions of romantic desire in moments of social and cultural criticism. As discussed above, Onoto Watanna's novels also center on "peculiar" girls who grow up strong-willed and tomboyish and who are candid and unfeminine at times in their social graces.

Sui Sin Far, as Kingston does later, displaces the more overt romantic themes of courtship anxieties and premarital drama by concentrating on the connection and camaraderie between men and women who fight injustice together. Thus, Sui Sin Far furthers an Asian brand of romantic heroine construction by outlining courage and faithfulness in a woman's service to a man she loves without having to resort to an anglo literary schema of proposals in drawing rooms and secret engagements. This Asian brand of romantic signification is, however, similar to late nineteenth-century African American literary practices of using marriage plots as representative of black domestic values and black identity—patterns discussed at length in the work of Ann duCille, Cheryl Wall, and Claudia Tate. In *Domestic Allegories of Political Desire,* Tate states "Black women's post-Reconstruction domestic novels aspired to intervene in the racial and sexual schemes of the public world of the turn-of-the-century United States by plotting new stories about the personal lives of black women and men" (9). I do not deny that similar negotiations of political and public identities inform the representation of Asian American private life in Sui Sin Far's fiction, and I agree with Patricia Chu that Sui Sin Far's use of domestic feminism plays a role in signifying "viable Asian American subject positions" to white readers (97). Yet, my point here (one which I will continue to build upon) is that turn-of-the century Asian American and African American fiction and contemporary literary criticism articulate ethnic femininity in remarkably similar terms for ethnic subject positions from such dissimilar historic contexts and for two traditions kept separate from each other in academia. While ethnic heroine construction and ethnic narratives work to destabilize the cultural biases and political injustices enacted by the dominant society, ethnic identities perform these tasks by participating in some common narrative reversals. Thus, Sui Sin Far combines political intrigue with romantic language in stories like "Tian Shan's Kindred Spirit," which perform female ethnic subjectivity in poetic strategies similar to those shared by black writers like Frances Harper and Pauline Hopkins who also employ romantic narratives to highlight reformatory politics. These narratives achieve the narration of culture-specific politics and the articulation of ethnic female identity through common manipulations of signs. While ethnic studies scholarship emphasizes the ways in which romance is a political sign in these narratives, the emphasis on the specific "politics" of these tales tends to draw attention away from the similar investments ethnic writers have in conventional forms like romance—investments which ultimately reveal complex relationships between narrative signs that do not always warrant assignations of culturally-specific ethnic identities.

Facing these patterns, I assert once again that we must examine the potential of less political tensions in works of fiction that also help to shape political ideas like ethnicity and race. White-Parks observes that Sui Sin Far was at one point preoccupied by demonstrating to her editor-mentors that she could in fact write stories on "non-Chinese subjects"—a fact that suggests not only anxieties of ethnic self-assertion, but anxieties about writing itself (44). Although the elder sister negotiated her conflicting desires to write anglo or Chinese stories, Onoto Watanna also second-guessed her own chosen narrative mode of romance. Both sisters' narrative articulations of ethnicity thus evince conflicts between subject matter and narrative mode that shed light on the narrativity of ethnicity itself. To solidify these observations I will turn once again to the more conventionally romantic writing of the more commercially successful sister of this pair—Onoto Watanna— to discuss the paradoxically liberating effects of narrating heroine development in accordance with the language of sentimentalism, before concluding with an explanation of Sui Sin Far's more limited expressions of romance.

THE HEART OF HYACINTH: ONOTO WATANNA ONCE MORE

The Heart of Hyacinth (1903), Onoto Watanna's later novel, employs much of the same romantic fantasy as her first novel, similarly eliminating a strong patriarchal presence by the death and emigration of male parental figures and drawing from the template of her willful, passionate, and impetuous heroines. Hyacinth is an orphaned white American girl who is raised by a Japanese widow who has a son by her late English husband. This time, Watanna's narrative allows the realization of a sanctioned marital match between two children regarded as likely partners in the beginning of the novel. Reversing the mismatch between Orito and Numè in her first novel, Watanna uses plot twists and a slow, meaningful evolution of romantic feelings to construct the loving regard between the white girl with the Japanese heart and the youth she looks up to as a brother, the "half-caste," Western-educated but Japanese-born Komo. The novel uses free-indirect discourse to detail Hyacinth's growing consciousness of and conflicted feelings towards her whiteness, her "Japanese" psyche, and her terror of leaving her foster mother and country to return to her biological father. The novel's language of heroine characterization also inscribes the gaze of a young American consulate officer who falls in love with Hyacinth's "strange beauty" (124). Watanna introduces and then suffuses a subplot involving Komo (who is absent for the bulk of the novel's first section) and his indecision regarding which country—the England of his schooling or the Japan of his birth—to call his home. After much of the novel has discussed Hyacinth's development, Watanna skillfully positions Komo's reentry in the plot: he leaves England to return to Japan and his mother's house the very minute Hyacinth's real father has arranged to come to Japan to claim her. Through another twist characteristic to the domestic genre, Komo has returned with the very people both mother and foster daughter fear—the Lorrimers, Hyacinth's biological father and stepmother.

Although the novel blends elements of the courtship novel, the adventure/mystery tale, and domestic fiction as a whole, Komo's return to Japan marks a moment in the narrative at which Watanna's writing adopts a purely romantic language. When Hyacinth runs away from her American biological father and stepmother to the hills near Matsushima to hide near the Buddhist priests, Watanna prepares the reader for an adventurous drama among the hills. Yet, rather than drawing out the mystery and suspense involving Hyacinth's flight and the search party (including two American officials and the racist Reverend Blount), Watanna slows down the narrative pace with sensory details and tonal effects evoking romantic gratification. Watanna has Hyacinth pause at the entrance to a cavern that will surely protect her, causing the heroine to ponder the moon and stars and to fall asleep outside, not entirely as hidden as will keep her safe from those who pursue her. Like a Snow White just short of the seven dwarves' hut, Hyacinth falls asleep in a spot where her predestined mate, the newly returned and matured Komo, will find her. Komo decides to go into the hills after his foster sister out of concern for her safety, and, out of loyalty to his mother and chosen country, he refuses to go in a search party with the American Lorrimers. Thus, instead of the game of hide-and-seek amidst the Japanese landscape or the dramatic family confrontation we expect, Komo searches the hills, grows frightened when he cannot find Hyacinth, finally beholds her sleeping form on top of a moonlit rock, and relaxes into the calm of instant, paralyzing, romantic love.

From this moment on the novel focuses almost exclusively on the growing love between the two youths, cultivating the match with pages of fleeting "tremulous" glances, whispers, sly "coy" questions, caught breaths, several flickering instances of the male gaze upon Hyacinth's form, and brief, meaningful exchanges between the two lovers before they use the direct language of matrimonial accord. Watanna only obliquely suggests that a marriage between the two actually occurs at the end of the novel by highlighting the following details: a description of the couple's travels to their transcultural places of worship and benediction, a passing mention of a promise secured by formerly-prejudiced but newly-reformed Reverend Blount, a final hesitation upon "the missionary's doorstep," and a conclusive word indicative of the couple's new journey: "Come" (251). In an effort to reach this conventional ending by way of enough gratifying detail of the growing love and understanding in Hyacinth's heart, the author forgoes reporting any specific details about Hyacinth's American admirer's proposal of marriage, and avoids mentioning both the Lorrimers's and Madame Aoi's reactions to this impending union. Watanna encloses the two lovers in a world of their own by displacing the language of their growing sensuous feelings for each other onto the Japanese landscape as each lover experiences the terrain of his/her chosen country again through love's eyes, internalizing a rejuvenated Japanese loyalty. The pair float dreamily in a boat on a lake before confessing their love for each other.

Yet, the convoluted turn of events in the second half of the narrative evidences the efforts Watanna makes to talk about romantic love in surprising, unconventional ways. One scene involves Hyacinth's rejection of her own betrothed, Yamashiro Yoshida, and the other scene details Hyacinth's request to her biological father to stay in Japan for one more month. Both scenes involve Hyacinth's use of an inchoate, romantic language to express her budding feelings for Komo. After rejecting Yoshida, she torments Komo by threatening to keep all of the gifts from her betrothed. The ensuing dialogue between the two, which Watanna continues into an immediate second chapter, is less sentimental than it is significantly charged with romantic meaning—a dialogue in which the object is not to state outright affection, but instead to wait for the other to betray such feelings. Komo insists that she give up all the fine gifts, but Hyacinth tries to refuse: "Could not do it. . . . Too great a sacrifice" (224). After these words Watanna codes the passage in terms of Hyacinth's dissolving innocence and Komo's double language of love, complete with the more obvious romantic signs of stammered words and coloring cheeks:

> "I will buy you all the things you want."
>
> She stared up at him amazedly.
>
> "You?"
>
> "Yes," he replied, flushing, "I—why not?" (224)

These narrative signs (double entendres, dramatic irony) are common features of Western or anglo romance, but in Watanna's case, the language of romance is uniquely interwoven with ideals of Japanese cultural identity. While Watanna prepares readers for the fruition of romance between Hyacinth and Komo, she emphasizes Hyacinth's observance of Japanese female codes of hospitality and propriety. At this moment, the writings of both Eaton sisters seem remarkably similar in that the language of romance is coded with references to cultural harmony. Like the cultural niceties involved in the matches made right by Sui Sin Far's Mrs. Spring Fragrance, Watanna constructs a transcultural, transnational (Asian/American) female romantic heroine by signifying her white protagonist's subjective worth as a proper romantic match for the half-white Komo. When Hyacinth prostrates herself and weeps emotionally in front of her biological father and asks him (after Komo asks her to) if she can stay in Japan for another month, her actions and internal dialogue indicate a conflicted familial love but more strongly suggest her growth into romantic love. It is while she is asking her "august parent" for permission to stay another month that Hyacinth grows emotional: "She could not tell why, but a flood of emotions seemed to fill her heart, so that she could no longer contain herself if she must look into the face of her father" (237). Dominika Ferens observes the ways in which Watanna provides cultural balance in her romantic match:

> Paradoxically, the white Hyacinth asserts her Japaneseness by breaking the long-standing Japanese tradition of filial piety and acting in defiance of her white father. The biracial Koma, in turn, chooses to remain in Japan to marry Hyacinth and thus places love for his family over the allure of life in the West. (*Edith and Winnifred Eaton* 163)

In this moment Hyacinth's actions announce her chosen subjective trajectory—to love Komo and remain in Japan instead of returning to her country of origin or marrying the upper-class Yoshida.

Hyacinth's emotional distress in this scene, shaped by the generic demands of sentimentalism and romance, provides evidence of her conventional heroism as she demonstrates filial loyalty and deference to her lover. Yet she maintains model conduct by demonstrating a cultural loyalty, which in this case Watanna matches with Komo's own forthright will and reevaluation of his maternal culture; thus, Watanna casts Hyacinth in a language of conduct-evaluation that is always matching her objectively with Komo, her foster brother and fated partner in romantic love. Ferens has noted the ways in which "we are asked to gauge the degree to which they have grown into or away from Japanese culture" (*Edith and Winnifred Eaton* 162). Hyacinth's subjective propriety and adherence to culturally dominant mores is thus encoded in a sentimental language, which then allows readers to consume *The Heart of Hyacinth* like an example of anglo fiction that narrates feminine development through courtship-to-marriage plots. These instances are similar to the character development deployed by Jane Austen in *Mansfield Park* (1814). Austen explicitly matches Fanny Price with her live-in cousin Edmund Bertram by characterizing them along the same morally scrupulous schema. Narrative commentary accompanies and enhances the subjective effects of characterization in *Mansfield Park*, but Fanny and Edmund's similarity of opinion in deciding how to resolve each moral crisis or impasse underscores their correctness for each other. For Watanna the appropriateness of a match between Komo and Hyacinth is signified along a scale of cultural balance that approximates Austen's scale of moral development. Hyacinth's development of heroism thus connects her performance of ethnic identity (her demonstration of Japanese values and training) to her realization of romantic love, as cultural identity forms a system of signification by which romantic love is recognized and communicated.

This system in which cultural identity, romantic fantasy, and ideal matches are interconnected is not dissimilar to the forces of order fastidiously maintained in the underlying language of harmony—the poetically appropriate unions—in the examples of Sui Sin Far's fiction discussed in the previous section. Like Sui Sin Far, Watanna also mediates the language of fiction and romance with an eye towards cultural balance that constructs ethnicity in relation to ideas of Americaness, Westerness, and culturally syncretic subjectivity. Seen as distinct and separate because of differing levels of political subject matter, we might instead read the works of the Eaton sisters in light of each writer's comfort with generic conventions. In her book-length study, Dominika Ferens destabilizes critical favoritism of Sui Sin Far's work by contextualizing the "commonalities" of the sisters' "literary practice" (*Edith and Winnifred* 5). Ferens locates this common ground in "the paradigm of ethnography," as she compares the ways both sisters significantly experimented with genre "in the production of . . . ethnographic knowledge for consumption" (1). One of Ferens's main premises in this study is that the works of both sisters were read and appreciated by a turn-of-the-century audience for their native-informant detailing of Asian cultures rather than valued for their formal, literary qualities (1–18, 50–51). Although her "archival," "cross-disciplinary approach" focuses specifically on ethnography, her analysis of the effects of "production" and "consumption" opens up questions of genre and provides my observations here with a foundation for an alternative model in reading the sisters' works. Why should we not, for example, read Sui Sin Far's "Mrs. Spring Fragrance," "The Inferior Woman," and "The Smuggling of Tie-Co" as romantic stories that present moments of direct political commentary? The author does not allow them to be purely romantic—purely compliant to generic standards or formulas. Instead, Sui Sin Far's more romantic stories stop short of overt expression of romance, as the brevity of the short story form and the demands of political and ethical commentary compete with the structural energies of her works. While Watanna's novels are able to at once adhere to conventional generic standards and offer a perspective in favor of Japanese culture, Sui Sin Far's stories are unable to transgress further than a superficial boundary of romance. By pointing to Watanna's generic dexterity here, I mean to point to a limitation in our critical interpretations of both women's works. Rather than continuing to suggest that one sister is more politically sensitive, more skilled, or more imaginative than the other, I think it cannot be stressed enough that both sisters, marginalized by their biracial identities, were similarly conscious of the ways in which their works would not be successful unless they attempted unique blends of genre and subject matter.[19]

As both sisters self-consciously negotiate genre and audience, they provide evidence that works of Asian American fiction significantly, though often obliquely and ambivalently, express romantic themes and are not as limited to the realm of political critique as we are taught to read them. This ambivalence is best expressed in a quotation from Onoto Watanna's anonymous autobiography cited by Amy Ling in "Ethnic Chameleon." In the same biblical reference employed by James Weldon Johnson in *The Autobiography of An Ex-Colored Man,* Watanna muses regretfully on her literary career,

"Oh, I had sold my birthright for a mess of pottage" (Ling 12). The Eaton sisters' ideals of cultural balance are more easily realized in idealized romance and marriage than in the material realities of immigrant America. For Sui Sin Far the ideal is less obvious except in those stories (like "Mrs. Spring Fragrance" and "The Inferior Woman"), which focus overtly on themes of matchmaking. It is while reading her more fantastic romantic/adventure stories like "Tian Shan" that we see a revealing trace of desire, hidden in a body of works interpreted most commonly in political terms.

The search for the perfect match in the Eaton sisters' writings is a feature of their shared investments in romance—investments which challenge the political stringency assigned to the scope of Asian American literature. Just as the works of fiction discussed in this chapter employ narrative codes like cross-dressing and cultural match-making to represent, re-envision, and create concepts of ethnic identity, the mechanics of heroine construction are involved in intertextual, transcultural, and relational articulations of femininity. In the next chapter I will build upon the depoliticizing readings of ethnic fiction conducted in this first chapter and continue to look at rhetorical features in a survey of both African American and Asian American narrative practices of objectifying heroines in relation to each other. The language of heroine objectification in ethnic women's fiction is a more visible site of the force of relational female subjectivity as the protagonist navigates between cultural ideas, social pressure, and ideas of individual self worth. I hope to cleave through layers of heroine characterization and excavate the overarching structural common ground between anglo and ethnic heroines and to contextualize encoded language and adherence to genre as more generative of tradition than cultural essentialism in American women's fiction. The subsequent investigation of the language of heroine objectification will move through more comparisons of late-nineteenth and early-twentieth-century women's texts, drawing out the self-conscious, competitive, and even anxious forces found in narrative configurations of female ethnicity.

Chapter Two
The Fairest of Them All:
Ethnicity, Heroines, and the Objectifying Lens

Feminine propriety and social mobility are two dominant themes in nineteenth-century anglo women's fiction, and these narratives engage with social issues such as industrialization, class stratification, and gender roles via the conventional marriage plot.[1] In responding to these issues, nineteenth-century American and British fiction about women inscribes a language that performs what I term as an "objectification" of femininity, or heroine objectification, while producing heroines whose social prospects readers may easily discern. Readers thus become familiar with certain narrative codes, which become part of a linguistic system that serves as an objectifying lens of feminine potential. Countless examples of nineteenth-century fiction configure beauty and moral fortitude as feminine characteristics representing the potential for social mobility, and this formula creates familiar and predictable patterns within the construction of heroines such as those found in Onoto Watanna's novels, which were discussed in chapter 1.[2] This system of signification is, in many ways, superficial and problematic because it compels readers to evaluate the ways in which female protagonists measure up to conventional aesthetic standards and behavioral mores, and it thereby helps to maintain dominant cultural ideals; it approximates the sort of two-dimensional representation of female subjects known as "the objectification of women" pervading contemporary visual media, by which sexualized and stylized parts of the female anatomy are emphasized visually instead of more complex signifiers of feminine identity.

In this chapter, I will trace signs of heroine objectification from canonical examples of anglo fiction into early twentieth-century African American and Asian American fiction to underscore the ways in which ethnic writers configure and reconfigure this language into subjective performances of female ethnicity. I will focus my discussion of heroine objectification on two African American novels, *Four Girls at Cottage City* (1898) and *Plum Bun* (1928) and then briefly consider the short fiction of the Asian American author Hisaye Yamamoto, in order to locate sites of relational heroine construction that cannot ultimately configure culturally distinctive articulations of female ethnicity. The term "relational" is a crucial part of my analysis here, and my aim in using it is to emphasize the dynamic, symbiotic, and intertextual processes involved in the narrative construction of identities. Regardless of racial or national heritage, all of the writers discussed in this section characterize female protagonists in relation to other heroines and in relation to cultural ideals of exemplary feminine subjectivity. Ethnic female identity, like anglo feminine identity, I argue, is configured and expressed in anxious and competitive ways as heroines self-consciously accommodate and strive to master dominant cultural mores within societies that maintain rigid systems of racialized and classed social hierarchies. As they struggle within these systems and combat social ills involving ideas of class, race, and national identity, transcultural heroines are objectified and characterized relationally in ways that reveal the structural and poetic limitations of female narratives and the commonalities between writers divided for reasons of cultural politics. My observations in this section build upon the project begun in the previous chapter's investigation of ambivalent articulations of romance in the Eaton sisters' fiction and my challenging of critical assumptions that ethnic fiction is more political than anglo fiction.

The language of heroine objectification exposes a text's investment in the value of subjective difference—a value maintained by the narrative's vacillation between a "fear of sameness" and "fear of difference." I take these phrases from Helena Michie's *Sororophobia: Differences Among Women in Literature and Culture,* which exposes the dynamics of relational female characterization in nineteenth- and twentieth-century transatlantic fiction. Contextualizing her work in light of the "Deceased Widow's Sister" acts of nineteenth-century England, Michie analyzes forced moments of unity between the female characters of Brontë, Eliot, and Hardy as the texts perform ambivalent, anxious acts of "sisterhood." Along with Michie's descriptions of "sororophobia as a prevailing narrative tension," Claudia Tate's discussion of "the semiotic of beautiful objects" in her reading of Emma D. Kelley-Hawkins's *Megda* (1891) informs my conceptualization of heroine objectification (Michie 19; Tate, *Psychoanalysis* 37). As we will explore later in this chapter, Tate traces the movement of this "semiotic of beautiful objects" in Kelley-Hawkins's characterization of young women who are represented in relation to standards of "bourgeois marriageability"(37). Like Michie and Tate, Lorna Ellis, in *Appearing to*

Diminish, suggests that heroines profit socially from feminine self-consciousness and behavior modification expressed through the narrative codes akin to heroine objectification. These works support an investigation of the mechanics of heroine objectification and its complex role in self-construction.

I view the objectification of heroines in the anglo and ethnic women's texts discussed in this chapter as the result of women authors' and their heroines' ambivalent interaction with the vague and often conflated demands of marriage markets and anxieties of publishing, as well as more general fears of markets in the midst of industrialization, modernization, and the resulting systems of class-stratification.[3] Several well-known transatlantic heroines acknowledge their awareness of contexts of female competition in scenes of social debut as they go to public balls and private parties and thus announce that they are entering into the marriage market. In many ways, these acts of market debut typify authorial consciousness of publishing market competition, and several of the heroines discussed in this chapter are cast in a language that suggests their authors' sensitivity to the demands of both marriageability and marketability. To highlight this complex system of market anxieties as a backdrop for the processes of relational, transcultural heroine construction, I will first provide an introduction to the language of heroine objectification as it operates across different genres in some notable transatlantic anglo texts, including examples found in juvenile literature, and significant instances informing Edith Wharton's characterization of Lily Bart in *The House of Mirth* (1905).

Jane Austen provides readers with a useful model for understanding female subjective potential as it is informed by the mechanics of the marriage market. In her characterization of fifteen-year-old Lydia Bennett in *Pride and Prejudice* (1813), Austen satirizes the effects of uncontrolled market exposure on the development of a young woman who makes her social debut—who is "out"—too early. Lydia mistakes permission for early entry into the market as evidence of her advanced ability to find a superlative marriage partner. She thus forgoes the maturation, identity-construction, and careful self-evaluation necessary for a more proper development into a truly marketable object in the marriage market of Austen's literary universe. Austen characterizes Lydia in terms of excess—obvious flirtation, frivolity, and social heedlessness. Demonstrating the potential chaos and circumstantial fluctuations of market dynamics which demystify romance's role in marriage, Austen emphasizes this anxiety of market pressures by having Wickham make an ill-informed decision to marry a woman he does not love. Wickham marries Lydia because she is simply available, not because he appreciates her unique charms or personality traits. Internalizing the more superficial mandates that privilege feminine gaiety and beauty, Lydia fixates on the need to become a woman who has the most dance partners at balls instead of developing into the type of woman whom men are willing to marry. In this portrait of Lydia's lack of social subtlety, Austen suggests a difference between an unproductive, undifferentiating system of formulating female identity and the more successful self-fashioning demonstrated by Elizabeth and Jane Bennett's negotiations between individual desire and conduct codes permeating the marriage market system. Austen's study of female identity in a localized marriage market and her characterization of the five Bennett sisters employ a language of heroine objectification; we are encouraged to read Elizabeth's finer qualities in relation to other "silly and ignorant" young women like Lydia (Austen 3).

Like Lydia Bennett, Thomas Hardy's heroine, Bathsheba Everdene, in *Far From the Madding Crowd* (1874), demonstrates a keen but ultimately misguided awareness of market dynamics and her relational subjective potential as she makes her first trip to the town's market square:

> However, the interest was general, and this Saturday's debut in the forum, whatever it may have been to Bathsheba as the buying and selling farmer, was unquestionably a triumph to her as a maiden. Indeed, the sensation was so pronounced that her instinct on two or three occasions was merely to walk as a queen among these gods of the fallow, like a little sister of a little Jove. . . . The numerous evidences of her power to attract were only thrown into greater relief by a marked exception. Women seem to have eyes in their ribbons for such matters as these. (92)

Despite the obvious satire on female vanity in this passage, Hardy highlights one young woman's self-consciousness of her ability to be attractive in a heterosexual context and in a heterosocial market. The passage provides a metanarrative examination on heroine construction itself as it illustrates the weight of comeliness, grace, and self-confidence in the midst of watching eyes. Yet, because modesty is also a virtue of the marriage market system, nineteenth- and early twentieth-century heroines only hint that they are conscious of how they measure in relation to other young women.

Jane Eyre (1847) provides a sort of counter-aesthetic paradigm to the system outlined above. Charlotte Brontë's use of the language of heroine objectification emphasizes physical plainness over conventional beauty through a thematic system that prescribes the amelioration of one's social circumstances and marriage marketability by first improving and enriching one's inner spirit.[4] More obvious executions of this system are found in turn-of-the-century juvenile novels, and in these texts the languate of heroine onjectification serves as an agent of Western/Christian ideals and patriarchal mores of domesticity. *The Secret Garden* (1911) by Frances Burnett, a classic children's novel focusing on a pre-adolescent heroine, incorporates language suggesting that Mary Lennox, originally a plain and impoverished child, will ultimately do well in marriage. Like Jane Eyre, Mary experiences sudden fluctuations between wealth and poverty and is also left to the care of virtually indifferent wealthy relatives. Both heroines discover the mysteries lurking within the secluded wings of each grand household. The explorative journeys of development undertaken by both orphans resonate in similar rhetorical cues, which are driven by loosely similar plot structures. These cues include references to physical plainness and subtle appraisals of increasing physical beauty. The first line of Burnett's novel informs us that Mary Lennox "was the most disagreeable-looking child ever seen" who "had a little thin face and a little thin body, thin light hair and a sour expression" (1). As she spends more and more time in the garden, the novel emphasizes Mary's improved spirits and looks through the narrator's commentary and through third-party comments in dialogue. She first evinces "such red cheeks and such bright eyes"; then the head gardener tells her in his Yorkshire dialect that "Tha's a bit fatter than tha' was an' thas' not quite so yeller. Tha' looked like a young plucked crow when tha' first came into this garden" (98, 109). As an illustration of Mary's healthy sense of modesty, the narrator reports that Mary's response to this comment about her looks shows that she "was not vain and as she had never thought much of her looks she was not greatly disturbed" (109). Ultimately, Mary's new guardians pronounce her as "downright pretty since she's filled out and lost her ugly little sour look" (312). This passage of dialogue also comments suggestively on Mary's promising future in the realm of heterosocial and heterosexual relationships as Mrs. Medlock reports that the newly attractive Mary "and Master Colin laugh together like a pair of crazy young ones" (312). In *Jane Eyre* the reader experiences Jane's improved physical appearance in Mr. Rochester's growing passion for her. His gaze is the radar not only for Jane's strengths as a character but also for her increasing marketability (she also secures the marriage proposal of the handsome yet stoic St. John Rivers), and Frances Burnett's trajectory is analogous with its symbolism of the dark and barren garden, which ultimately blooms.

Although *Jane Eyre* and *The Secret Garden* are tonally, thematically, and overall generically different, the textual effect of the language of heroine objective appraisal remains, with few modifications, virtually the same. Juvenile novels like Burnett's employ but diffuse the marriage plot requirement for commercial success and concentrate instead on the positive ramifications of mental courage, inner strength, and endurance signified by passages highlighting the improved physical being of these young girls.[5] In such novels, the language of heroine objectification moves readers forward towards the heroine's increasingly positive social prospects, a motion that holds a double meaning, which we read as improved marital prospects, higher status, and significance in a collectively understood market for subjective worth. Thus, both Mary Lennox's success at rejuvenating the broken family and community unit at the end of the novel, and the fact that she helps to shape a new home and family of her own, signifies as much positive marital potential as it is able to do so within the space of a child's novel.[6] The language of objectification then points to those rhetorical codes used in describing heroines who, like Cinderella, are housed in narratives that promise a progressive movement towards a heroine's increased fortune and self-consequence.

THE HOUSE OF MIRTH: TESTING THE LIMITS OF HEROINE OBJECTIFICATION

As evidenced by my allusions to the fiction of Austen, Hardy, and Brontë above, formulaic narrative elements like the objectifying language of heroine construction are not exclusive to domestic fiction or juvenile literature. Using the aegis of a sophisticated use of irony, novelists like Henry James and Edith Wharton also interact with late nineteenth- and early twentieth-century cultural assignations of female marketability. In James's *Washington Square* (1881), Dr. Sloper's cold and clinically objective perspective cannot accept the incongruous love-match between his plain, unremarkable daughter and the handsome and educated Morris Townsend. In Edith Wharton's *The House of Mirth* (1905), the dividing line between economy and romance is faintly drawn in Lily Bart's mind because she considers herself a lover of beauty more than a consumer of goods. Fine linens, expensive crystal, opera box seats, and weekends of leisure at palatial country homes provide the backdrop for Lily's growth and development as a heroine. The novel exercises the subtlety of economic gradations permeating society, which are masked as aesthetic sensibilities. Wharton's use of irony targets obvious cultural formulations of female beauty and social success as Lily represents the limits of this formula's guarantees. Lily is so beautiful, so charming, and so worthy, it seems, of a good marriage that she is considered dangerous to her suitors because of her skills in the marriage game. Her expertise rings of insincerity and threatens to dispel the myth of love veiling the economic security guaranteed by marriage.

Lily is so acutely aware of economic inequity that she learns to rationalize her own elite position and her materialism by thinking of herself as an object on display[7] As the following passage indicates, Lily consistently compares herself to other women: "Ah, it was good to be young, to be radiant, to glow with the sense of slenderness, strength and elasticity, of well-poised lines and happy tints, to feel one's self lifted to a height apart by that incommunicable grace which is the bodily counterpart of genius!" (111). As Amy Kaplan tells us, "Lily's identity is described in relation to a background against which she can outline herself, or a mirror in which she can be viewed"(Kaplan 91). Rather than shirking objectification in the budding stages of her self-actualization, Lily embraces her training in elitist mores of femininity and justifies her expensive taste by claiming to have indeed the finest sensibilities. She is aware of her charms as she poses in the sunlight for Percy Gryce, and she is gratified fully by her victory in arranging herself into the most stunning tableau-vivant at a New York evening party (Wharton 128-129). These scenes depict the keenness of Lily's competitive spirit. When she is certain that Percy will propose marriage to her, she loses interest in the marriage game. Life for her is not a party even when it could be— it is being sent to market.

Wharton's characterization of Lily exemplifies the experiential limits to an existence underlined by society's participation in an objectifying game perpetuated by social evaluations. Even after Lily learns the worst about this system and decides to drop out of her former social universe, she continues to have the same need for social approbation. The crucial penultimate scene between Seldon and Lily at the Benedick finally presents an intermingled relationship between romance, sentimentalism, and economics as Lily drops incriminating and therefore financially valuable letters from Bertha into Seldon's fireplace. As she does so, Lily makes an impassioned speech about leaving her "best self" behind with Seldon. However, she finally realizes that she needs her best self image with her, and this acknowledgement delineates Lily's ultimate system of self-objectification, one that has evolved from the idea of draping herself in the best dresses to understanding herself as a wronged yet virtuous woman.

Lily's subjective redemption at the end of the novel demonstrates an alternate schema of heroine objectification, one which emphasizes an evaluation of moral, ethical, or spiritual behavior. Her need to secure her "best self" to preserve her sense of integrity represents a significant change of focus from self-consequence through marriage towards the achievement of independent self-actualization and individual self-expression. Wharton wants us to know that Lily has a soul. Lily is so exemplary that she cannot take the easy road to comfort and cannot ultimately pursue marriage as ruthlessly as the system warrants. Somewhere along the way, Lily's taste apprehends the vulgarity of economic comfort, and while she appears to be only searching for work and survival at the end of the novel, she is really salvaging the romantic from the "dinginess" of economy. The romantic and sentimental language that objectifies Lily thus preserves a link between Lily's new model of self-actualization and the success in marriage markets achieved by her literary predecessors. However, Lily's suicide at the end of the novel underscores her obsession with having to be the "best." She dies as a result of following the precepts of her new system of seeing herself as a wronged woman. Her tragic death represents the limits of the system of heroine objectification, which emphasizes personal distinction in relation to conventional mores. In the way that this ending rings as sentimental, Lily Bart's death thus mirrors the suicides of the figure of the "tragic mulatto" found in nineteenth-century African American literature.[8]

The works of ethnic studies scholars like Ann duCille and Lisa Lowe, however, compel us to remember that nineteenth- and turn-of-the-century anglo narratives, and, I would add, *The House of Mirth,* say very little about people of other races. According to postcolonial critics like Gayatri Spivak and Edward Said, this emphatic whiteness maintains cultural hegemony without having to refer to other races, nations, or cultures.[9] The upper-class world of Lily Bart, for example, is actually built upon many types of hidden and overlapping social restrictions, including those of race, class, religion, and national identity. But the narrative cannot house all of these forms of exclusion. These connections, however, suggest that we can read ethnic female identity as analogous to the narrative representation of socially-displaced anglo women; this narrative inscribes the class-critiques implicit in much of nineteenth- and early twentieth-century novels of female development and evolves, in contemporary fiction, towards critiques of racism and cultural alienation. By examining the objectification of heroines in both ethnic and anglo novels, I will draw out sites of heightened self-consciousness and subjective anxiety, which reveal the interconnectedness of race and class and determine the narrative role of ethnicity in twentieth-century female characterization.

LITTLE WOMEN EVERYWHERE: FEMALE OBJECTIFICATION, BANDS OF WOMEN, AND ETHNICITY

The structural relationship between two nineteenth-century texts in particular evinces hidden desires and fantasies common to the creation of marketable heroines, both anglo and ethnic, as they battle dominant norms and aesthetic ideals. Thematic and poetic similarities between Louisa May Alcott's *Little Women* (1868–1869) and Emma D. Kelley-Hawkins's *Four Girls at Cottage City* (1898) far surpass those shared by their titles. Both texts share the narrative mode of domestic sentimentalism that offers moral instruction in Christian female propriety. *Little Women* maintains ties to John Bunyan's 1678 *The Pilgrim's Progress,* beginning with the novel's preface and continuing in the first chapter, "Playing Pilgrims." The preface, "adapted from John Bunyan," introduces the reader to the March sisters with the words: "For little tripping maids may follow God /Along the ways which saintly feet have trod" (1). Likewise, Kelley's *Four Girls* incorporates the tone of conversion narratives by blending it with typical elements of domestic fiction and marriage plots.[10] Almost one third of the novel progresses without serious mention of its Christian subplot, a plot carried by the entrance of the devout Charlotte Hood and her son Robin. Kelley's preface also makes mention of "the Mission" of the narrative and invites the reader to continue a relationship with "my four girls" (5). These girls are described in loving detail by a narrator who holds them up as instructional models of feminine propriety and spiritual integrity throughout the course of the novel. Both Alcott and Kelley-Hawkins construct Christian virtue and domestic sensibility by characterizing young women who make the most of whatever little their material prospects promise them. Like Alcott's figure of the rich, fashionable coquette Meg March chooses not to emulate at Annie Moffat's ball (in a chapter appropriately entitled "Meg Goes to Vanity Fair"), these books offer counter-aesthetics of the imaginative temperance and industry of the new heroine (Alcott 94-112).[11] The ideals both novels offer in place of a leisured (and thereby morally compromised) lifestyle demand that these young women offer strength of character and other stalwart traits of true heroism to their readers. Both authors construct and demonstrate these characteristics of femininity through use of an objectifying language that describes "our girls" and the "playing pilgrims" in relation to cultural ideals of heroines in other novels.

The narrators of *Little Women* and *Four Girls* offer readers an alternate world inhabited by socially-responsible female protagonists as a substitute for the queenly circumstances enjoyed by more affluent heroines from the eighteenth and nineteenth centuries like Clarissa, Evelina, and Emma. In the first line of Alcott's novel, Jo March, the central heroine, alludes to the problem of her family's diminished material wealth during the festive Christmas season. Meg, the eldest sister, complains outright: "It's so dreadful to be poor!" (9). In Kelley's first chapter of *Four Girls at Cottage City,* she also alerts the reader that "our girls were far from being rich girls" (23). To cushion the realities of poverty, however, both writers use a tone and narrative emphasis to suggest comfort, domestic contentment, and richness of spirit and mind. For example, the first page of both novels begins with one of the characters complaining about concerns of little societal importance. Jo March remarks ungraciously that "Christmas won't be Christmas without any presents" and Kelley's central heroine, Jessie Dare, younger and livelier than her sister Garnet, makes a similarly plaintive observation by declaring, "What a shame it should rain this day, of all days, Net!" (9). "This day" refers to the first day of the four girls' three-week long stay at the resort locale known as Cottage City. Even as this seemingly threatening rain falls, elder sister Garnet remains "snugly down between the sheets" for "a few more minutes sleep." Luring readers into this safe spot shared by the two sisters, the narrator then highlights the girls' other wholesome prospects by characterizing their benevolent, beloved mother who remarks "sympathizingly" in a genteel language, "It is too bad you have not a better day for your journey, my dears" (10). The March girls, too, seem comfortable enough on the rug by "firelight," and from "her corner" saintly Beth "contentedly" reminds the grumbling sisters that they have "father and mother and each other" (3). Both writers also create a sense of pleasant, familial harmony by outlining almost immediately the personality differences between the sisters who are all situated within a unified physical place (home) and who are all affirmed as unique characters through the narrator's nurturing tone.

The characterization of these groups of young women requires, their narrators suggest, a vigilant yet approving eye towards identity differentiation. On the second page of Alcott's novel, the narrator has already pinpointed Jo as having "gentlemanly" habits and as being a "bookworm." Alcott also attempts to distinguish "little Amy" whose nose "isn't nice" from the rest of the girls by italicizing words misused by this youngest sister (4–5). Both Alcott and Kelley lay out differences of character in the girls' dialogues with each other, tonally maintaining innocent impatience and impertinence in the speeches of Jessie Dare and Amy March. Alcott uses conversation between the sisters to allow for their obvious personality differences until the fourth page when she evokes the partnership between heroines and their readers in order to justify a physical description of her characters. She writes, "As young readers like to know 'how people look,' we will take this moment to give them a little sketch of the four sisters" (6). Kelley, on the other hand, carries specific physical modifiers for each girl throughout the novel, as in her constant reference to Garnet's "plump little form," and Jessie's "dark eyes" and "girlish voice"—rhetorical cues that obviate any full-length discussion of their physical persons. Their objectified features and attributes follow a formula wherein the reader learns to attribute certain stereotypes of female behavior and female archetypes with each of the girls. Both writers' tactics demonstrate that physical descriptions are essential not only for readers to have a differentiated image of each girl and sister but also because each writes in relation to cultural standards of ideal heroines.

Deborah McDowell reminds us in her introduction to the Schomburg Library's edition of Kelley's text that the characterization and story of the four light-skinned black girls "forgoes the dramatic possibilities that the material realities of race and class suggest, subsuming them under the larger spiritual vision that collapses all social distinctions in the interest of Christian egalitarianism" (xxxvi). Kelley invokes the politics of institutionalized racism outright only once, when Jessie alludes to having to sit in the "nigger heaven" section in public theatres (81). At this moment, Garnet, shocked by her younger sister's crude speech, casts an "indignant" tone, mindful of conventions of propriety, over the lived material inequities of segregation. The subject of the girls' conversation at this point involves a mixture of classical references, instructions on decorous speech, as well a discussion of the morality of going to the theatre, all of which exemplify the tensions between politics and sentimentalism that exist at the narrative's core.

While the novel does not, as McDowell remarks, fly "the racial banner," for Kelley the novel involves a more significant project of positive imaging in the characterization of black heroines who are equal to white girls in terms of the social benefits of education, aesthetic cultivation, and moral integrity. Kelley attempts to suffuse obvious markers of race in the narrative by substituting in the dynamics of class. Thus, the girls must demonstrate the poise, presence, and breadth of cultural knowledge of richer, "whiter" girls without, of course, compromising their moral principles. The result of such language in Kelley's text is that the novel reads (like *Little Women*) more like a critique of class dynamics and not of racism. In fact, the emphasis on propriety and gentility in the novel's enactment of femininity suggests that the dynamics of class distinctions and class markers help create concepts of race. The debate in academic circles which surround novels like *Four Girls*, (novels which putatively champion whiteness as an ideal), centers predominantly on divergent readings of the novel's use of the language of heroine objectification. Either these young women are catering to a class-informed performance of light-skinned blackness that highlights "Kelley's capitulation to the era's race-prejudiced theology, which saw blackness as synonymous with evil" or this language inscribes Kelley's active project of humanizing black heroines for turn-of-the-century America (*Four Girls*, McDowell xxxvii).

As McDowell's introduction asserts, it is less productive to differentiate between the agendas mentioned above than to look at what these ambiguities and contradictions can teach us about the construction of race and ethnicity. For example, the cultivation of upper-class sensibilities in *Four Girls* and the themes it shares with *Little Women* reveal telling similarities between race-based and class-based social critiques as they create and respond to ideals of gentility and whiteness. It is no accident that all eight girls must be opposites of each other in personality, and that in both novels, the younger girls are paired with older girls who, though different in temperament, help to balance out character flaws. Jo's boyish ways and hot temper are softened by her favoritism of sweet-tempered and pious Beth. In *Four Girls,* the eldest and most respected girl, Vera Earle, makes a pet out of the youngest and often silliest girl, Jessie. Both authors, in order to solve the problem of choosing a personality type which will garner the most amount of reader sympathy in a publishing market saturated with fiction for girls and women, decide to focus instead on sisterhood, on feminine archetypes which cohere around a common spirit of goodness—a "golden chain" of women (McDowell xxxvii).

By employing a language of heroine objectification, both authors are able to compare and to relate each of their individual characters to ideal heroines in literature; thus, Alcott can bemusedly allude to girl readers who need to know what their heroines look like, and Kelley must constantly assess her heroines' physical competitiveness by mention of "rosy lips," "laughing eyes," and a "sweet, pretty smile." Oddly enough, it is Kelley's unmitigated use of hyperbolic physical modifiers that indicates to readers the fact that these heroines are perhaps not beautiful in a conventional sense but in fact beautiful in relation to classed and racialized aesthetic standards. For example, Kelley introduces readers to Allie Hunt by describing her as a "slender, blue-eyed girl" who has a "low, lady-like laugh" (10–11). Such descriptors are meaningless unless they respond to pre-existent standards, in this case standards that posit a hierarchical relationship between whiteness and blackness. Kelley's act of characterizing the "lady-like" laughter of Allie announces a cultural system of prejudice under which one might assume that because of her class or race that Allie is not ladylike.

Claudia Tate's *Psychoanalysis and Black Novels* discusses Emma D. Kelley-Hawkins's earlier novel, *Megda,* at length. Tate's analysis seeks to decipher the gray area between "political" and "private," and "black" and "white" novels by pointing to the role of personal desire in configuring political commentary in black literature. Writing to the issue of Kelley's resistance to "traditional racial paradigms," Tate ponders whether "we should read *Megda* as we read *Little Women,* since we cannot read *Megda* like *Iola Leroy*" (Tate 23). Noting that Kelley's work "already presumes as gratified the political objectives of racial equality," and that it "idealizes the domestic sphere," Tate uses the text to move beyond "conventional racial reading-models" as well as a "typical feminist reading" (24). Tate contextualizes her reading of the text within late nineteenth-century ideas of "racial hybrids" and "the black Irish" and asserts that Kelley-Hawkins and other black women writers of her time knew that "racial privilege was not automatically associated with white skin color." Read in this light, Kelley demonstrates "the arbitrariness of racial categories" while describing her light-skinned black characters as having "textualized white bodies," which serve as "specular objects" (24–25). Through an explication of *Megda's* "complex libidinal semiotic of romantic settings, clothing, and sensory perceptions" that "nurture" Kelley-Hawkins's heroines, Tate reads the novel psychoanalytically and considers it an exercise in "fantasizing plentitude" and "wholeness" (27, 45). Calling *Megda* a "utopian novel," Tate asserts that the text's "presumptions of racelessness in connection with exaggerated whiteness deconstruct the privilege associated with fetishized white skin" (45). My discussion of heroine objectification in Kelley-Hawkins's *Four Girls* and Alcott's *Little Women* works in conjunction with Tate's analyses of semiotic manifestations of desire in *Megda*. While Tate connects Alcott's and Kelley's novels by discussing their shared "pre-oedipal fantasy of wholeness," her pairing of the texts in this way also points to ways in which we can read the narrative interconnectedness between concerns of class and race.

Alcott and Kelley both use similar strategies in garnering subjective power for their outcast heroines. Beyond sentimental descriptions of beauty and moral fortitude, both authors use more indirect methods of heroine objectification to establish their heroines as worthy of social distinction, and more particularly, to indicate that their little women have acquired and achieved intellectual prowess and cultural training despite nineteenth-century social mores and exclusionary constructs of "culture." In *Little Women* and *Four Girls*, intriguing processes of dissemblance occur in scenes that highlight the charm and aesthetic cultivation of the girls while they "pretend" to be more powerful and more genteel than circumstances allow. These activities allow them to parody dominant cultural ideals while also showing mastery of conventional assumptions about arts and social ideas, which are racialized, classed, and gendered. The most notable example of this process in *Little Women* occurs in an early chapter entitled "The P.C. and P.O.," which describes the March sisters' game of dressing like, and pretending to be, members of Charles Dickens's "Pickwick Club." The chapter includes an edition of "The Pickwick Portfolio," a newspaper in which the girls report on the goings-on of the week in formal and ironic language. The "Portfolio" includes "A Lament" which, in overstated language, mourns "the loss of our little pet" (S.B. Pat Paw) and eulogizes the deceased cat's strength at hunting and playing with an "airy grace" (115–116). Another report, "A Sad Accident," details an ordinary basement mishap involving Meg ("our beloved president") who had "fallen while getting wood for domestic purposes" and whose fall had created a "perfect scene of ruin" (116). Besides being amusing, the irony embellishing these stories of common occurrences at the March household evidences a level of sophistication in the girls' ability to use their imaginations and wit. Alcott's detailed attention to the typography and layout of the "Portfolio" demands reader admiration for her own ability to use an irony comparable to Dickens. Alcott's and Kelley's heroines are aware of the vast publishing world as they allude constantly to their readings of Dickens, Tennyson and domestic sentimental novels like *Uncle Tom's Cabin* and *Megda*.[12]

The consumption of literature, in fact, enables all of the girls to demonstrate their cultivation of Taste. In an early chapter in *Four Girls* entitled "An Afternoon with Tennyson," Vera Earle helps the girls pass a rainy afternoon by discussing "The Lady of Shalott." Not only does the chapter narrate the events in the poem, it also incorporates the girls' opinions on "moral weakness" and heroine construction. The girls discuss Tennyson in a passage that demonstrates their cultural education and cultivated aesthetic sensibilities:

> "Ugh! His poetry is too ancient for me," replied Jessie.
>
> "Ah, that is just the beauty of it. And he expresses himself so prettily. There is only one fault I can find with him."
>
> "What is that?" asked Garnet.
>
> "He makes his women too weak."
>
> "Physically, intellectually, or morally?"
>
> "Oh, morally. His description of them as they are physically, suits me exactly. Tall, slender, fair, proud! But weak—too weak." (60)

By incorporating the discussion of established male literary figureheads into their texts, Kelley and Alcott, like their heroines, enact a type of literary cross-dressing that seeks to critique the division of power by gender and class. Sharing the same target (the white masculine literary establishment) both writers choose to counter the exclusion they feel as women writers of domestic fiction by emulating the standards of and engaging with culturally dominant ideals of sophistication and taste in a sort of parody of the establishment. The commentary on Tennyson's "weak" heroines allows a moment of political rereading that demonstrates familiarity with, mastery of, and a critique of racialized and classed dominant cultural ideals. This dynamic also occurs in Jessie Fauset's *Plum Bun* when the

Murray sisters playact conventions of gentility in their "Mrs. Henrietta Jones" skits. These instances begin to indicate the affinity between class and race critiques in female narratives, an affinity that exposes those moments when ethnicity in female narratives is less of a culturally distinctive quality and more of an advancement of the critique of class. In the next section, I will trace more of these linked ideas of class and ethnicity in twentieth-century African American heroine construction as I examine the language of heroine objectification in Fauset's *Plum Bun.*

"TO MARKET, TO MARKET": JESSIE FAUSET'S *PLUM BUN*

The mechanics of heroine construction shaping African American novelist Jessie Fauset's central character, Angela Murray, demonstrate the quintessential challenge of feminine representation under the weight of tradition. In chapter 1 of this project, we noted the ways in which Onoto Watanna comments resignedly about her authorial frustration in describing the conventionally coquettish Cleo in *Miss Numè of Japan.* Fauset similarly employs this type of metanarrative technique, calling attention to a culturally sanctioned marriage market by ironically entitling her novel's sub-books with lines from a nursery rhyme that plots a journey to market, as well as female subjective ripening. Written in the third person, *Plum Bun* (1928), like most other female bildungsromane of the nineteenth and early twentieth centuries, has a marriage plot and a coming-of-age story that deploys the language of heroine objectification. Fauset's clever title and subtitles, however, provide insight into the conventional nature of female developmental narratives. Her choice of words implies that the traditional conclusion of a female bildungsroman (in which marital or vocational success signifies the self's integration with society) perpetuates social dynamics of a market economy of desire, negotiation, and consumption. The novel's romantic resolution playfully calls attention to consumerist associations of long-sought rewards when Anthony Cross shows up in Paris as a surprise Christmas gift for the heartsick Angela. Sitting in a snug "five foot square drawing-room," Anthony claims humorously that there "ought to be a tag on me somewhere . . . but anyhow Virginia and Matthew sent me with their love" (378–379).

The lighthearted language of gift-giving and exchange here mitigates the force of the sentimentalism in this ending by using humor to soften the novel's more serious though subtly deployed themes of institutionalized racism, materialism, and sororophobia, which disrupt a tight social circle of family and friends. Fauset has prepared readers for a traditional double-wedding for the two sisters all along, and yet Anthony's sheepishness and Angela's surprise at seeing him are depicted in a language that is tonally modern, or post-sentimentally self-conscious. Yet, it is a also a language that, though couched in modern dialect and ironic distance, conjures up associations of romantic denouements simply by using the setting of Paris in winter and suggestively equating men and women as gifts for each other. In keeping with a more modern narrative structure, Fauset does not overtly mention future nuptials for our central couple but refers obliquely to its likelihood by alluding jointly to the parallel lovers, Virginia and Matthew. Illustrating a full cycle of actualized female subjectivity and reintegration back into the social unit, the imaginary tag to which Anthony alludes links Angela's subjective worthiness to community approbation via the message of love from a sister. Any discomfort the writer may have had when envisioning a "happily ever after" ending abates itself with this language of softened sentimentality, which is a self-conscious narrative nod to generic convention within the literary marketplace and its high traffic area of heroine production.

Such language demonstrates Fauset's working sense of systems of heroine objectification. Fauset attempts an exhaustive meditation on the process of self-construction, which is informed and complicated by a network of generational differences, the dynamics of race and class, and sexual mores. At the outset, our narrator explains the differences of perspectives and positions on racial politics held between the Murray parents, the Murray children, and white elite society by using the symbolism of domestic interiors and architecture. By contrasting the black middle-class Opal Street with the shops and hotels of richer, whiter areas like Bellevue Stratford, and by setting up Angela's dislike for her small home in contrast to her parents' feelings of domestic tranquility, Fauset introduces a lexicon of relational selfhood early in the novel. In this first section, "Home," Fauset differentiates between Angela and her sister Virginia's characters by outlining their antithetical feeling for the middle-class domestic bliss worked towards and maintained by the Murray parents. In *"The Changing Same": Black Women's Literature, Criticism, and Theory,* Deborah McDowell notes that Fauset's own "ambivalent stance" on "the program of racial uplift" functions "in the opposition between Angela Murray . . . and her sister, Jinny, between whom the narrative divides its sympathies" (McDowell 63). Virginia eagerly helps her mother with the kitchen preparations for Sunday dinner while Angela tolerates the day's rituals because "she liked the luxuriousness of being 'dressed up' two consecutive days" (Fauset 20–21). At this point, the narrator has already described certain exclusive Saturday pleasures shared by Angela and her mother as they "pass" for white women in the finer boutiques and hotels of Philadelphia.

The question of inner worth versus social rank is penned in racial terms through the disparity between Angela and her mother's perspectives on ideas of personal success and failure. Unlike the March sisters or the "four girls" of Cottage City, Angela feels threatened by class and race hierarchies; however, like these other female protagonists, Angela attempts to circumvent the limitations imposed by a racist social hierarchy through her cultivation of upper-class sensibilities that approximate subjective whiteness in the novel. Mrs. Murray, as described in the free-indirect-discursive narration of her husband's point-of-view, harmlessly entertains her inner world fantasies of being rich and at leisure by roaming through high-class settings whenever she has some free time. Mrs. Murray herself refers to this practice as "playacting," and never suspects that her dramatic proclivities are being misinterpreted by her similarly light-skinned daughter. To Angela's mother, these strolls in the realm of high fashion are simply a matter of aesthetic taste that transcends racial categories and which demonstrates her "essentially feminine" qualities (Fauset 15). The narrator attempts to counterbalance this description of Mrs. Murray's potentially reprehensible acts of passing or "disclaiming" by stating that "her infrequent occupation of orchestra seats was due merely to a mischievous determination to flout a silly and unjust law." Fauset seems overhasty in her comparisons of mother and daughter as she uses the language of aesthetic cultivation to gloss too conveniently over issues of both class and race while promoting a distinctively feminine sensibility. Mrs. Murray, writes Fauset, "liked shops devoted to the service of women" (15). In the same paragraph Fauset sums up Mrs. Murray's defining impulse, an impulse excused because Fauset envisions this habit as distinctively feminine: "A satisfaction that was almost ecstatic seized her when she drank tea in the midst of modishly gowned women in a stylish tea-room." Mrs. Murray's excitement is similar to that sense of satisfaction Angela feels in her "third story front" room as she practices "Drawing and French" (37). Just as Mrs. Murray cannot explain her love of fashionable tearooms, her daughter feels a vague "secret subconscious ambition (sic) resolve" while she enjoys the "element of fine ladyism" in the act of learning French. Through "playacting" and "drawing," Fauset connects mother and daughter in a bond of material dissatisfaction encoded in astute aesthetic training.

To the narrator, the essential difference is that Angela associates taste and "Art" with whiteness while her mother's aesthetic preferences are purportedly de-racialized. However, both women's yearning for the finer things in life serves a larger purpose of providing the main character the justification for following a specific narrative topography—the romantic female bildungsroman—a form usually reserved for anglo women and anglo heroines. Describing the "fortuities" which pave the way for Angela's increasingly materialistic and self-serving outlook (dark-skinned Virginia's lack of interest in fashion and style and the death of their mother), the narrator goes on to depict Angela's misguided journey towards fulfillment and self-actualization. Readers are encouraged to think of the late Mrs. Murray's acts of passing as innocent and occasional subversions of unjust social codes; whereas Angela's phase of passing in New York represents a more insidious obsession with a life of seeming. Read along the lines of material desire, Angela Murray betrays the same fixation with objectification that plagues Lily Bart in *The House of Mirth*.

Thus, the narrative of longing and internal conflict can evolve neatly in the daughter who has internalized false, though culturally-sanctioned, estimates of personal character and success. Exploring diverging ideas of self-fulfillment and self-consequence, Fauset uses collective estimations of black and white potential for upward mobility as a backdrop from which to offset this account of superlative romantic and vocational success. In the early chapters, race (in Angela's point-of-view) is drawn as just another personal quality (like education, physical appearance, and talent) that factors into one's chances for happiness (or lack thereof). The concept of race becomes part of a paradigmatic formula for personal success in which a woman's potential for fulfillment is based on superficial qualities and categories:

> Certain fortuitous endowments, great physical beauty, unusual strength, a certain unswerving singleness of mind,—gifts bestowed quite blindly and disproportionately by the forces which control life,—these were the qualities which contributed toward a glowing and pleasant existence. (12–13)

The adjectives used in this passage like "great," "unusual," and "glowing," are telling elements of the novel's thematic and poetic engagement with female subjectivity's relational struggle. These adjectives may indicate that Angela is consumed by an envious yearning for a specific antagonist's better personal qualities or lifestyle. Like the disparity of municipal resources between middle-class neighborhoods and wealthier sections of Philadelphia upon which Fauset's novel occasionally comments, Angela's struggle for selfhood is also tied up with her competitive awareness of the nameless masses around her, against whom she must strive for the best urban existence a woman of her talents might attain. The tension encapsulated within her impersonal yearning is captured by the juxtaposition of the unrelated words "glowing" and "pleasant"—"glowing" a relational but vague referent for superlative standing amongst one's peers, and "pleasant," a marker of a more practical and domestic comfort.

By the time Angela arrives in New York, the narrator no longer has qualms about presenting us with a familiar story—that of our protagonist as the modern, urban young woman who faces an intimidating impersonal "Market" in which and against which to define her subjective potential and identity. Angela's budding artistic ambition serves as a useful narrative device in which to analogize a young woman's struggle for "self-expression" (Fauset 37). As Lee Edwards outlines in her seminal text on heroine construction, *Psyche as Hero,* the "portrait of the hero as a female artist" emerges in later twentieth-century transatlantic fiction to displace a generic demand for heterosexual romance in a plot's conclusion with alternative, self-affirming models of vocational excellence (Edwards 189). The latter schema, according to Edwards, replaces seemingly innocuous narrative templates deployed by novels like Austen's *Emma,* which actually limit female potential by circumscribing it within the mores of propriety and domesticity of a patriarchal society. The female artist hero is motivated by "her yearning to construct a self independent of culturally constructed norms" (Edwards 237). Significantly, Fauset makes no grand claims about Angela's artistic ability and instead uses this motivation to make some observations about the relationship between aesthetics, subjectivity, race, class, gender and an overwhelming urban maelstrom in which all of these systems of denoting and signifying self-consequence struggle for notice and evaluation. Accounting for Angela's initially effusive thoughts about New York street life, Fauset writes:

> "A great picture!" she thought. "I'll make a great picture of these people some day and call them 'Fourteenth Street types.'" And suddenly a vast sadness invaded her; she wondered if there were people more alive, more sentient to the joy, the adventure of living, even than she, to whom she would also be a 'type.'" (89)

Suddenly, Angela's fastidious sense of style, her discomfort with the mediocrity of Opal Street life, and even her need for the subjective freedom from racial constraints converge and form a driving need for subjective distinction. Such a motivation complicates any notions about preconceived racial or ethnic essence; much like Lily Bart, Angela struggles against almost every narrative identity and trajectory she might claim. Hesitant, like her mother, even to assume outright whiteness, she lets others think what they will about her origin, responding "I don't think so" when she is asked if her new assumed surname "Mory" is Spanish. "Angèle," her assumed first name, evokes a Western European identity as it sounds French but captures a sense of transcultural possibility (95). Rather than pick a name easily identifiable with one given race or national origin, Angela employs her creative ingenuity and aesthetic sensibility to avoid becoming a "type."

Properly assessing Angela's subjective motivation is a challenging task particularly because, unlike heroines with which she is contemporary, the thought of marriage occurs to her almost as an afterthought, and even then, as a practical consideration as opposed to a romantic notion. Her characterization offers some insight into the dynamics of heroine objectification in fiction, both ethnic and anglo. Like Lily Bart, young Angela is indoctrinated into a materialistic system and infused with an inner world that allows her to appraise herself in relation to other young women and to cultural standards of superlative femininity. Although the "gentlemen beaux" gather at her house every Sunday, the narrator goes to no length to sentimentalize their presence as possible lovers; instead, they appear initially as part of an ongoing discussion on race politics kept up by Virginia and Mr. Murray. Interestingly, Angela's first potential romantic male lead, "Matthew Henson," appears as almost a comical figure in light of her overdetermined lack of interest in him. Fauset plays with stock elements of romantic and sentimental female development narratives even while she makes a more modern inner subjective journey her real focus. Matthew's early presence in the novel and the way in which he is configured as a male lead by the different ways the two sisters regard him serves as a mechanical nod to convention. An uninteresting character, Matthew must at least be introduced into Virginia's (Jinny's) thoughts early on if the reader is to believe later that the two will marry. McDowell reminds us that although Fauset's novels "deploy a range of generic conventions—the romance, novel of manners, fairytales," her narrative style is "comprised of plots within plots and texts within texts that refer to and comment upon one another in multiple and intricate combinations" (McDowell, *The Changing Same* 65).

The novel's most conventional feature, however, is its characterization of its central female protagonist, who in the sentimental mode employed in the work of Alcott, Watanna, and Kelley, ultimately outshines every other female in terms of intelligence, talent, and physical appearance. Fauset renders Angela, as Edith Wharton represents Lily, as the superior beauty object with an anxious inner self. This narrative decision enables both the literary conventions of romance (arguably making the novel more marketable as a woman's text) as well as a social commentary on the superficiality of market forces. The superior qualities of both Lily and Angela are predominantly physical. Angela's sister Virginia, with her goodness and graciousness, has more the character fitting the nineteenth-century domestic heroine. Heroines like Lily Bart and Angela Murray evoke a template not unlike that used by Onoto Watanna in her portrait of Cleo Barnard in *Miss Numè of Japan*. These physically superior women are appealing to the readers of this time period in which mass production, commerce, increased consumption and social Darwinism fueled a culture of competition. In a post-sentimental reading, however, many of these outwardly beautiful female characters (and the narrators who describe them) are hyper-conscious about the physical demands marketable heroines must meet. Heroine objectification thus moves ambivalently through these texts as authors attempt to meet readers' expectations while simultaneously striving for socially-conscious poetics. In the final section of this chapter I will locate heroine objectification within mid-twentieth-century Asian American fiction (after the era of the Eaton sisters.) By looking at heroine construction in a few of Hisaye Yamamoto's short stories, I will point to an alternative pattern of heroine objectification in Asian American female subjectivity, which destabilizes the weight of physical beauty by focusing on the inner world of a heroine's memories and anxieties.

RELUCTANT STARDOM: ASIAN AMERICAN HEROINES AND OBJECTIFICATION

"The Legend of Miss Sasagawara," Hisaye Yamamoto's 1950 short story about a misunderstood Japanese American woman who has been relocated to an internment camp, presents an alternative system of heroine objectification. This system attempts to move beyond conventional anglo heroine objectification in notable ways, which I will point to later in this section. The stories passed on in the camp about Mari Sasagawara's putative madness in "The Legend of Miss Sasagawara" finally give way to the truth about her "troublous" and lonely life with her ascetic father. Out of the handful of Yamamoto's stories that are read and studied today, "The Legend" is unique in its commentary on female identity-construction and heroines who are produced by community lore.

"The word 'legend' implies a heroine," claims Esther Mikyung Ghymn in her interpretation of Yamamoto's text as a story created to "ensure sympathy" for "mentally ill characters" who are the manifestations of "Asian American womanhood with all its pain and sadness" (Ghymn 129, 131). Ghymn's analysis of "The Legend" attempts to contextualize Asian American heroine construction in contradistinction to anglo feminine novels, represented chiefly by Ghymn's reference to Charlotte Brontë's unsympathetic portrait of Bertha Mason's madness in *Jane Eyre*. Unlike those heroines found in nineteenth-century anglo women's fiction, Yamamoto's female narrators and main characters are almost always described in non-corporeal terms, and their incipiently self-assertive voices are more provocative in the texts than descriptions of their physical beings. In this section, I will discuss "The Legend" in relation to the patterns of objectification discussed thus far, and I attribute the movements and displacements of the narrative emphasis on inner life in mid-century to contemporary Asian American heroine construction to its relationship with an anglo female narrative tradition.

Yamamoto introduces us to Miss Sasagawara through the first-person perspective of Kiku, a twenty-year-old Japanese American woman. Right away, our narrator employs the language of heroine objectification to set Miss Sasagawara apart from the rest of the camp community: "it was easy to imagine Miss Sasagawara a decorative ingredient of some ballet . . . her shining hair so long it wound twice about her head to form a coronet; her face was delicate and pale, with a fine nose, pouting bright mouth, and glittering eyes" (20). In the remainder of the story, Yamamoto describes no other woman in such detail. As Kiku tells us, Miss Sasagawara's notoriety in the community is a result not only of her beauty and flamboyant style but also from her standoffish social behavior. In keeping with the themes of many of Yamamoto's stories, Miss Sasagawara's behavior seems to hold the secret to a sexual mystery. Camp "legend" documents her strange habit of sneaking into a young man's room to watch him sleep (31–32). Kiku encounters her one midnight in the camp showers and Miss Sasagawara, "under the full needling force of a steamy spray," "turns away reservedly instead of speaking" (22). Kiku's friend Elsie relates another story about the heroine's idiosyncratic behavior; this time, again, the symbolic use of water highlights Miss Sasagawara's fear of sexuality, the sexual gaze, and invasion. A neighbor, Mr. Sasaki, attempts to enter the Sasagawara apartment while offering to hose out the barrack floor. Miss Sasagawara, who is cleaning out the apartment "with a pail of water and a broom," screams hysterically at the neighbor: "What are you trying to do? Spy on me? Get out of here or I'll throw this water on you!" (21). Yamamoto experiments with water as a metaphor for ideas of sexuality and its transgressive power while working through a tension between order and chaos, restraint and passion, sanity and madness.

The puzzle of "the legend" is Miss Sasagawara's pervasively anti-social behavior, which occurs simultaneously with her seemingly exhibitionist tendencies. The narrator informs us of her history as a ballet dancer and attributes this past vocation as reason for her flashy skirts of "arrestingly rich colors" and her poised way of walking (20). Miss Sasagawara's unfriendly rebukes and guarded actions when she is confronted with the proximity of any stranger imply that she feels she is the target of a sexualized gaze, if not lust. Kiku manages to glimpse Miss Sasagawara's body in the shower and inadvertently describes the older woman's body in a language of sexual appeal: "I hoped my body would be as smooth and spare and well-turned when I was thirty-nine" (22). Miss Sasagawara's physical distinction and social reserve highlight her "temperamental" stage presence. When she goes to the hospital for treatment, escapes, and returns again, all of the doctors and nurses rush to her ward to have a look the renowned patient. Kiku, too, sneaks to the ward to watch the antics of this older but young looking woman, and as she looks, she becomes aware of Miss Sasagawara's own consciousness of the spectacle she is creating: "I knew she must be aware of that concentrated gaze. . . . smilingly immune . . . to tactless gawking" (26–27).

Reports of Miss Sasagawara's madness and mysteriously brief period of sociability (when she choreographs a ballet dance for little girls dancing in the Christmas pageant) flow through the story by the force of community shock, mockery, and via the language of gossip. An unmarried, beautiful and talented woman (we discover later that she is a poet as well), does not, in this case, accord the language of admiration. Yamamoto's choice to focus on a community's construction of a heroine that rests on half-truths, dubious assessments of her mental stability, and the objectifying gaze on her body serves as social commentary on the power of societal expectations and standards of normalcy. This power is maintained within a community of Japanese Americans who are collectively experiencing more insidious and institutionalized forms of discrimination while they are relocated and interned during World War II. Yamamoto's story thus critiques the normalizing power of culturally dominant ideals within the camp while also subtly hinting at the power of cultural policing by the American government.[13]

Like "The Legend," Yamamoto's other stories are not sentimental portraits of idealized femininity. Her 1948 story, "The High-Heeled Shoes: A Memoir," subverts the expectations conjured by its title and focuses instead on the construction of femininity in a society that leaves women vulnerable to the sexual whimsy of a perverse masculinity and institutionalized patriarchy. The story's central protagonist becomes unhinged one morning after receiving a suggestive phone call from a man she does not know, and the incident triggers the suppressed memory of other similar incidents, including one involving a naked man wearing high-heeled shoes who attempts to lure women to his car. "Seventeen Syllables" and "Yoneko's Earthquake," two frequently anthologized stories, also emphasize female vulnerability and internal suffering as two young girls awaken suddenly into cynical adulthoods after hearing of their mothers' sexual transgressions. These stories all indict patriarchal conventions as the primary reasons for the unhappiness of mothers and daughters who have to accommodate the realities of suppressed individual liberties into their formerly dream-filled and innocent world views.

Like the representation of objectively superior female characters in the works previously discussed in this chapter, the creation of a relational feminine distinction in Yamamoto's stories exposes exclusionary social and cultural standards; however, Yamamoto's characterizations operate without the accompaniment of marriage plots and conventionally romantic or sentimental language. She and other contemporary Asian American writers usually reserve objectifying descriptions of physical beauty for secondary personae, displacing the criteria for conventional heroines away from the central female character. One could argue, for example, that the real heroine of "The Legend" is the nondescript Kiku who narrates the tale and of whom we know even less about than Miss Sasagawara. As an alternative to conventional forms of heroine construction, Asian American heroine objectification often highlights the unhealthy consequences of feminine passivity while also allowing the narrator or central protagonist to explore her own feelings of insecurity for not being able to meet dominant cultural ideals of femininity. These narrators may then use descriptions of feminine distinction to highlight the traditional, conventional values of their communities, values that are represented as threatening to the female narrators' scope for self-expression and self-actualization. Stan Yogi notes in his essay, "Rebels and Heroines," that Yamamoto characterizes "unlikely outlaws who violate cultural rules" from the perspective of young female second-generation (Nisei) narrators who regard the outcast women with a "compassion" that "indicates that they reject the subjugation of women dictated by Issei [first generation] culture" (Yogi 146). Thus, Yamamoto's stories share the feminist purview of many of the works already discussed, including *Little Women, Four Girls, Plum Bun* and *The House of Mirth,* but her heroines challenge social conventions without having to be extraordinary themselves.

In the developments within Asian American literature since the turn-of-the-century writing of the Eaton sisters, the poetics of heroine construction shift the focus away from superlative being to an inner ordinariness of subjectivity. These seemingly everyday heroines remember and reflect upon extraordinary, haunting events. Yoneko Hosoume in Yamamoto's "Yoneko's Earthquake" is the first-person narrator in a story about adultery, patriarchal Issei mores, abortion, death, and the destabilization of religious faith. The adult Yoneko, remembering events that took place during her childhood, does not emphasize her physical person in any way, choosing instead to describe other characters in detail while delineating the painful realities absorbed by her inner world as a child turning into an adult. Like Kiku in "Miss Sasagawara," Yoneko expounds upon the physical attractiveness and talents of another central character, this time a man, who ultimately exposes the domestic instabilities within the Hosoume household. The weight of the past, in these more contemporary Asian American female narratives, overpowers women who wrestle with repressed memories. Like the heroines of gothic novels, many female protagonists of Asian American fiction are potential victims of seemingly mysterious forces that are not exactly supernatural, but are instead complex webs of secrets; the goal of narrative recollection and report in these stories and novels involves the heroine's ability to solve a mystery of her past.[14]

This interiority, accessible via the first-person narration of contemporary Asian American fiction, stemming from Yamamoto's stories to more recent versions of female Asian American subjectivity, offers a counter-aesthetic pattern of heroine construction, one which might nevertheless remind readers of fiercely interior anglo first-person heroines like Brontë's Jane Eyre or Lucy Snowe. The fact that much of contemporary Asian American fiction refuses to participate in conventional forms of narrative resolution, however, does not change the visibility of its investments in its own patterns and systems of signifying the social or material prospects of its heroines. Although Asian American narratives like Yamamoto's stories resist the "happy endings" found in obvious courtship-to-marriage plots found in *Plum Bun,* or *Four Girls at Cottage City* by limiting the associations of romance evoked by the language of heroine objectification, the alternative emphasis on female subjective interiority in light of strained material conditions is what Lily Bart achieves in the last chapters of Wharton's *The House of Mirth.* Thus, the "tragic paradigm" found within women's texts, as discussed by Lorna Ellis in her work on British women's fiction, is not limited to ethnic fiction but is in fact the fate waiting also for several strong-willed anglo heroines who refuse to compromise their beliefs to meet conventional standards of behavior (Ellis 162).

As this chapter has explored, female subjective development, whether anglo or ethnic, involves the mediation of intertextual and relational performances of identities. In keeping with the dominant conventions of late nineteenth-century women's fiction found within the works of the Eaton sisters, early twentieth-century American women's texts evince a consciousness of market forces, both at the level of marriage plot thematics and within the poetics of heroine objectification, which help to make heroines familiar to readers. Ethnic and anglo heroines remain characterized in remarkably similar ways as these objectified characterizations straddle the binaries of beautiful and plain, rich and poor, feminine and unfeminine. Thus, Alcott's little women share a common language of feminine characterization with Kelley-Hawkins's four girls; Jessie Fauset's heroine Angela exemplifies a subjective longing for distinction similar to Edith Wharton's Lily Bart. This Cinderellaesque narrative motion towards subjective redemption from social exclusion evolves to more complex and subtle articulations of female development with the emergence of heroines, who, like Yamamoto's characters, search for new ways to critique social displacement and sexism. However, the advancement of cultural politics is not always accompanied by

radically different poetics due to the ways in which heroines maintain significant transcultural relationships. In the subsequent two chapters, I will look
at the developments within more recent examples of ethnic heroine construction in an effort to demonstrate that the evolving contemporary heroine continues to reference conventional structural trajectories. In the next
chapter, I will incorporate this section's examination of relational identity
and heroine objectification into a discussion of subjective negotiations of
space and place as heroines attempt to move beyond the constrictive parameters of the marriage market into rooms of their own.

Chapter Three
Cinderella's Understudies:
Marginality, Ethnicity, and the Negotiated Spaces of Heroine Desire

Over the years, anglo feminist literary tradition has built a shared understanding of the symbolism of space and architecture as representative of gender roles within society and the domestic familial unit. Perhaps the most famous example of scholarly work on gender and space is Gilbert and Gubar's *The Madwoman in the Attic* (1979), a text that has elicited widespread recognition of a paradigmatically female literal and figurative circumscription.[1] Highlighting claustrophobia and anxiety as two psychological drives influencing the narrative tensions and ambiguities within much of nineteenth-century women's fiction, Gilbert and Gubar ground their conclusions in an assumption that women writers of the nineteenth century share a tradition of searching for space and affirmation in a literary marketplace dominated by men. This seminal study characterizes female writing as an explorative yet often dangerous endeavor—a volatile craft, informed by fear of rejection and success, guilt, and the anxiety of representation. *The Madwoman in the Attic* put forth the idea that a feminine tradition, if not biologically determined, may at least incorporate a system of anxious signs as a set of psycho-social responses to writing under the weight of male authorial production and an often exclusive marketplace. To write, under these circumstances, is to evacuate the confined attic space, to risk the label of madness, and to invade the parlor, the drawing room, and even outdoor public spaces with the will of a general staking lost territory; it is to enter battle within the literary marketplace as well as attempting to reorder the spatial politics of narrative itself.

In this chapter, I will concentrate on space as it is conceptualized and symbolized in African American and Asian American women's novels in the twentieth century as a means of discussing a heroine's self-affirming search for place within society. I will show that the symbolic use of space in women's writing is another site of transcultural heroine production that challenges divisions between ethnic and anglo women's fiction. Beginning with an analysis of Jade Snow Wong's *Fifth Chinese Daughter* (1950) and then Jamaica Kincaid's *Lucy* (1991), I will trace their immigrant heroines' navigations towards self-actualization through the spaces of their adopted countries. I will also discuss their pursuit of vocational success as representative of their spatial conceptualizations of identity and the search for place or position. Finally, I will conclude with Paule Marshall's *Brown Girl, Brownstones* (1959), a novel that, more conspicuously than the others, employs a symbolism of architecture to demonstrate the relationship between ideas of space and self.

I will refer to conceptualizations of space outlined by Gaston Bachelard in *The Poetics of Space* (1964) and Yi-Fu Tuan in *Space and Place* (1977). The language of space permeates descriptions of physical structures like houses and rooms and provides a figurative model for critiquing the gradations of class and racial hierarchies. Space, in the texts at hand, also often signifies social position. Both anglo and ethnic women's texts maintain textual relationships with each other through a shared preoccupation with space while their heroines assert individual identities by demonstrating their places within their societies. I will challenge the model of claustrophobia associated with female writing and will instead explicate instances of a figurative, subjective agoraphobia within identity-formation similar to the ambivalence characterizing negotiations of marriage plots and heroine objectification outlined in the previous chapters. This agoraphobia often involves the overwhelming challenge for ethnic female subjects to construct self-actualized as well as unique identities within their bicultural communities, a challenge shared by their authors who battle the dynamics of production and consumption of female heroines and their stories in the literary marketplace.[2] Yi-Fu Tuan, in differentiating between ideas of space and place notes that although space "is more abstract than place," both concepts "require each other for definition" as "place" offers us a "security and stability" from which "we are aware of the openness, freedom, and threat of space, and vice versa" (Tuan 6).

Feminist criticism has also demonstrated over the years that physical confinement does not always prohibit or even restrict women's creativity. Second-wave feminist readings of domestic fiction discuss examples of subversive creativity even in the midst of gender-based social constriction. Even Virginia Woolf's famous treatise on the economic factors of female creativity,

A Room of One's Own, espouses a symbolically closed space that should be set apart specifically for a woman writer. Significantly, Woolf's prescription of privacy for the female writer involves a spatial language that attempts to remedy a stifling paradigm of marriage by offering another form of enclosure as an alternative to this convention. In tandem with this type of theoretical model of feminine creative freedom, this chapter explores heroines' relationships to space as transcultural narratives of female development attempt to offer new alternatives to the marriage plot. My reading of spatial language configures enclosed space as somehow empowering to the female protagonist who searches for a place within society.

Consider briefly the example of young Nanda Brookenham, who, in Henry James's novel *The Awkward Age*, cultivates a sense of individual self-consequence by burrowing in the space of her tastefully decorated boudoir. James suggests that Nanda's refuge in this room is a natural alternative to marriage after she realizes that the man she wants to marry will not, in fact, marry her. Other examples in literature and criticism point to tensions and contradictions within concepts of space that inspire the type of observation one character makes about Victorian femininity in A.S. Byatt's 1990 novel *Possession*:

> I wrote a paper on Victorian women's imagination of space. *Marginal Beings and Liminal Poetry*. About agoraphobia and claustrophobia and the paradoxical desire to be let out into unconfined space, the wild moorland, the open ground, and at the same time to be closed into tighter and tighter impenetrable small spaces—like Emily Dickinson's voluntary confinement, like the Sibyl's jar. (61)

Emily Dickinson offers a prototypical figure for the creative force and impact deployed from closed quarters; she also lends the notion of cloistered womanhood a meaningful sense of agency. Dickinson chose not to leave her house and even her room for much of her life. Her history is intriguing in light of contemporary evaluations of space, the novel, and femininity. As countless works of feminist scholarship evince, nineteenth-century American women were expected to think of themselves as objects and agents of domestic tranquility, and if women chose to write at all, they were to write in the inoffensive language of sentimentality. Read in this context, Emily Dickinson's poetry and identity (the sheltered daughter of New England who was always clothed in virginal white) configures and repositions all of these norms into a powerfully individuated voice.[4]

If we consider that Dickinson was voluntarily penned off from the rest of the physical world, then we have the beginnings of a model for envisioning female narrative identity as a response to agoraphobia instead of claustrophobia. Dickinson's deliberate though ironic use of closed physical space also provides us with a model for the symbolic pleasures offered by nurturing and self-affirming closed spaces. Several examples of nineteenth- and early twentieth-century anglo fiction provide us with meaningful interpretations of space in relation to identity. In Theodore Dreiser's *Sister Carrie* (1900), the narrative trajectory of female development highlights an ordinary woman's search for space, place, and vocational success in an urban marketplace ridden with other talented individuals. In this system, the heroine can succor her desire for self-consequence and social recognition only by using the hyperreal space of the stage. Jane Austen's *Mansfield Park* also contributes to an understanding of symbolic space because of the disjunction between the Bertram's comfortable domestic situation and Fanny's secondary position as the charity cousin. The Bertram family relegates her to the removed quarters of the small east room which never has a fire, and Fanny serves more as a handmaid to Mrs. Bertram than as a member of the family. Nevertheless, within the thematic world of Austen's fiction, in which urban values falter morally in relation to more localized country mores, Fanny's characterization offers an appealing reworking of fairy tale dynamics, which redeem domestic servants and traveling female vagrants by positioning them as true princesses worthy of the love and domestic security resulting from marriage to a prince. (Fanny wins the contest between herself and the worldly Mary Crawford for Edmund's love.)[5] As we will find in this chapter, different narrative modes, such as the naturalism informing Sister Carrie's negotiation of agoraphobic self-construction as well as Austen's narrative combination of realism and romance, are both involved in the transcultural spatial charting of developmental potential for ethnic heroines.

OLD WORLD, NEW WORLD: IMMIGRATION, SPACE, AND THE NEW VILLAGE

Because they re-articulate the American promise of self-made success and the struggle for a place within the country's countless networks of thriving markets, narratives of immigration offer perhaps the best models of the dynamism of space in the construction of female ethnicity. In fact, spatial metaphors pervade much of early and contemporary American immigrant fiction as narrators and protagonists express a sense of disjointed existence between the felt presence of the old world in the new world. David Leiwei Li tells us that some of "these narratives invariably engage the feelings of home and belonging not only in the present but also throughout the long processes through which subjective identifications with geocultural space are formed" (Li 126). The narrator of Maxine Hong Kingston's *The Woman Warrior* (1976) claims, "I could not figure out what was my village" (Kingston 45). Frank Chin's *Donald Duk* (1991) also makes evocative use of the Chinatown space while depicting the protagonist's sense of being suspended between two different cultural worlds. On the first page of Jade Snow Wong's autobiographical novel, *Fifth Chinese Daughter* (1950), our narrator introduces Chinatown as "one of the unique spots of this continent" (1). Emphasizing Chinatown's smallness within the San Francisco neighborhood of Nob Hill, within the city itself, and even within the "continent," the narrator highlights its "narrow, congested streets," and its "compact" quality. In the second paragraph, we read about the dissonant cultural spaces pervading Chinatown's "atmosphere," and this tension parallels the protagonist's later developmental challenge of negotiating the cultural expectations of two worlds. Using the gradations of landscape as a natural analogy to the syncretism present in Chinatown, Wong writes: "The same Pacific Ocean laves the shores of both worlds, a tangible link between old and new, past and present, Orient and Occident."

Like the other narratives discussed in this project, *Fifth Chinese Daughter* creates its own version of ethnic subjectivity by characterizing one female's cultural identity in relation to a dominant system of mores and aesthetic ideals. At the time of its publication in 1950, the ethnic category of "Asian American" had little meaning or currency; accordingly, *Fifth Chinese Daughter* makes no significant mention of any other Asian national group, relying instead on the creation of racialized distinctions between "Caucasian," "Chinese," and "Negro." The novel fosters a discussion of relational femininity in which the young female protagonist's greatest subjective challenge is to find self-affirmation within the network of patriarchal forces present in Chinatown and the ethnocentrism of mainstream American society. As Xiao-huang Yin notes, young Wong's search for self is driven by a "longing and passionate admiration for life in the outside world," as well as the burden of "redefining Chinese heritage to fit certain expectations of the American public" (Yin 142, 148). Jade Snow, like other ethnic immigrant heroines, understands that her need to rebel is informed by the disjunction between old world and new world ideas; yet these differences are often expressed in simple terms, which effect larger narrative similarities between characters like Jade Snow and more canonical heroines like Jane Eyre and Lucy Snowe. Similar to the paradoxes defining many of the actions undertaken by Brontë's female characters, Jade Snow does not decide to leave the constricting space of Chinatown to seek her fortune within the presumably more liberated space of the Western world. Rather than mere escape, Jade

Snow continues to search for a place within her community, choosing to work within the space of Chinatown instead of leaping out into the wide world. Claustrophobia provides an incomplete model for explaining the movements towards self-actualization of such heroines. More powerful than constriction, Wong implies, is the fear of rejection, loneliness, and isolation offered by the open world, where one is alone and without community, without a "mesh of tradition," and without a collective order within which and from which to achieve and express a unique identity and life (Wong 110).

Both Jade Snow Wong and Frank Chin fashion protagonists who are initially tempted out of the space of Chinatown because of the relative freedom of subjective experience offered in mainstream white America. Chin's Donald walks around grumbling about "dinky Portsmouth Square" and other spaces within Chinatown. Jade Snow seeks self betterment and independence by doing domestic work in the grand households of white America, but these glimpses of a non-Chinatown life and higher socioeconomic positions seem less than appealing in the narrator's accompanying descriptions of bourgeois materialism and elitism. Though Xiao-huang Yin claims that Wong idealizes American life in these sections, Wong's descriptions are actually far more ambivalent about the manifestations of white American prosperity (Yin 135–140). Wong uses the architecture of interior spaces in these sections to suggest her distaste with the visible structure of a class economy: "the perpetually darkened 'front room' with its heavy velvet drapes, drawn to keep the sun from fading the plush furniture" (104). About another family's house, Wong writes somewhat judgmentally: "They owned a large house patterned after English cottage architecture, which the mother tried to keep in perfect order as a setting for her daughters' activities" (105). The discussion of space here contributes to a critique of an exclusive, materialistic white culture, a feature common to both *Fifth Chinese Daughter* as well as *Donald Duk;* these and other elements of critique carry the narrative justification for the decisions both protagonists make in favor of their fathers' abilities to maintain ties to Chinese culture. Like Donald's self-taught appreciation for and understanding of his father's idea of being a Chinese-American without losing his Chinese heritage, Jade Snow similarly looks for a way to express a unique blend of two cultures. After a successful college career that she undertakes to be free of the constrictions of traditional nineteenth-century Chinese mores, Jade Snow develops her artistic talent and sets up a shop in Chinatown for sculpture and pottery as a way to win parental approval through acts of deliberate cultural compromise prescribed by her father.

Chin and Wong also both perform subjective mediations between communal pressure and individual desires in their spatial manipulations of point-of-view, which blur first-and third-person perspectives. Wong explains in her foreword that her use of the third-person point-of- view to discuss one central heroine is in keeping with traditional Chinese narrative form and cultural order. The fusion of perspective in both cases explores the spatial parameters of narrative form as each first-person voice is contained within the larger space of third-person, collective existence. Demure but defiant, self-assertive but cushioned ultimately by growing parental approval and respect, Jade Snow learns to carve a unique place of her own within the overlapping spaces between "Caucasian" and "Chinese" culture. Moving along the path towards educational and artistic success, she becomes the daughter—the self—of a text of her own creation. As space and place configure ontological possibilities and identity roles in the novel, the narrative fosters, sustains, and nurtures Jade Snow's developing sense of individual self.

This exploratory narrative perspective works to demonstrate the complex, relational process of self-formation for the Chinese American subject, and in Jade Snow's case, the mantle of authority cloaking her expression of individuality is a deliberate tool of balance between the divergent authorities which guide her self-construction. Her expression of American identity incorporates the Chinese cultural tenets of respect, order, and personal humility; in the text's prefatory words Jade Snow describes the stages of her young life with a "psychological detachment" used to detract from her "personal importance"(vii). Most of her assertions of independence in the text are cushioned within her respect for tradition and the discipline of moderation or balance. When Jade faces the threat of a humiliating corporal punishment in Chinese school after she is unjustly singled out for having passed notes in class, she deflects the punishment by vocalizing her rights as an individual. As she speaks to Mr. Dong, she chooses to defer to another patriarchal authority—her father—in defying Mr. Dong's orders: "I speak only for what is right, and I will always question wrong in the way my Daddy has taught me. I am willing to bring him here to submit this matter to his judgment. Until then, I hold out no hand" (64).

Such impassioned eloquence for justice reminds us of another surprisingly strong-willed heroine—Jane Eyre—who also uses the collective plight of the weak and oppressed within which to situate her own rebellion against authority figures like Aunt Reed and Mr. Brocklehurst. Both Jane and Jade Snow use form and structural order of the first-person autobiographical narrative in which to highlight their unique stories of displaced feminine development. The heroines' stories are also similar in that they share a need to project an unconventional, non-frivolous type of femininity in the pages of their narratives—an emphatic seriousness—characterized by diligent pursuit of education and self-betterment and self-affirmation, perhaps as a defensive measure against the secondary consideration they both receive within their larger familial units. A reliance on ideas of providence and a belief in the redemption servicing the virtues of fortitude, patience, and hope is another common thread between the two texts. While situating her personal goal of bicultural success and self-improvement, Jade Snow narrates that she "left it to God to take care of His share in bringing her college education to reality" (111) which is evocative of Brontë's famous concluding apostrophe, "Amen, even so, come, Lord Jesus!'" Both texts, though driven by the characterization of independently-minded women, take special pains to demonstrate larger cultural or religious orders that seem to sanction the rebellion of the heroines.

Wong titles her last chapter with the words of a Chinese Proverb and concludes her account of her creative and cultural success in Chinatown by first noting the surprise about her accomplishments in "the eyes of the Western world"(244). She notes the pervasive skepticism of the larger Chinatown community:

> Chinatown was agog. A woman in the window, her legs astride a potter's wheel, her hair in braids, her hands perpetually messy with sticky California clay, her finished products such things as coolies used in China, the daughter of a conservative family, running a business alone— such a combination was sure to fail! (244)

The passage attempts to signify our heroine's bicultural identity through a culturally syncretic description of her physical form in the window. Like Jane Eyre's fierce self-assertion of physical plainness, Jade Snow wears braids instead of curling her hair in the Western fashion to which her sisters adhere (89). This observance of conservative style helps her balance her more internal rebellion against patriarchy. She works alone, and she has no qualms about putting her body on public display, "Western" style, while working to hone her craft, "Chinese" style. Her success as a young woman here is thus highlighted in terms of resourcefulness, labor, and creative ability rather than foregrounding her value as a marriageable person. And yet, Jade's creative efforts—her signification of an individual voice and identity—still demand and elicit public commendation in the conventional sense.

Wong suffuses the doubts evidenced by the Chinatown community by recognizing the familial approval and respect Jade Snow wins with this show of her industriousness and respect for discipline. Mr. Wong expresses his support for his daughter in a conclusive "narrative, unusual in nature and length," in which he praises the American "Christian concept" which "allows women their freedom and individuality" (246). Like Brontë's Jane,

Jade Snow too feels compelled to conclude her personal story of self-construction and growth within the larger order of Christianity. If the search for a self-affirming place within the larger grasp of tradition were not clear enough, Jade Snow congratulates herself on being able finally to "stop searching for that niche that would be hers alone." As the cover of the first edition of the text illustrates, with its depiction of the back of a young woman walking alone through what is presumably the empty space of San Francisco's Chinatown, Jade Snow tells us that she "had found herself and struck her speed."

The search for a personal place within a community, city, and national culture—"that niche"—shapes Wong's narrative. Her autobiographical novel balances chapters emphasizing lessons she has learned personally with the stock plot elements of Western narrated self. Wong's first chapter, "The World Was New," situates young Jade Snow, innocent, youthfully flawed, and new to language and general rules of social living. Subsequent chapters such as "Learning to Be a Chinese Housewife," and "The Taste of Independence," cohere around the novel's underlying theme of the complex, tense relationship between personal freedom and societal mores. Like the individual chapters of slave narratives and other nineteenth-century autobiographies, each section offers the protagonist a personal place in the collective narrative of Western cultural selfhood. The writer of this record of self-formation is aware of narrative expectations and formal conventions as she crafts each section.[6] Thus, halfway through the story of the first twenty-four years of Jade Snow Wong's life, she labels a chapter "Girl Meets Boy," with an eye towards the literary convention of the heterosexual romantic subplot. The chapter itself is mild in terms of romance. Wong situates the encounter between Joe and Jade Snow by pointing out Jade Snow's previous romantic experience in relation to a white American norm: "Jade Snow had not even gone out on her first date" (114). In her dry, matter-of-fact style, Wong describes Jade Snow's growing uneasiness about "missing something obviously very desirable" (115).

Through an insincere and forced structural organization, Wong attempts to construct a clean narrative of sectional development, suggesting that it is only in this "Girl Meets Boy" chapter that Jade Snow has suddenly started to question her lifestyle in relation to "normal" teenage female experiences.[7] Wong writes: "It was then that she began to wonder whether getting the highest grades was the most important accomplishment in school after all." The claim is disingenuous, yet appropriate for autobiographical writing. Fiction allows space for nameless longings and motifs of unfulfilled dreams and visions. The classic autobiography, the earliest examples focusing on self-betterment, places subjective goals and experiences in declarative language, and most of the narrative action of character development fits squarely within the parameters of chapters. Wong's text adheres to this demonstrative language and order in keeping with the autobiographic mode, a mode that tends to limit the exploration of topics and characters unrelated to the lessons learned by the self. Such formal deliberation accounts for Wong's easy dismissal of sibling rivalry between all the Wong daughters. In the earlier chapter, "With Eyes on China," which begins with a discussion of the Chinese marital customs and their implications for female behavior, Jade Snow examines the differences between herself and her younger sister, Jade Precious Stone. By using empirical statements that objectively characterize both girls as polar opposites in two brief paragraphs, Jade Snow contrasts her own industrious, active self to her prettier sister's "frivolous" and passive temperament, simplistically diffusing the narrative weight of a potentially significant rivalry between the two girls (88-89). Wong never discusses this difference in personality again, a practice that adds to the effect of order and structure in a search for identity via the causative language of self-improvement. Thus, Wong's readers are invited to experience Jade Snow's early life in relation to dominant norms and forms that make it easy to equate plainness and intelligence with quintessential narratives of plain and romantically inexperienced women.

However, Wong inserts an important difference—an ethnicized difference—into this narrative of first romance. This difference asserts itself as an emphatic practicality (Chineseness) as Jade Snow the narrator uses the mode of autoethnography to explain to her white audience the reasons why her version of American girlhood cannot be separated from its Chinese context. "Girl Meets Boy," does not wax poetic on first love and passion but discusses instead an oddly desexualized relationship between Joe and Jade Snow, as Joe gives Jade advice about college. Several pages later in an another chapter, Wong diffuses the emotional import of Jade Snow's first kiss with Joe by having Jade Snow analyze her lack of passionate feelings for him. "After all, he was twenty-three and probably too old for her anyway," she thinks, filing away the episode as another piece of experience to be subsumed within her larger narrative project of Chinese-American female expression (130). The placement of these incidents demonstrate Wong's understanding that heterosexual subplots are crucial to the marketability of her narrative; she manages to include all of the structural elements of a strong coming-of-age novel without using the rhetorical play of fiction. Her adaptation and "ethnicization" of the conventional female bildungsroman involves her substitution of matrimony with creative success and community recognition.

Wong's narrative goal—"the purpose of creating better understanding of the Chinese culture on the part of the Americans"—mediates her ethnographic consciousness, and consequently, her development of heroine construction explores cultural confusion compounded by institutional racism in proffering a sense of otherness. However, she cannot offer a truly distinctive and culturally determined sense of ethnicity. Rather, Wong's maneuverings between the narrative space of classic American autobiography, transatlantic women's bildingsromane, and a seemingly culturally-informed performance of a Chinese, third-person "I," depict a female subjectivity that employs the space and structure of conventional narratives in a desperate attempt to highlight the cultural syncretism of her own voice. Frank Chin condemns Wong's text for catering to a "white Christian imagination," especially in the characterization of Jade's father (Chin 24). While I disagree with Chin's dismissal of the text, Wong's voice does indeed mediate the forms of Western autobiography as well as the bildungsroman. The text's integration of these traditional anglo elements mirrors Jade Snow's own subjective navigation through the developmental possibilities offered in the world outside Chinatown, as well as the world within.

Jade Snow's identity, which she attributes to cultural blending, demonstrates the narrative shape of ethnic subjectivity. Jade Snow does not so much put forth an Asian American identity as much as she modulates the space between "Chinese" and "American." Ultimately, her success is professional, and it represents simply another version of the American success story. Her vocational success employs a revised narrative formula discussed by Lee Edwards in *Psyche as Hero;* Edwards explains that the marriage plot informing the narratives of writers like Jane Austen is replaced in the twentieth century by more liberated schemas of female self-actualization, like the quest for vocational and/or artistic success and recognition. She identifies an alternative transcultural template of the artist heroine, whose creative triumphs displace the previous structural condition of a heroine having to find a mate. I refer to Edwards here to point out that the model of vocational or artistic success occurs within anglo as well as ethnic fiction. Edwards's discussion of artistic and personal fulfillment for heroines examines the fiction of both Virginia Woolf and Maxine Hong Kingston, for example. This 1984 study suggests that ethnic identity shares significant structural features with anglo identity as heroines evolve in the twentieth century.

Wong's text serves as a sort of apprenticeship—an intermediary ground between non-fictional memoir devoted to ethnography and actualized fictional heroinism. Her story seems to hover in the wings of the stage of fictional expression as Jade must first model herself as an integrated bi-cultural self, before she and other immigrant heroines can garner the subjective power to set a new stage for ethnic heroinism in novels. As *Fifth Chinese Daughter* illustrates, vocational or artistic heroinism enacts a diligent search for a self-affirming place within society as the female protagonist initially experiences an understudy, or subservient role, usually in the form of domestic servitude. Self-actualized artistic expression may come, as Jade Snow's and Jane Eyre's stories show us, after an experiment with more regular work, which places the socially-displaced female protagonist in proximity to people who have more power and consequence. Service in the form of domestic work, tutoring, or teaching, however, offers socially-displaced women a relational power in terms of access to the physical spaces of domestic comfort as well as the benefits of class-distinction, which are configured by educational standards.[8]

By bridging *Fifth Chinese Daughter*'s culturally indistinct conceptualization of ethnic identity to heroines in African-American immigration texts, I will explicate further the ways in which female ethnic selfhood is articulated through the symbolism of space and place and the pursuit of vocational and artistic heroinism. In the following section, I will highlight the mechanics of a "governess syndrome" operating in the transcultural project of heroine construction, a structural element that is the result of anglo and ethnic writers' investigation of the spatial unrest experienced by their heroines. While exploring the overwhelming loneliness experienced by heroines in societies dominated by class and racial hierarchies, the governess syndrome enables a relational female identity-construction that allows the socially-displaced heroine access to the structures of cultural power while giving her a place from which to discuss her crucial difference and self-worth.

THE GOVERNESS SYNDROME: VOCATIONAL HEROINISM AND TWO LUCY'S

In her fiction, Charlotte Brontë removes the heroine from the privileged space of the drawing room and relegates her to the boarding school and classroom, with only provisional access to the grander interior spaces of wealth, power, and lavish comfort. While *Jane Eyre* represents, for many, the prototypical governess heroine and the founding text of a transatlantic tradition of governess heroines, Lucy Snowe, the more cynical and anti-social heroine of Brontë's *Villette*, explores this narrative tension of spatial inclusion and exclusion to its most extreme, most isolated level. Lucy Snowe makes no mention of her parents or any real family. In fact, she anchors her story of personal development in a series of long-lived encounters that converge coincidentally around her relationship with her godmother's family, a family living happily in adequate comfort in a spacious home within which she begins her story. "Villette," a fictional name for Brussels and the town to which she sets sail to make her fortune, represents the site at which all of Lucy's unrealized longings, fears, and lessons of self interplay as she compares herself and her potential for happiness and intimacy with others around her. In Villette, Lucy reunites with the Brettons, her godmother's family, and she faces her own unrequited love for the son of this household, a man whose social prospects do not, in Lucy's opinion, match her own.

Plain, poor, and unconnected, Lucy Snowe takes Jane Eyre's story into the darker spaces of irremediable loneliness. Her one bright epoch takes place in a school in which she becomes an instructor and slowly falls in love with a male teacher (who eventually dies in a shipwreck). Probing the depths of self-doubt and self-projection, Brontë pairs Lucy with Madame Beck, the owner of the house and school in Villette, and employer to which Lucy is indebted for employing her when she is most in need. Madame Beck's mysterious, all knowing, and invasive character serves as a lens for Lucy' worst fears and doubts about her own ability to be happy in society. The relationship between employer and employee here involves an uncomfortable knowledge of hierarchy. This relationship mutes the benefits of the governess perspective as related by *Jane Eyre;* Lucy never feels like one of the family or like an affirmed member of the school. Her conflicted, paranoid character offers readers a unique perspective on the construct of a happy life. *Villette*'s refusal to grant its heroine any lasting redemption or any truly self-affirming place in society introduces a later nineteenth-century "tragic paradigm" in anglo women's literature (Ellis 162).[9] Its pessimistic critique of class-based exclusion makes it the perfect backdrop from which to highlight the narrative dynamics of racial and cultural social displacement configuring ethnic heroine construction in Jamaica Kincaid's *Lucy,* the story of a modern West-Indian au pair in urban America. As Brontë and Kincaid focus on the governess position in their representations of marginalized feminine development, the similarities in their shared strategies of characterizing heroine development reveal the spatial qualities of both anglo and ethnic identity construction, as the female protagonists, attempting to move beyond the marital paradigm for self-affirmation, search for secondary positions and places within stable familial units.

Both heroines' stories exemplify figurative tensions between ideas of space and place,"space" representing amorphous ontological possibilities in a lonely, exclusionary world and "place" offering a sense of home—a feeling of belonging and affirmed identity resulting from attaining an individual role or position within a household, or social unit. As Tuan notes in his study of space, "What begins as undifferentiated space becomes place as we get to know it better and endow it with value" (6). In the following passage, which poetically demarcates the space between a human being and the surrounding universe, Bachelard offers a similar insight into the appeal of place, which works against an occasionally overwhelming sense of space, creating a form of subjective agoraphobia: "How terrible the world seems to those who do not know themselves! When you felt so alone and abandoned in the presence of the sea, imagine what solitude the waters must have felt in the night, or the night's own solitude in a universe without end!" (189).

In *The Poetics of Space,* Bachelard discusses the meaning of "intimate space" as he claims that "whenever space is a value—there is no greater value than intimacy" (202). In their pursuit of intimacy and their explorations of identity, both Lucy's share a quest for place that is narrated in terms of a similar language of marginalization that transcends race and class as well as time. As *Lucy* explores the thematics of social exclusion and cultural alienation, it incorporates the structure of Brontë's governess story. The text's exploration of the spatial politics of social position enables not only a discussion of class-based social exclusion, but extends its spatialized geopolitical critique to colonialism and neocolonialism.

The female protagonist of Kincaid's *Lucy* (1991) steps into the literary potential of governess narratives at the end of a century teeming with the ready language of postcolonialism and feminism. Less than twenty pages from the end of Kincaid's short novel of movingly understated self-reflection, Lucy describes the origin of her name and dances lightly around her barely articulate feelings of indignation and anger at the British colonialism pervading the cultural history of her homeland of Antigua. Lucy alludes sweepingly to the country's complex legacy of institutionalized and cultural patriarchy in a description of a rich uncle whose name she must take as a middle name and a last name which "must have come from the Englishman who owned my ancestors when they were slaves" (149).

In this same paragraph, Kincaid invokes the canonical names of nineteenth-century British women writers as Lucy explains her desire to be named "Emily, Charlotte, Jane . . . the names of authoresses whose books . . . [she] loved." While Lucy Potter's story shares thematic and structural similarities with the story of Lucy Snowe's life in *Villette,* Kincaid's Lucy chooses to identify her name with Lucifer after her mother irritatingly tells Lucy she has named her after "Satan himself" (152). The delight with which Lucy accepts this explanation, and her later identification with Satan's figure in the Bible and "Paradise Lost," typify her postcolonial relationship to grand narratives of culture and literature. Lucy harbors anger towards daffodils in the American northeastern spring because she remembers the injustice of having to learn Wordsworth's poem in a school system designed to rear proper British subjects (29–30). She envisions her life as "a book of blank pages," and tries fiercely to avoid the narrative patterns, constructs, and "untruths" that she learns to associate with a "life with mother, father, and some children" (77).

To avoid living a life of domestic unhappiness and cultural servitude like the life Lucy sees her mother leading, Lucy leaves her island of perpetual sunshine to come to the United States as an au pair, a retreat she conceptualizes in terms of space. About the difference she now feels in her new life as a domestic servant, Lucy offers the following spatial relationship:

> I was no longer in a tropical zone, and this realization now entered my life like a flow of water diving formerly dry and solid ground, creating two banks, one of which was my past—so familiar and predictable that even my unhappiness then made me happy now just to think of it—the other my future, a gray blank, an overcast seascape on which the rain was falling and no boats were in sight. (5–6)

These beginning pages of the novel are rich with spatial imagery as Lucy attempts to reckon with her inchoate feelings of homesickness even while she is in the midst of defending her emigration from Antigua to herself and to her readers. She reflects upon the fact that the American cityscapes she sees on the night of her arrival are the very places about which she used to day dream: "all these places were lifeboats to my small drowning soul, for I would imagine myself entering and leaving them . . . through a bad feeling I did not have a name for" (1). As the longer passage above indicates, Lucy's arrival and subsequent acclimation into the American life involves a process of constant referential living, towards her past, her home country and her new home as she deflects and dodges the personal limitations and obstacles offered in each space she navigates towards.

Lucy's growing homesickness causes her to remember her vision of a future when she was safe in Anitgua: "If I had to draw a picture of my future then, it would have been a large gray patch surrounded by black, blacker, blackest" (6). On the next page, Lucy describes her room in her new American home, "a small room just off the kitchen—the maid's room." She clarifies her new image of herself to her readers: "I was only an unhappy young woman living in a maid's room, and I was not even the maid" (7). This admission dissolves, like all other of Lucy's thoughts, in the stream of her incessant evaluation of good and bad, happiness and unhappiness, both for herself and for the people around her. She dreams of a nightgown made in Australia, and awakens with the household's "actual maid" looking down at her. The word "Australia" reminds her of this continent's spatial (and colonial) relationship to the rest of the world, a relationship, which set in context to Lucy's deep rumination about the spaces of her past and present, Antigua and America, suggest her own unarticulated sense of individual and cultural violation and shame as a colonized person and an expatriate. Australia, she thinks, "was settled as a prison for bad people, people so bad that they couldn't be put in a prison in their own country" (9).

Eleanor Ty maintains that Lucy's ruptured relationship with her mother and her subsequent emigration from her motherland demonstrates the postcolonial version of the psychoanalytic conflict of "becoming a gendered subject," a process that entails "a splitting off from the pre-oedipal, maternal bond and embracing the Law of the Father" (Ty 120). While I believe that this type of reading is productive in contextualizing the decolonizing role of ethnic and minority fiction, I feel that it ignores the ways in which a novel like Lucy engages with the narrative structures it reputedly critiques. Lucy tells us explicitly that she has "loved" the fiction of Charlotte Brontë, and this "love" is manifested in the structural similarities between *Villette* and *Lucy*. Both novels are narrated by heroines who cannot stop comparing themselves to those around them.

Kincaid's heroine charts the traditional territory of the anglo-woman's first-person narrative by destabilizing, through her pent-up frustration and cynicism, the "untruths" of "made up" storybook white domestic ideals (77, 12). From the perspective of the outsider or "Visitor," Lucy evaluates her employers and their privileged and seemingly liberated lifestyle towards which the rest of the civilized world is supposed to aspire. Having caught that "lifeboat" to get to such freedom, Lucy begins to understand the connections between her country's history of exploitation and the mental luxury and the comfort enjoyed by people who can sincerely believe in causes (environmentalism) and truths (a mother's love for her children), all of which Lucy finds remarkable (71, 26). Her refrain is telling: "How do you get to be that way?" As the children of this comfortable urban apartment watch the rain in wonder, and as the emotions of those around her soar and thrive on changes in climate, Lucy questions: "How do you get to be a person who is made miserable . . . because the weather doesn't live up to your expectations?" (13, 20). The question is only almost rhetorical; it contains a subtle but earnest request for instruction. Lucy leaves Antigua to become a better, freer person, but the pages that follow indicate that she feels that there may be something embedded in the core of her self that makes her irreconcilable to positive thinking and to happiness. As with Lucy Snowe, the reasons for Lucy Potter's internalization of hopelessness stem from her constant reference to the differences between her cultural identity as a woman from Antigua and rich white people in the United States. Like Lucy Snowe, who views her own personality and prospects as objectively weak and substandard in relation to the happier, richer, more loveable people around her, Lucy Potter attributes her isolation to her sense of self that is enmeshed in the hard, indisputable facts of colonialist and racist history.

Both heroines' stories are similar not only because of the connections between class hierarchy and racial exploitation, but also because they are defiant personae who insist upon finding places in society where they can be recognized and loved for themselves. This common thread is startlingly clear in the last paragraph of *Lucy,* when she finally begins to construct a tangible narrative for herself in the pages of a blank book. Breaking down with emotion her readers have not seen in her until this point, she writes: "I wish I could love someone so much that I would die from it" (164). These enigmatic, conclusive words offer readers some insight into the emotional need driving Lucy's movements through her life. Her retreat from Antigua and her mother and then her subsequent refusal to tie herself to her employer Mariah's family are defense mechanisms against the confusing emotional bonds between mother and daughter, employer and employee, colonizer and colonized. When it is time to leave the house on the Great Lake where she has gone for the summer with Mariah and the children, Lucy staves off her disappointment by detaching herself from the things she would most love:

> I would not miss the lake; it stank anyway, and the fish that lived in it were dying from living in it. I would not miss the long hot days, I would not miss the cool shaded woods, I would not miss the strange birds, I would not miss animals that came at dusk looking for food—I would not miss anything, for I long ago had decided not to miss anything. I sang songs; they were all about no pot of gold at the end of the rainbow, no good deed going unpunished, and unrequited love. (82)

Similarly, Brontë's Lucy Snowe cultivates a sensibility of ambivalent "Reason" in a chapter entitled "Reaction," which accounts her agonizing wait for a letter from Dr. Bretton, the man she loves without hope of reciprocation. In a language that describes an internal battle between the forces of "Reason," "Imagination," and "Hope," Lucy Snowe describes her own characteristic process of self-effacement and calm cynicism, and the passage below resonates with the same forced suppression against emotion captured in Lucy Potter's lyrical though insincere celebration of detachment:

> My mind, calmer and stronger now than last night, made for itself some
> imperious rules, prohibiting under deadly penalties all weak retrospect
> of happiness past; commanding a patient journeying through the wilder-
> ness of the present . . . checking the longing out-look for a far-off prom-
> ised land whose rivers are, perhaps never to be reached save in dying
> dreams. . . . (Brontë 289)

Kincaid's *Lucy,* like Brontë's *Villette,* constructs a relational feminine narrative which is meant to refract the narrative force of ultimate redemption,
peace, reward, love and social warmth, onto a cooler plane of concrete reality. Both narratives test formulas and schemas of personal success and societal inclusion by characterizing heroines who evaluate their prospects in a
material world and settle finally for secondary positions in which they feel
trapped but dare not leave for fear of failure, rejection, and the mean va-
garies of chance. While Lucy Snowe enters Villette society through the position of governess or in-house teacher, a perspective that offers a counter
narrative of poverty and isolation, Lucy Potter enters the American space
and presents a challenge to its cultural narratives of fulfillment from her position as a racial and national Other. She, too, must work for her place in the
space of a household as well as for her basic sustenance in the United States.

As Lucy Potter's relational narrative inserts this difference, it creates a
sense of ethnicity while using the governess narrative template of nineteenth-
century anglo fiction. Along with specific passages of social commentary critiquing the white bourgeois elitism of Mariah's friends who all "had fun" on
a trip to Antigua and the passages discussing Lucy's homeland's colonial
legacy, she asserts her difference from a white ideal by continuously displacing the object of her narrative search. Stream-of-consciousness judgments
about other people and references to lessons learned ultimately account for
Lucy's second retreat from Mariah's household, but instead of finding a better place for herself, Lucy finds an apartment with a roommate who does little to ease her sense of isolation. Instead of abating our heroine's sense of
spatial unrest and rootlessness, the novel evokes a more familiar narrative
structure (the search for a self-affirming place) to depict an unsatisfied quest
for self-actualization that attempts to undermine conventions of narrative resolution. However, Lucy Potter's emotional expression of her inability to "love
someone" on the last page of the novel unhinges the narrative's reserved, critical tone, dispelling at last the frightening power of a story of a self that seems
to refuse to connect to any place or person along the path of development.

Lucy learns cultural lessons and asks questions that loosely perform
Gayatri Spivak's discussion of "tangential narratives" in "Three Women's
Texts and a Critique of Imperialism." Spivak argues that canonical novels

like the ones written by Brontë, Shelley, and other nineteenth-century women displace the figures of racial "Others," and function according to narrative truths that maintain that "the other cannot be selfed" (Spivak 277). Through her portrait of Lucy's unhappiness, Kincaid enacts the exclusion of an elitist and racist narrative trajectory similar to nineteenth-century female development and concedes that sometimes the racial others cannot be "selfed" according to the comfortable narrative preoccupations of colonial culture. She explores the tension between the storybook narrative of a house with kids, a mother and father, and their domestic servant or nanny and Lucy's angst-ridden responsive feelings of betrayal and isolation to construct and narrate a relational model of ethnic selfhood.

Though Lucy re-articulates the governess position and perspective from the Other's point of view and thus occupies the central space of a narrative system previously reserved for anglo females, Kincaid's emphasis on Lucy's cynicism and guarded intimacy suggests that the material history of Lucy's subjective identity ultimately prevents her from finding a place in both American and Antiguan society, and from experiencing any sort of a "happy ending." However, as we have seen, Lucy Potter's isolation mirrors Lucy Snowe's, a heroine who is Jane Eyre's less popular, brooding sister, and who hails from a supposedly more idyllic, pre-postcolonial, anglo narrative realm. Lucy Potter's ethnicized sense of self thus integrates the structural space of the unhappy governess narrative in Kincaid's attempt to extend a critique of class to a critique of race. This structural integration, embodied by Lucy Potter's vocational explorations and immigration, does not articulate a sense of social displacement and marginalization that is remarkably distinct from a paradigm of class exclusion employed by Charlotte Brontë more than a hundred years earlier. That is, though Lucy Potter's material hardships and emotional angst are every bit as palpable as Lucy Snowe's, the specificities of her cultural anguish match the shape and tone of Lucy Snowe's non-ethnicized inferiority complex. Like the similarities in heroine objectification common to both Angela Murray in *Plum Bun* and Lily Bart in *The House of Mirth*, the search for place exemplified by the governess position employed by both Brontë and Kincaid articulates themes of gender, class, and racial exclusion through the use of shared narrative elements. The distinctions between anglo and ethnic fiction thus obscure the narrative project of self-expression as heroines articulate identity in relation to each other. These relationships between texts demonstrate the ethnic subject's investment in narrative templates, even as she attempts to find a new place for herself in fiction.

A comparison of the structural similarities shared by *Villette* and *Lucy* thus demonstrates poetic and thematic manipulations of space and place, which configure elements of class, race, as well as gender. Both texts use the position of the governess perspective in their narratives as a substitute for the traditional marriage plot; the stories of both Lucy's also thus represent a structural mediation between the space of the marriage plot and a place or sounding board for those women who cannot or choose not to marry. As both marginalized heroines search for a place within society through pursuit of domestic work, their stories are versions of female development and self-actualization that function in relation to the bourgeois familial unit and dominant cultural standards of self-consequence. The poetics of their shared need for love and affirmation demonstrate the role of a subjective longing for inclusion analogous to an outsider who looks in on the "material paradise" of people "bathed in nourishment, as though" they "were gratified with all the essential benefits" (Bachelard 7). The delineation of insider and outsider is expressed in even more concrete terms of space in the next section as houses provide meaning for immigrant subjectivities. We will find here that the exploration of spatial possibilities veers similarly away from the marriage plot and moves from the structural incorporation of the governess plot to the development of the artist heroine who searches for a place that will nurture her identity and self-expression.

THE SPACE OF SELF: SELINA BOYCE

The title of Paule Marshall's 1959 novel, *Brown Girl, Brownstones,* pairs elements of ontology and architecture succinctly, with equal emphasis, like words chanted in a children's rhyme in the rudimentary articulation of youth struggling to learn concepts of an adult world. Such a title, however, simplifies the relationship between the two elements, suggesting to some readers perhaps that the color of both skin and stone signify a unique racialized amity. Marshall never belabors a point of a strict racial connection between the two concepts; feminine development, like the history of the brownstone itself, involves a deeply complex mediation between shifting reference points and the subjective lessons learned from a more universal passing of time. "Brown girl," in Marshall's story, is a signifier referring to difference from the male norm, in terms of nationality and race as well as gender. Yet unlike Fauset's *Plum Bun,* there are hardly any white people in this novel until the last section, implying that a narrative of this type of difference and social displacement is relational and referential without ever once having to offer conventional comparisons between whiteness and blackness.

This section will contextualize Marshall's novel in light of her uniquely non-racialized meditation on racial and national identity as an exploration of spatialized and compartmentalized identity—or identity (individual and collective) as a series of spatially envisioned relationships; I argue that Marshall's vision of space and identity engenders a loose reordering of the bildungsroman format as the protagonist's development ultimately calls into question ideas of belonging and actualized identity. While Dorothy Hamer Denniston asserts that Marshall's novel "moves beyond Western literary paradigms to unveil a distinctly African orientation" that portrays the "black community as empowering to the individual," I see Marshall's re-configurations of these structures as indicative of her ambivalent feelings to-wards the anglo literary forms as well as convenient systems of identification, which fuel her heroine's own insatiable search for enclosure and defined parameters of self (Denniston 7). Denniston, and other ethnic-studies feminist scholars like Pin-chia Feng similarly offer culture-specific readings of narrative form that envision African American and Asian American narratives as somehow actively resistant to Western literary struc-tures. Although I believe that *Brown Girl, Brownstones* does ultimately en-gage with the structural requirements of bildungsromane, I will narrow my focus and primarily discuss the symbolism of space in the novel.

The novel's preoccupation with spatial dynamics is more apparent than in Wong's and Kincaid's accounts of their immigrant heroines' search for place and position. More than these other texts, Marshall's novel exem-plifies the pleasures of spatial limits in the formation of self because this text most adheres to the structure of the bildungsroman. Spatial and structural relationships thus allow Marshall to discuss racial identity without having to discuss blackness and whiteness in depth; we understand, as we begin reading the novel, that Selina's story is another version of female develop-ment and the quest for belonging in relation to a norm of white middle-class American citizenship. We comprehend Selina's desire for a place in society easily, precisely because Marshall's story incorporates the themes of identity-formation and intergenerational and intra-community conflict without dis-rupting conventional narratives of female development. I read Selina Boyce's restless movements between safe, enclosed places and intimidating open space as emblematic of her quest for an individuated, self-affirming place, a search that ultimately takes her beyond the spaces of her home, her commu-nity, and even her adopted country.

For Marshall, selfhood, or subjectivity, involves the navigation be-tween figurative and literal space. The brownstone, in Marshall's world, symbolizes Selina Boyce's incipient concept of self and being. Gaston Bachelard maintains that the house "is our first universe, a real cosmos in every sense of the word" (Bachelard 4). However, Selina experiences inner conflict with regards to her home; she develops into a young woman who understands her community's obsession with material advancement and the acquisition of property, which are signifiers of self-consequence in a class-stratified society. While the narrative charts her development, Selina searches for a meaningful place in society, a place outside her brownstone house, and even outside the confines of her Barbadian community's stifling social standards. Her search for a self-affirming place within her community involves her search for identity as well. Rejecting the domestic mores emphasized by her family and community, Selina looks to the world outside of her house to form her own values and sense of self. Yet, Selina does not suffer from a simple case of claustrophobia, as would fit most paradigms of feminist literary scholarship. Her manipulations of closed and open spaces within the novel enacts a complex schematization of abstract and physical space, one which symbolically outlines a young person's desperate movements between safety and danger, freedom and comfort, solitude and intimacy—movements driving her need to test out new spatial parameters in order to find a sense of well-being within a specific, nourishing place. As Yi-Fu Tuan notes, "Human lives are a dialectical movement between shelter and venture, attachment and freedom" (Tuan 54).

This section will explore Selina's restless negotiation of space in Marshall's novel as emblematic of subjectivity's entanglements with different societal categories and classifications of being: race, nation, class, and vocational position. For example, instead of choosing to be a governess like Lucy Potter or Lucy Snowe, Selina trains herself as an artist similarly to Jade Snow Wong's development as a sculptress. This decision involves a narrative trajectory similar to all three novels discussed previously in that these narratives emphasize vocational development as a meaningful alternative to marriage as the path towards self-actualization. Thus, Marshall delineates selfhood through a series of spatial relationships that span geographic concerns of space for immigrant persons striving to succeed within a foreign urban setting, as well as the limitless possibilities and subject positions available to second-generation Americans who, nevertheless, feel trapped by networks of social exclusion based on race, nation, class, or gender.

Marshall introduces the reader to the relationship between self and space in the beginning pages of the novel, first with the description of the brownstones on Chauncey Street, next by filtering the focus to the brownstone in which Selina lives, and finally arriving at the spot on the landing on which Selina sits in a dreamlike state. The role of houses as introductory symbols in novels of development has a particular nineteenth-century ring as we are reminded of Jane Eyre's description of Gateshead Hall and her reclusive window seat behind the red curtain, Lucy Snowe's choice of the

Bretton house as a starting subject point for her life story, as well as David Copperfield's famous description of his birth home. The tradition lives on in twentieth- century discussions of self and society, apparent for example in the beginning of novels like *Plum Bun*. In every instance mentioned above, the narrator compares the larger physical structure to the main protagonist at hand, usually using the language of materialism and aesthetics to situate an initial place, indicative of the hero or heroine's spatial/social unrest. As in the case with Lucy Snowe and Jane Eyre, Selina's housing structure reminds her of her own intrusion, her invasion of a space not truly reserved for her, according to the aesthetic codes of gentility determined by class and race. Selina wanders the formerly all-white inhabited brownstone, enjoying a clandestine appreciation for the Victorian furniture, which her family does not truly own. The descriptions of the finery of the interior surfaces serve as a contrast to the young female subject who feels inferior to the potential grandeur of the house and its furnishings, and who feels like a racial Other, as well as undeveloped, impotent, and unenlightened:

> A truculent face and eyes too large and old, a flat blouse, dirty shorts, and socks that always worked down into the heel of her sneakers. That was all she was. She did not belong here. She was something vulgar in a holy place. The room was theirs, she knew, glancing up at the frieze of cherubs and angels on the ceiling; it belonged to the ghost shapes hovering in the shadows. But not to her. (6)

The house in which she lives as an outsider thus embodies Selina's worst feelings of inferiority and second-class status. At this point in her life, Selina internalizes the exclusionary aesthetics of white colonialist culture, teaching herself that the "holy" classical-themed decorating scheme of the house does not represent her "vulgar" self. However, Marshall introduces the reader to Selina's self-loathing in terms of a more general pre-adolescent awkwardness and self-consciousness in her description of "eyes too large and old" and "a flat blouse" with "socks that always worked down into the heels of her sneakers"(6). As Selina develops into a young woman with talent and self-confidence, the house continues to evoke her feelings of shame and rootlessness. While Bachelard maintains that the space of the house is a positive site for social beings and discusses its "enclosed" and "protected" qualities ("all warm in the bosom of the house"), Selina's ambivalent relationship with the brownstone exemplifies her restless search for place in her bicultural community (Bachelard 7).

The spatial divisions within the brownstone are also analogous to the Boyces's tenuous position in white American society as the family feels displaced by immigration as well as race. Dorothy Denniston states, "The buildings, the rooms, the streets, the very silences cry out in sympathy with the exigencies of the black immigrants' plight in America" (Denniston 8). The Boyces hold the bottom rooms of the house, and the kitchen or main center of their household is situated in the basement. The owner of the house, an old white servant, dies slowly upstairs amidst finer yet dusty objects, much like Miss Havisham's interiors in *Great Expectations*. Space also determines the gender politics of the story, which present a matriarchal alternative to a patriarchal society ("man country") in which "the mother" has the strongest voice of all. The kitchen serves as the primary social marketplace, transformed from a private domestic realm to the most public room of the house. The father, Deighton, daydreams in a sun parlor, useless and impotent in Marshall's cosmology. And like every family of the Barbadian-American community and African American community of Brooklyn, the brownstones serve as indicators of familial consequence and identity.[10] While they share "the same brown monotony," each brownstone strives to preserve uniqueness—"something distinctively its own" (3).

Space, even when it seems to be a site for individual and collective transformation in Marshall's novel, implodes and explodes by way of the Selina's restive sense of urban realism. Marshall makes it relatively clear that Selina's (and her community's) quest for a safe, nurturing place rests upon a crumbling foundation of "scuffling" and scraping pennies—a sense of social stratification similar to Wharton's description of "dinginess," in *The House of Mirth* and F. Scott Fitzgerald's observation of the "ash heaps" between the glittering city of New York and the working class outskirts in *The Great Gatsby*. Readers may notice that after Silla Boyce attains her dream of having a brownstone, she cannot wait to acquire a second one in Crown Heights, the upscale neighborhood in which the rest of her community has already been buying up old houses. Thus, the meaning of any space changes and often evolves. Only on Saturday nights, for example, does Silla Boyce's kitchen transform itself from a space of drudgery and domestic dispute to a forum for feminocentric discussion and the exchange of ideas. We first experience the mother's awe inspiring oratory power in this room, through Selina's ambivalent perspective and her fear that her mother's often violent convictions will harm her and her father's dreamlike, fragile world. Her mother's words, to a ten-year-old Selina, are "living things . . . bestriding the air and charging the room with strong colors" (71).

The significant though indeterminate movements between safe and unsafe space in the novel may be best exemplified by the novel's initial description of Selina's movements inside the house and through her neighborhood.

If we understand this initial chapter's role in the novel as a prelude to the narration of her search for her place within society, and if we allow that each stop she makes within this first chapter, entitled "A Long Day and a Long Night," serves as a metaphor for a force and influence over her budding subjectivity, then we can begin to see the restless quality of her development. An analysis of Selina's preliminary movements illustrate that restlessness and confusion are overriding factors in Marshall's conceptualization of ethnic identity. When the novel begins, Selina is sitting on a landing, the most public interior space of the house, and the space least connected to any of the various cultural categories typified by the brownstone's inhabitants. In a passage noted above, she moves from the stairs to the most formal room of the house where she experiences the disillusionment of her own reflection as an inferior person in the parlor with its "hushed dimness" and "ponderous furniture and potted ferns which the whites had left" (5). Marshall weaves together these explorations of space with the narrator's description of Selina's changing moods. Her walk down the stairs towards the parlor, for example, is a walk of imaginative transformation: "she was no longer a dark girl alone and dreaming at the top of an old house, but one of them, [white people], invested with their beauty and gentility." She moves next to the basement where she and her sister sleep, and to the dining room, which houses nice but seldom-used things. Here, Selina sees a family photograph that does not include her. Her frustration upon seeing this picture underlines her need "to declare herself" against the ghostly image of a family that has not taken a family picture in ten years, and in an enigma of a home in which space is invested with secret meaning (6).

Selina's next movement is significant in that it involves some degree of sororophobia[11] When Selina, after seeing the family picture that shows everybody (including her now dead brother) but herself, impulsively feels the need to be heard in this "inviolate silence," she decides to burst in on the quiet enjoyed by her reclining, softly feminine (and menstruating) sister. Here in the bedroom, Marshall demonstrates the relationship between self and space as Selina, finding no solace in the exclusive quiet of the white and genteel parlor, glimpsing her absence and seeming insignificance in her family portrait within the unused tomblike dining room, invades the spatial harmony her sister Ina has created for herself on the bed. Fusing the now absent masculine power of the dead brother with her own sense of rough "awkwardness," Selina tries to assert herself in her shared bedroom by marring the quietude and conspicuous femininity embodied by her more passive, prettier and more proper older sister (4-7). Later in the novel, Marshall indicates that while young Selina feels intimidated by Ina's graceful development and meek obeisance to her parents, Ina, because she misinterprets strength as an unfeminine trait, and precisely because she always does what she is told, is far less developed and doomed to more unhappiness than Selina. Her name, "Ina," is itself only a part of Selina's name, and it signifies Ina's stunted subjective development. Nevertheless, until the novel's conclusive scenes, Ina's character and the possibilities of life she represents and experiences herself (early physical development, physical attractiveness, religious faith, and early engagement to a boy of whom her parents would approve) threaten Selina's still unrealized sense of self-affirmation and identity. In this initial bedroom encounter between sisters, Marshall demonstrates the power of conventional mores in distorting one's sense of self and space. Saddened and angered that her family does not envision a clear place and role for herself, Selina displaces her emotion onto a sister by whom she feels threatened. She accuses Ina of being an "ugly" baby, demonstrating her youthful corrective of violence and anger to remedy her own insecurity. Ina finds the statement laughable, rolls over in her pillow, and responds that Selina is growing "uglier" as she gets older (7).

The remainder of the chapter follows Selina's intermittent ramblings between closed spaces and open spaces. "After the house, Selina loved the park," Marshall writes (13). She sees the park not however as a simple open area, but as "the perfect boundary for her world. . . . the fitting buffer between Chauncey Street's gentility and Fulton Street's raucousness." The open green space is to Selina a mediation of spatial possibilities, a compromise between the proper world and the sinful one, and most importantly, a space where the "lovers met and murmured at night" (13). The amorous activity at the park is conjured in Selina's mind every time she thinks of the park. After she and her best friend Beryl are able to spend many evenings there confiding in each other, the conflation of love and acceptance with personal space is complete. Marshall plays subtly with a conventional pairing of romantic love and personal space as the true signifiers of self-consequence as she also introduces the reader to Selina's prepubescent undefined longings for sexual conventionality. Fulton Street, on the other hand, represents at this early stage, the amorphous, wide world, a force Selina regards with some ambivalence. She feels secure and snug on the landing in the brownstone and yet longs for the world "beyond the dark hall" full of "challenge" and "turbulence" (4, 13). This tension works ceaselessly in the novel as the protagonist becomes more and more aware of her loneliness, like *Plum Bun's* Angela Murray's sense of alienation in the crowded city of New York.

Near the park and Fulton Street, away from the rooms that had upset her just minutes before, Selina again glimpses the intimacy of a closed space formed by a band of girls (including her best friend Beryl) walking close to-gether without her. Selina feels envious and excluded because they have just spent time together "in the dark theater," and when they taunt her with de-tails about the movie, she thinks to herself that "she would be leaving them soon to live in a big house in a sweet land and that they would miss her" (15). As she thinks about another separate place as redemption for the ex-clusion she feels at this moment, Selina, the narrator tell us, "walked faster." After finally getting over her anger with Beryl, the two make a promise to spend the evening together sharing a secret, and Selina retreats once more in a state of happiness. She goes back to the parlor, the only awake member of her family in the brownstone, and finds repose in the parlor that would not comfort her before. Like Jane Eyre and the red curtain with the book of Bewick's birds, Selina takes her candy behind the window seat and thinks "warm thoughts of the secret she would share with Beryl" (16). Snug in her clandestine space of comfort, the hidden window of an exclusively formal room, the glass between her and the unpredictable world of emotion out-side, she sits and waits for the next obstacle of the day.[12] Gaston Bachelard's following description of enclosure and movement offers a spatial paradigm paralleling Selina's movement through space in search of an intimate sense of place: "It is a strange situation. The space we love is unwilling to remain permanently enclosed. It deploys and appears to move elsewhere without difficulty" (Bachelard 53).

Selina's typically adolescent search for self is dominated by her literal and figurative search for a cultural identity—a place or role—within her im-migrant community. While setting her heroine's development apart from a white norm, Marshall employs a symbolic register of displacement in the contrast between darkness and single rays of sunshine, the open spaces of freedom and possibility and the safe parameters of intimacy and nurturing, and the upper-class neighborhoods with magnificent new houses and poor neighborhoods of second-hand brownstones—"each generation unraveling in a quiet skein of years behind the green shades" (4). As she develops and searches earnestly for a self-affirming place within society, the metaphoric il-lustration of homelessness and rootlessness captures Selina's compounded alienation. Her subjective development is hinged precariously in the arrangement of culturally understood differences between black and white, Barbadian and "American Negro," girl and boy. The final movements of the novel's plot illustrate the sweep of her adolescent journey from an insular immigrant ethos, cutting through socioeconomic barriers by the force of her artistic talent, and arriving finally at stardom, center stage, superior, in tal-ent, to her white dancer peers.

Selina finds herself at last leading a battalion of movement all her own as she and her dancer friends troop "through the East side, bearing toward the river" to her white friend Margaret Benton's "greystone" house. In these moments after our heroine achieves artistic self-actualization, Marshall depicts the thrill of self-consequence and identity as the now fully grown and confidant Selina Boyce moves with a steady resolve to her destination. No longer chased and pursued by discomfort and alienation from unfriendly, threatening spaces, Selina marches with her group "in bold formation down the street, spanning the entire sidewalk . . . carrying their exhilaration in a warning to the other pedestrians" (283). Selina's band is a spectrum of feminine and feminist archetypes forging their way through bourgeois urban life, and Marshall tells us that Selina is the trained fighter, "a cavalier," next to the "fabulous sprite" and "Wagnerian heroine." The formation of this group of friends exemplifies a sense of belonging within "felicitous space" as Selina has, at least temporarily, found a place amongst her group of dancer friends, a place that simultaneously offers her freedom of movement and expression, but one in which she also experiences an "inner pressure" of "physically dominant intimacy" (Bachelard xxxi, 101). Thus, even during Selina's most gratifying moments of self-actualization, her sense of self mediates the dynamism between ideas of open freedom and experiences of intimacy, a relationship Marshall figuratively explores in the tension between closed and open space.

This self-assured forward propulsion and projection into adulthood is ultimately shaky, Marshall tells us. The first in a series of climactic exits and retreats, Selina's encounter with the fundamental racism practiced by Mrs. Benton and the members of her social class forces Selina to probe the layers of identity she has been constructing as she reflects upon "her own dark depth" (291). Marshall's mirror scene is crucial here because it lays out the unique feature of Selina's subjective angst—that even after surviving adolescence's regular tests of fortitude, and even after finding an outlet in which her true self can express itself—even with "the fierce struggle of her humanity she must also battle illusions!" (292). Marshall suggests that Selina has learned, similarly to Ralph Ellison's *Invisible Man*, that subjective essence and identity are realized and recognized through differing interpretations. In the midst of her self-actualization, Selina learns the lesson of appearances—that impenetrable surface that forms when others see her as an illusion—the fact of her blackness. For a novel entitled, *Brown Girl, Brownstones*, our narrator allows our heroine to experience the overt frustration of racialized alienation only two times, first at the beginning of the novel when Selina feels like an intruder in the parlor of her own home, and then this last time as she confronts a woman who underhandedly takes away the glory of Selina's first dance performance by attributing her artistic talent to her "race's natural talent for dancing and music" (288). As I mentioned at the beginning of this section, white characters enter the narrative only in the last section of the novel. Marshall's carefully structured exploration of a female self's movements and navigation between safe and unsafe spaces somehow evokes all of the feeling of a compounded isolation without introducing white characters until the end. We are left to assume, after reading Selina's epiphany in the mirror, and after evaluating the fact of the narrative's sparse white-black interaction, that much of the antagonism threatening her free subjective development comes from the "battle" necessary for identity formation within any community. Her greatest challenges have come from within her community and within herself.

Selina's character offers us a demonstration for the ceaseless motion and nameless longing experienced by the developing "I." This motion though does not follow the theoretical model developed by feminism and its description of claustrophobia as a result of gender and racial role limitations, but evokes instead a more general subjective agoraphobia, or a fear of subjective possibilities in an unwelcoming, isolating social universe. Marshall's spatial explorations capture the dynamism of modern possibilities, the world of opportunity presented by the illusion of unlimited options for individual development. For Selina, the challenge of leaving one's home and one's neighborhood to explore Fulton Street and Manhattan is simply a matter of taking the chance to do so. Such opportunities, however, cause internal conflict in Marshall's characters. Silla Boyce upbraids her husband Deighton for his conflicted, inconsistent behavior: "It's that you was always looking for something big and praying hard not to find it" (174). Clive, Selina's boyfriend later in book four, represents the inertia of subjective possibility felt less keenly by Selina and her father; Clive's motivation, after all, is the quest for "nothing." Like *Plum Bun*, Marshall's story of individual development gravitates around certain crucial scenes of agoraphobic, nostalgic critiques of urban and industrial forces. One of the most revelatory scenes in the novel comments on industrialism's role in creating an "overwhelming" sense of loneliness, a scene which demarcates the subtle heroism of Silla Boyce in her strident quest for wages in the midst of a whirring network of machinery:

> They had built it, but ironically, it had overreached them, so that now they were only small insignificant shapes against its overwhelming complexity. . . . And no one talked. Like the men loading the trailer trucks in the streets, they performed a pantomime role in a drama in which only the machines had a voice. (99)

The descriptions of smallness in the face of a threatening larger presence exemplifies the impersonal and alienating space of early twentieth-century New York City to its inhabitants who search for a place from which to sound an individual "voice" amidst the throng.

Both the first and last scenes of the novel contextualize Selina's relationship to the architecture of a brownstone, beginning with a description of a lonely ten-year-old girl sitting on a landing shared by her brownstone's boarders, and ending with her flight from the basement of an old brownstone (the office for the Barbadian association) and her conclusive, self-reflexive amble through the ruins of old brownstone neighborhoods as she reflects on her place in the "cairn of stone and silence"(310). But Selina's manner of dodging and maneuvering for a significant nurturing place in her home and society at large begs the question of the role of race in the development of her "Brown girl" heroine construction. It demands our attention not only because of the dyad set up in the novel's title but also, as I will argue, because such a title diffuses the complexities and specificities of name and place markers of identity in general, hinting at the novel's more understated national, ethnic, and racial narrative project. The project of narrating race, Marshall suggests in this novel that avoids "this tired race theme," involves unsettled tensions and ceaseless shifts in culturally accepted and understood divisions of space, place, and position in a stratified social economy (Marshall 253). Marshall indicts American society for its class hierarchy in spatial terms through Silla's few impassioned speeches about the "man country" in which people have to "claw their way to the top" and "scuffle to stay there" (225). Keenly critical of her mother's and her community's world-view, Selina challenges this paradigm by scheming to win the Barbadian association's scholarship money for her own purposes through feigned dedication and indoctrination of this "dog-eat-dog" creed. Yet she experiences the limitations over her potential that stem not only from her community but also by white America's "illusions" about her own subjectivity. In the final pages of the novel, Selina realizes that she has been searching for place within the "center of life" throughout her development as she walks through the old neighborhoods of Brooklyn: "What was at the center?—love, a clearer vision, a place" (308). This sought-for space, symbolized by motifs of darkness and light, closed and open spaces, drives the quest for feminine self-actualization in this ethnic novel while actually diffusing, or perhaps sublimating, an experiential racial essence. Race, the novel suggests, is a result of a culturally-realized space, a relational place within the hierarchy.

Thus, racial identity is the result of an individual or group performance of selfhood that is spatially removed and referentially recognized as distinct to a performance of a dominant norm or standard. A wealthy Barbadian woman can be accused of "playing white in truth" (246) in a tone of mixed disapprobation as well as admiration, and a young Barbadian woman can signify her self-consequence within the community by acquiring a new bedroom with her family's new house in a new neighborhood. Selina's best friend Beryl, the daughter of the successful business man, invites her teenaged friends over to a "pre-evening soiree and housewarming" to celebrate her new bedroom, an event young girls in Selina's peer group, who have to share basement bedrooms with their sisters, all anticipate excitedly (190). When the reluctant Selina arrives, she views a strange, ritualistic, class-conditioned phenomenon in the sight of four girls in Beryl's new bedroom, which is "all pale pink and virginal white, with Beryl's old dolls arrayed on the bed." The entire event is a target of Marshall's satire on class-based posturing in that the girls are old enough to discuss college majors and professions, but the celebration of the bedroom, (even if it takes place after the young girl is almost a woman) is a necessity to a community dedicated to "playing white." Not only is the entire household (and most of the Bajan community) involved in the construction of whiteness and blackness as differentiated spaces configured by class distinctions, but Beryl and her friends are playing at a construction of adulthood that also fetishizes whiteness (and virginity) in dreams of professional vocations. The use of "soiree" and "pre-evening" highlights the young womens' provisional position in relation to adulthood and adult activities.

In this scene, Marshall complicates social roles and spaces by using the focal point of the coveted elegant interior of the new bedroom to highlight the inanity of Beryl and her friends' goals, which perpetuate the patriarchal (and neocolonial) agendas of their fathers. The personal freedom this new space might offer, Marshall suggests, is overshadowed by the fierce need of each young subject to conform to a social pattern, as if each girl is fearful of unbridled subjective freedom. Selina walks waveringly around these possibilities in her youth, seeking freedom but safety and intimacy as well. On a few but significant instances, the author uses a description of Selina's longing for romantic love to also hint at her need for the nurturing and affirmation that comes from enclosure. As she matures, for example, Selina avoids the brownstone and the park and goes to the public library to be safe "behind the stacks" (154). Marshall also tells us that Selina associates these spaces, in her mind with the romantic love of a "quiet boy who would read with her in the library," this vague need growing stronger until she can see him "in the darkness beyond her bed" (189). Selina's vision of a boy in the library speaks to her pairing of personal space with personal affirmation—the prince and the castle that come together in fairy tales and the grand house that comes with marriage to a gentleman. Selina's vague longings, after the bedroom soiree, transform into goals as she becomes more active and learns to measure herself productively in relation to the other members of her community.

As she develops, Selina feels that her mother (along with the rest of the Bajan women) distorts the significance of house-holding, turning it into an act of class posturing. As Silla Boyce points out, "the Jews" in the "man country" learned long before the West Indians that material acquisition leads to class-distinction, which then leads to gentrification when ethnic groups help construct a sense of achievable whiteness (17, 38). Silla respects her Jewish employers for this business acumen, noting the dedication required to transform an entire cultural group into an economic power. Her admiration, however, enacts the true narrative of ethnicity in Marshall's vision: group by group, each identity sees itself in relation to socioeconomic whiteness, defined by abandoning Brooklyn brownstones and living in Manhattan and having leisure time to spend without having to worry about collecting revenue. The Barbadian Association's president makes this theme clear in his opening speeches, which prescribe a consolidation of business power, or the use of accumulated capital and brain power and professionalism to set West Indians apart from the "American Negro," to achieve like "the Jew" (222). Marshall's concept of ethnicity here conflates and complicates nationality, ethnicity, and class, which is evident in passages describing the association meetings in which members are scandalized when they hear from one liberal member that they should admit "regular" nonimmigrant black Americans.

These place-markers of cultural identity attempt to demarcate tangible divisions in the larger shared space of American citizenship; however, Marshall shows us that these labels can no more pin down identity than people can maintain comfortable, nurturing places for themselves in society. Her vision also offers a materialist critique of such classifications as it illustrates the economic foundation at the formation of each category and the fact that Jewishness, a religious classification, somehow parallels the national classification of Barbadian only in that it is a self-proclaimed "other" category within the lived American performance of identity. Silla confuses Religion with Nation as she compares Jew to Barbadian while leaving out the black American. This illogical carving out of place within American citizenship demonstrates the conceptual flaws in commonly-held ideas about ethnic identity.

The novel thematically presents ethnic identity and the movements of its search for collective recognition and place as inherently illogical and, ultimately, deeply unsatisfying. For men like Deighton Boyce, Clive Springer, and even more successful community leaders like Bajan spokesman Cecil Osborne, self-development involves a choice between paralyzing hopelessness in the face of an all-powerful white masculinity or an artificial, self-effacing zeal for membership within another group, like the religious cult Deighton joins. Clive, Selina's lover, scorns Selina's "enthusiasm" and "artiness" in her chosen form of dance as personal expression. Walking by the beach, Selina watches Clive stop himself from falling head on into the crashing waves, so much a victim to his own inertia that he cannot even get caught up in the natural momentum of his person and body (266). Selina compares his trapped self-projection to her own father's mysterious fall into the ocean near Barbados and his ultimate drowning. It is at this moment that Selina forms her first real plan—her first deliberate decision as an autonomous self instead of a person guided by reactionary behavior, chance, and the desperate movements and retreats between threatening and nurturing spaces. She decides that she and Clive must collect enough money to go "far enough away," and she decides to convince her community that she is the best subject, the most promising and proper young Barbadian-American citizen worthy of its scholarship (266).

The goal of self-consequence and personal place merge at this moment in an interesting act of duplicity. Such conventional striving, Marshall suggests, is alien to the real Selina and somehow unfulfilling in the long run. Successful finally in this quest as well as in her truer goal of artistic self-actualization, Selina confronts her selves in the mirror, after experiencing Mrs. Benton's racist remarks, and can no longer continue with her original plan. Selina wins and relinquishes the Association's scholarship, apologizing eloquently though vaguely to her community for fooling them with her false devotion to their philosophy of arduous, competitive living (303). The fruits of the formulaic, culturally-sanctioned economic advancement prescribed by the Bajan rendition of white middle-class domestic bliss are ultimately unsatisfying not only to Selina but to Silla and Ina as well. Silla, caught up in the mechanics of her own material obsession, loses her husband's love and is ultimately unsatisfied with the possession of just one brownstone. Ina, the ideal Barbadian-American young woman who is on the verge of marriage with the ideal Barbadian young man, talks about her future in a "flat tone" of "abstraction" (299). Selina compares her own needs with her sister's:

> Did Ina glimpse the sad tinge to that happiness—in the sanctioned embrace two nights a week, the burgeoning stomach, the neat dark children, the modest homeon Long Island . . . the slow blurring of the self, the steady attrition of the soul over all those long complacent years. (300)

This stark picture clearly expresses Marshall's critique of conventional feminine narratives of self-actualization, which involve the dynamics of marriage

markets and self-fashioning in keeping with codes of propriety and professional development. Personal space, in Ina's eyes, involves a journey to the
idealized suburban existence—the house of the happily ever after. As young
female protagonists, the sisters understand that their years of development
must take them to some space of arrival, which is why Marshall ends the
novel when she does, with Ina engaged and Selina as a stowaway to the
mother country. Ultimately, the novel's spatial demarcations (between safe
and unsafe, closed and open, darkness and light, complete and incomplete
development) involve our more traditional cultural engagements with and
reconfigurations of a young woman's search for place in society. In the thematics and poetics of the novel, space provides Marshall's ethnic heroine
construction with a most productive model for articulating identity construction. This model allows Marshall to represent ethnic identity as a set of
figuratively spatial relationships to the norm of whiteness—the distance
from Fulton Street to Crown Heights to Manhattan's upper-east side.
Selina's search for place thus mediates geographical space, the levels of class
hierarchy, and the subjective stages towards finding a fulfilling position, or
role, within the American marketplace.

However, Marshall also explores space narratively, by adhering ambivalently to the structure of the bildingsroman to discuss Selina's ethnic
subjectivity. *Like Fifth Chinese Daughter,* and *Lucy, Brown Girl,
Brownstones* incorporates recognizable elements of Western narratives of
development. These features include the search for vocation, the critique of
class dynamics, the expression of artistic talent or a unique voice, the
metaphoric use of houses, and a redirection of marriage plot energies, all of
which are inscribed within several anglo novels already discussed in this
study. In *Brown Girl, Brownstones,* the overlap between the space, or structure, of conventional anglo heroine development and the struggle for place
forged by ethnic identity embodies Selina's own ambivalent negotiation of
open and closed spaces as she searches for a place outside of the brownstone that is not really her home. Thus, the novel expresses an ambivalence
towards both traditional and new trajectories of female development as it
invokes the traditional plot of an outcast heroine searching for acceptance,
but underscores the complications arising from differing meanings of identity as far as race and nation. At the end of the novel, Marshall seems to de-
struct the formal elements of bildungsromane, but cannot offer a formal
alternative to this structure. Her heroine does not find her personal place
within her community and understands that the search will not end with the
conventional place markers of marriage or professional or even artistic success. On the contrary, Selina has "no idea of what the years held," and our

narrator prohibits the picture of a happy ending by alluding to Selina's death, "long years" down the road (285).

As Selina infiltrates different spaces and places in her search for iden-tity within a community, her story modulates the more typical structure of the female developmental narrative, displacing a happy ending and in gen-eral disquieting the potential for softer, happier scripts of female behavior. Read in these terms, Selina's story seems to belong to a later paradigm (the "tragic paradigm" mentioned at the end of chapter 2) of female actualiza-tion discussed by Lorna Ellis, who groups novels like George Eliot's *A Mill on the Floss,* Kate Chopin's *The Awakening,* and (I would add) Nella Larsen's novel *Quicksand* together in the fact that they all have heroines who fail to find a satisfying place within society. Yet in her afterword to the Feminist Press edition of the *Brown Girl, Brownstones,* Mary Helen Washington claims that Selina's final decision makes the text "one of the most optimistic texts in Afro-American literature, for it assigns even to an oppressed people the power of conscious political choice" (322). Unlike the heroine development outlined by Ellis's study *Appearing to Diminish,* Selina's scope of self-actualization does not necessitate the pattern of em-powerment through socially-accommodative behavior described by Ellis. Selina's reconciliation with her community does not occur as a result of her compromising herself or refashioning herself in terms of her community's stifling mimicry of white middle-class mores. She feels reintegrated into her community as she decides to leave it, after her realization and celebration of her place within an organic cohesion of fragmented selves and experiences. Thus, the novel engages with the "paradigm" of irresolution Ellis discusses in her study of female bildungsromane without formulating the dire circum-stances of death or madness resulting in other novels that conclude with the heroine's unfulfilled search for belonging and actualization. *Brown, Girl Brownstones* is thus unable to commit structurally to a new alternative, or new schema of ethnic female self-actualization and remains somewhat trapped within the space of the bildungsroman as the heroine will continue to explore new avenues towards the realization of personal place and be-longing. This lack of commitment results in a rich spatial language of iden-tity that offers a generalized description of the relationships between social norms and gradations from these ideals informing individual and collective articulations of self.

The last page of the novel is a marvel of spatial symbolism, casting over the import of the brownstone its true place within a capitalist ethos of creation and destruction. New houses loom "on the far perimeter of the plain," and the once small Selina, frightened of Fulton Street's constant display of wild and unchecked human behavior, now faces the entire city boldly as it "seemed to draw near, the lighted windows spangling the sky like a new constellation" (310). Something between entrapment and the fear of "utter silence" in the last line moves our heroine continuously. To announce finally her understanding of her place in the "giant cairn," she takes off one of her two silver bangles (which identify her as a Barbadian-American girl) and tosses it into the void. The "frail sound" it makes perhaps testifies to the ways in which the angst of self-construction is relatively abysmal in a fragmented universe, or "wreckage" of identities (310).

As contemporary heroines like Selina begin to move through the possibilities of narrative space beyond the happy ending, past the marriage plot, and towards the plane of independent self-actualization, new literary strategies emerge as re-configurations of traditional textual structures. Another narrative pattern emerges as writers narrow their focus and highlight a brief span of years between the spaces of childhood and adulthood. These adolescent narratives, or coming-of-age novels, combine the structural energies of contemporary bildungsromane and traditional courtship-to-marriage plots as authors fashion heroines who both subscribe to and critique dominant cultural mores. Like Marshall's ambivalent negotiations of space, these attempts to introduce new subjective realities can unwittingly conform to literary conventions that challenge academic distinctions between anglo and ethnic fiction. In the next chapter I will conclude this examination of ethnic heroine construction by explicating the pattern and meanings of our investments in adolescent heroine construction and chart the ways in which the contemporary writer delves into the space—the frontier—of a woman's most formative years.

Chapter Four
Little Princesses: A New Generation of Ethnic, Adolescent Heroines

Literary and cultural scholars who work diligently to identify, critique, and deconstruct forces of racism and sexism subsisting in American cultural production might be pleased with recent developments in publication houses and film and television studios all over the country. The past decade has ushered in a significant increase in the creation and consumption of ethnic female narratives, resulting perhaps from the seeds of feminism and multiculturalism sprouting into mass-market culture after decades of germination within the academy. Consider, for example, the mainstream success enjoyed the 1998 Disney film *Mulan*, an adaptation of the Chinese folkloric story of Fa Mu Lan, which narrates the adventures of a young girl who joins the army disguised as a boy and fights with her countrymen against invasion. In his *Imagining the Nation: Asian American Literature and Cultural Consent*, David Leiwei Li suggests that this type of romanticized Disneyfication of an Asian text occurs as new ethnic narratives are created in opposition to "the 'radical left' project of ethnic nationalism in ways that were not possible a decade earlier" (222).[1] His allusion to the development of new types of ethnic narratives within the mainstream American marketplace brings to mind several questions surrounding the idea of cultural authenticity. Are comedic ethnic narratives inauthentic portraitures of ethnic culture? Must ethnic fiction necessarily address political concerns? Are contemporary works of ethnic fiction stringently decolonizing of "anglo" aesthetics? What if they are not?

In this chapter, I contextualize ethnic heroine construction in Asian American and African American novels with an eye towards these debated questions and reveal constructed heroine virtues that are in fact more traditional than feminism and ethnic studies criticism may deem productive in representations of contemporary female development. *Mulan's* significance, in that regard, involves interdisciplinary debates over representation and imaging within mass-media texts that leave almost everyone concerned about the implications of Disney's sugar-coated and romantic version of multiculturalism. The film's appeal not only represents a culmination of multiculturalism's popularity as a theme, it also exemplifies Disney's and other media conglomerates' growing interest in promulgating a specific brand of female adolescent narrative, one that is emphatically heterosexual and one that testily incorporates ethnic subjectivity through the inclusion of a minority character within a conventional narrative form.

Because stories about girls have become increasingly popular and marketable, this trend has been accompanied by a sort of cultural consent for the exploration of the lives of ethnic girls. Young readers today can walk into almost any bookstore and purchase editions of the hugely popular *American Girl* series, which chronicles the life of girls who represent different racial and national backgrounds (including one Swedish immigrant and one African American girl who escapes from slavery). Since the late 1980s, young female readers have also been able to follow the principle events in the life of Claudia Kishi, a second-generation Japanese American and original founding member of the Baby-Sitters Club in a series that in 1995 had already sold 130 million books (Inness 167). Significantly, the past decade has seen a paradigm altering shift in consumer power from adults to preteens; a new age-group label—"tween"—incorporates the heretofore disparate age groups between 9 and 12 into one lump target market.[2] These developments point to a blurring of narrative space between adulthood and childhood as adolescence becomes a palatable, even fetishized, outlet for the exploration of subjective possibility. In their television network, for example, Disney has created a separate programming entity ("Zoog") exclusively for prepubescent children and adolescents. Three noteworthy television shows within "Zoog" (*Lizzy Mcguire*, *That's So Raven*, and *The Pride Family*) explore not only white but black female adolescent subjectivity as well. The role of the ethnic best friend has also become a powerful subject position in pop-culture narratives. From this position, peppy Lane Kim, the adolescent Korean American and best friend of a white television-series heroine, subverts stereotypes and cultural mores for Asian American females by nursing a passion for popular music (instead of studying science) in the Warner Brother series *Gilmore Girls*. The series was in fact aired as a result of creative development ideas shared between the worlds of advertising and Warner Brothers network executives and funded by the "Family Friendly Forum," which is dedicated to "offer a greater array of compelling family programming on network television."[3] In light of these recent developments, we might ask a familiar question about social influence and mass media: To what extent is adolescent ethnicity commodified when these comedic narratives create well-adjusted, middle-class heroines to represent ethnic subject positions?

Within the academy, the realm of ethnic adolescence, which is studied and conceptualized in terms of material and cultural forces, seems incongruous to the tonally positive and comedic models offered in popular culture and more lighthearted scenarios of young-adult romance and peer-group based identity crises. Adolescence, a relatively recent topic explored in African American and, certainly, Asian American fiction, continues to be a site of ambivalence, especially in light of feminist critiques of gender-roles and social constructions of gender, ethnic-studies critiques of identity-formation, and academic debates about the generic parameters of the bildungsroman.[4] For example, in ones of the "Super Series" editions of the young-adult *Babysitters Club* books (which are written by a non-Asian author) Claudia Kishi, a Japanese American heroine of juvenile fiction mentioned already, falls in love with a Japanese American boy after the author notes their shared "punk" dressing style. Most writers of adult Asian American fiction and, certainly, most practitioners of Asian American literary theory conscientiously avoid the use and deny the existence of such themes and subject matters and would consider this scenario as too frivolous and comedic for the realm of Asian American subjectivity.[5]

Arguably, the creators of some contemporary literary ethnic heroines do present scenarios of hardship in realist modes to demonstrate, insightfully and productively, the compounded forces of racial discrimination and economic exploitation. One such heroine, Naomi Nakane, from the 1981 novel *Obasan* by Japanese Canadian writer Joy Kogawa, recollects her adolescence in Japanese internment camps in a tonal register that leaves little, if any, scope for the type of narrative resolution offered to ethnic protagonists in popular culture. In illustrating the differences between an idealized white middle-class youth and the material realities facing children in relocation camps, Kogawa has young Naomi Nakane seek psychological relief by reading classic Western novels of development in her camp. The material and political realities of Naomi's situation, however, prevent her from internalizing the positive and romantic messages of the novels she reads. She tells us, "No matter how I wish it, we do not go home" (Kogawa 126). Yet Kogawa's 1981 text was published before the developments in popular culture I have named above, and while many Asian American novels published since then achieve the same stark, moving decolonizing vision, several recently published ethnic novels offer opposing narrative outlooks as publishing houses develop greater interest in producing "chick lit" and other forms in the comedic vein.[6]

At the end of her 1985 survey on adolescent fiction, *Growing Up Female,* Barbara White forecasts a dire scope for contemporary female development, stating that though "the heroine does not clearly lose her identity, her ultimate fate is usually left undefined; she remains in conflict with society and divided within herself" (White 162). Pin-chia Feng's 1998 study of ethnicity in female bildungsromane explains these "difficult" processes of constructing ethnic subjectivities as heroines manage social pressures from a network of race, nation, class, and gender codes (Feng 2). Feng notes that ethnic female bildungsromane place more of an emphasis on the process, rather than the product, of selfhood (Feng 36). Both White and Feng discuss evolving genres that respond to changing social concepts of youth, femininity, and ethnicity.[7] In this chapter, I take their observations as starting points and apply them to a larger question of how social values of femininity and ethnicity are configured and reconfigured in novels by Toni Morrison, Lois-Ann Yamanaka, and Gish Jen. More particularly, I contextualize the representation of feminine virtues in contemporary ethnic heroine construction as another site of intertextual exchange between anglo and ethnic literary production.

I turn now to narrative similarities between A. J. Verdelle's *The Good Negress* (1995) and the international girls' classic *Anne of Green Gables* (1908) by the Canadian writer, L. M. Montgomery. The lesser-known former novel explores the adolescent development of an African American girl growing up during the Civil Rights era. Both novels depict the development of motivated, intelligent girls who are raised by women who are not their biological mothers. In addition, both novels engage with cultural expectations of female propriety and female training and do so by mediating the tension between a need to privilege individual expression, or personal will, and a need to maintain the more traditional feminine mores of their historical contexts. More particularly, both novels describe their heroine's abilities to self-visualize the steps to inner growth via the path of strong imaginations that signify the value of inner strength and individuated spirit to their readers. Consider both writers' similar employment of a positive, hopeful tone in the following passages from the novels. In *Anne of Green Gables,* Anne describes an imaginary friend found in the glass of an old bookcase, into which she gazes during her rare free moments from kitchen labor during her years as a foster child:

> We used to pretend that the bookcase was enchanted and that if I only knew the spell I could open the door and step right into the room where

> Katie Maurice lived . . . And then Katie Maurice would have taken me
> by the hand and led me out into a wonderful place, all flowers and sun-
> shine and fairies, and we would have lived there happy for ever after.
> (Montgomery 107)

The tone of the following passage from *The Good Negress* is remarkably
similar to Anne's descriptions of imaginative scope in the midst of domestic
drudgery:

> Over time I began to witness to this window, and to imagine the win-
> dow witnessed me. I watched myself grow in the black night reflections
> . . . That was my window. I was twelve and standing at the sink when
> we met. (Verdelle 100–101)

My intention in pairing the texts together in this manner is to introduce
some narrative possibilities inscribed by both texts' incorporation of a particular structural feature that evokes certain emotions, interpretations, and
expectations on the part of the reader. Despite their materially different circumstances and the history separating these two texts from each other, their
common use of female imagination and inner strength within a discussion of
female training asks that we consider the similarities and differences. The
contemporary novels discussed in this chapter similarly inscribe the feminine
values of traditional, anglo novels of feminine development.

In response to the increase in scholarship about female ethnicity and in
tandem with the rise in popularity of adolescent narratives, this chapter will
problematize the conceptualization of anglo and ethnic, as well as literary
fiction and pop-culture juvenile fiction, within the realm of narrated adolescence. This chapter seeks to go beyond both feminist and ethnic studies
scholarship evaluations and assessments of progressiveness versus conventionality in regards to representations of young girls. I insert my ideas here
into an expanding field of inquiry spanning sociology, literary criticism, an-
thropology, media studies, and women's studies.[8] Responding to debates on
girl culture, mass media, and reading, Angela Hubler surveys girl readers
and discovers an inexplicable shared reading habit, which compels adolescent girls to read *Sweet Valley High* series books, *Jane Eyre,* and *Caddie
Woodlawn* with similar enthusiasm and without tremendous differentiation.
The title of her article, "Can Anne Shirley Help Revive Ophelia?" responds
to Mary Pipher's now famous *Reviving Ophelia,* a significant recent study
on mental health crises among young women in the 1990s and the effects of
women's imaging within a "girl-poisoning" mass media (Pipher 12).
Pointing to increasing diagnoses of depression amongst women as they enter

mid-adolescence, Pipher includes Olive Schreiner and Sylvia Plath, among others, who are part of a literary tradition of women plunging into despair and wistful passivity around the age of fifteen (19).[9] Toni Morrison too comments upon this trend in female development in her characterization of Pauline Breedlove in *The Bluest Eye*, a text discussed later in this chapter. Morrison's description of Pauline involves a palpable personality change in the middle of Pauline's adolescence:

> Pauline was fifteen, still keeping house, but with less enthusiasm. Fantasies about men and love and touching were drawing her mind and hands away from her work. Changes in weather began to affect her, as did certain sights and sounds. Those feelings translated themselves to her in extreme melancholy. (Morrison 113)

Morrison then takes Pauline through the disillusionment of early adulthood, which stems from Pauline's internalization of white Hollywood narratives. "In equating physical beauty with virtue, she stripped her mind, bound it, and collected self-contempt by the heap," writes Morrison (122). The vulnerability of adolescent identity functions in this chapter as a point of entry into current debates about the impact of cultural forces and pressure on developing female subjectivity, a theme that is explored thoroughly by all three of the novels discussed in this chapter.

BEAUTY, INNER STRENGTH, AND WIT

The three novels covered in this chapter have heroines who wrangle with ideas of sameness and difference as they enter into adolescence and develop into young women.[10] While the previous chapters have dealt with structural tensions between the desire for unique, individual expression and the security of social acceptance and marital marketablility, this chapter's concentration on adolescence will allow us to delve further into the conflicted textual energies participating in the construction of ethnic female identity in contemporary fiction—specifically, the narrative cultivation of typically traditional, or anglo, feminine virtues and attributes. In the first two sections of this chapter, I will trace the dynamics of conventional virtues like beauty and inner strength in Toni Morrison's *The Bluest Eye* (1970) and Lois-Ann Yamanaka's *Wild Meat and the Bully Burgers* (1996), in which the heroines must learn to exchange beauty (equated with whiteness and anglo norms) for inner strength and self-confidence. The heroine of the next novel, Gish Jen's *Mona in the Promised Land* (1996), shapes her identity by dint of her superior wit and comedic prowess. I view the presence of these virtues and attributes in the characterization of these three heroines as forces of ambivalence resulting from the authors' relational and symbiotic negotiations of concepts of ethnicity and femininity within their projects of heroine construction in the literary marketplace. This anxiety manifests itself most obviously in the themes of identity-formation and cultural confusion driving these novels of adolescence. However, the ambivalence with which thematic tensions are structurally resolved in these novels suggests the force of relational heroine construction, and the authors attempt to perform individuated narrative voices in terms of ethnicity because ethnic identity furnishes a unique framework of development. Thus, I conceptualize each text's privileging of one virtue or attribute as its link to heroine construction within an anglo, or mainstream tradition.

The cultivation of typically feminine virtues and attributes performed by the heroines of these novels and championed by each novel's narrative voice ensures them a connection to and place within a transcultural heroine marketplace wherein heroines are consumed and admired for some specific propensity or unique trait. These networks function within a patriarchal heterosexual economy that creates and privileges certain virtues over others. However, I do not dwell on marriage plots and heterosexual energies in these novels in the same sense as in chapters 1 and 2. While certain instances of heterosexual desire and training do exist in these texts, I find it more productive to see these feminine virtues and attributes as symptomatic of an ambivalence that, instead of permitting frank and blatant explorations of romantic fantasies or scenarios, involves the authors' negotiations of cultural expectations for contemporary femininity and ethnicity. The premiums of beauty, inner strength, wit, and imagination in these examples of ethnic heroine construction then ensures a literary marketability as ethnic heroines and their stories become recognizable and more familiar to all readers in some ways. Characterization in these terms subtly suggests marriage market potential for these heroines even as their stories are in accord with contemporary feminist and ethnic studies' assumptions that romance in adolescence tends to victimize young women.

My need to investigate the ways in which these novels navigate through the current of these social, political, and generic expectations informs this discussion of ethnicity and femininity. I choose to conclude this project with these three novels because they challenge, even unconsciously, assertions and binaries discussed in feminist and ethnic studies criticism which evaluate some novels as frivolous and others as serious—all in the name of politics. By using textual tension, ambivalence, and anxiety as my guides in this investigation of adolescence and ethnic heroine construction, I am able to put narrative ahead of politics as I probe into the textual depths and limits of behavioral learning, identity-formation, and most importantly, conflict resolution.

BEAUTY, A PRIMER: TONI MORRISON'S *THE BLUEST EYE*

Toni Morrison's 1970 novel inaugurated a new, postmodern generation of awkward American adolescence that explores the youthful desire for social acceptance through the eyes of racial outsiders.[11] Morrison's female characters (nine-year-old Claudia MacTeer and eleven-year-old Pecola Breedlove) are reminiscent, in some ways, of Carson McCullers's Mick, the exuberant adolescent female character in *The Heart is a Lonely Hunter* (1940), as well as her later heroine, Frankie Addams, from *The Member of the Wedding* (1946). These heroines remain convincingly youthful and even innocent amidst an adult social infrastructure of limited opportunities, prejudice, and exclusion. And like twelve-year-old, tomboyish and awkward Frankie Addams, Morrison's heroine Pecola desires above all things love and acceptance—a feeling of true membership within her family and community. Note the similarity of the yearning and despair felt by both protagonists, which is narrated through the third-person point-of-view in both novels. McCullers's describes Frankie:

> She stood before the mirror and she was afraid. It was the summer of fear, for Frankie. . . . In the past year she had grown four inches . . . according to mathematics unless she could somehow stop herself, she would grow to be over nine feet tall. . . . She would be a Freak. (17)

A few pages later, the catalogue of Frankie's fears continues:

> She was afraid of these things that suddenly made her wonder who she was, and what she was going to be in the world, and why she was standing at that minute, seeing a light, or listening, or staring up into the sky: alone. (22)

In response to her growing awareness of social alienation, Morrison's Pecola Breedlove also experiences sudden mood swings wherein she transfers feelings of joy or sadness onto the natural world around her. After an elderly white shopkeeper treats the young girl as if she were invisible, Pecola glares in anger at some dandelions in her path, dandelions which just minutes before had made her feel "part of the world and the world a part of her" (Morrison 48–50). Though both heroines seek social acceptance, the language of Pecola's self-loathing implicates more insidious factors of social exclusion based upon Pecola's collective identity as a Breedlove and as a poor, African American girl:

> As long as she looked the way she did, as long as she was ugly, she would have to stay with these people. Somehow she belonged to them. Long

hours she sat looking in the mirror, trying to discover the secret of the ugliness, the ugliness that made her ignored or despised at school, by teachers and classmates alike. (45)

Both girls see immediate solutions to remedying their loneliness. Frankie finds hope in the fact that she will be "a member of the wedding" of her older brother, clinging to a fantasy that she will somehow share the love and unity between her brother and his new wife. Pecola, on the other hand, wishes and prays fervently to have blue eyes.

The significant tonal difference between *The Bluest Eye* and *The Member of the Wedding* results from Morrison's use of the female first-person pre-pubescent point-of-view. Claudia MacTeer, Pecola's younger peer, narrates much of Pecola's story. The power of the material desire driving Pecola's story and Claudia's innocent and distanced perspective engenders a sadness and tragic mood dissonant with less serious cultural associations of adolescence such as puppy-love, peer-group melodrama, and intergenerational conflict. In fact, Pecola's youthful desire for beauty and its implications for the exclusionary aesthetics of race and class are so forceful in the novel that they cannot be contained within a first-person narration but must instead be mediated by another narrator. Morrison has considered her use of a second narrator for Pecola as a flaw in her novel (211). Her self-critique is interesting in that it points to the ineffable and uncomfortable elements of youth desire within our cultural narratives. As it charts this new terrain of adolescence, Morrison's novel also paves the way for later discussions of socioeconomic inequities and their relationship to identity-formation and subjective potential through her experiments with the poetics of heroine construction.

Morrison's novel plays with children's narratives and the promise offered by fairy-tale redemption found in western parables and stories. The force of Pecola's yearning for beauty blasts the possibility for such positive conclusions by making the child long for a specific physical transformation that is impossible to achieve. The narrative also satirizes anglo norms of propriety and prosperity that are commonly deployed in American early learning primary readers. Our author belies the happy ending we might expect for our deserving female protagonist by including fragments of early-reader Dick and Jane stories. These fragments in the novel upset the promise of a positive ending by announcing themselves as banal words in a more heterogeneous, complex prosody. Morrison expects readers to note the disparity between Claudia's childhood memories of poverty, her account of Pecola's tragic circumstances, and the flat words of Dick and Jane stories that ring falsely in the midst of developed sentences and descriptions of brutal winters and broken households. She collects the narrative potential of a sort of national fairy tale (Dick, Jane, and Spot in their house), the hope of girlhood, and the simple though unattainable desire of a young black girl ultimately to critique the empty, even propagandistic promise of the American dream. A desire comprised by such unquenchable longing, like the wish for riches, love, or the return of the dead, seems to engage with mythic structures and parables which reward patience, humility, and devotion with the granting of such a dream. In this case, however, the extreme materiality of desire undermines such resolution. It is a wish only magic could grant in a tragically nonmagical world. Morrison's realism thereby critiques the conventionality of simplistic narratives like fairy tales and primary readers and their potency in molding the shape of our wishes and dreams, for introducing us to ideas like "romantic love" and "physical beauty": "Probably the most destructive ideas in the history of human thought" (122). To wish for blue eyes in this symbolic register of privileged whiteness is to bring disappointment and pain upon oneself.

As we read, we realize that Pecola's "internalization of the dominant ideology" of "white, middle-class discourse" is a result of her family's inability to "breed love" as her last name suggests (Feng 52–53, 62). Pecola's mother Pauline, discussed in the introduction of this chapter, as well as her father Cholly, are unable to move past a debilitating sense of social displacement and dehumanization caused by their past experiences with racial prejudice from white people and color discrimination within their own northern black communities. Cholly impregnates Pecola, and Pecola loses her sanity and believes that she finally has blue eyes at the end of the story. In depicting the tragedy of this young girl's life, Morrison sacrifices positive redemption in order to critique a cultural obsession that pits whiteness against blackness and which equates blackness as "the funkiness of nature" (83). No resolution is possible because the narrative of desire itself is flawed. While this instance of heroine construction critiques the racist and elitist predominance of beauty as a feminine virtue, it offers no other virtue or attribute as an alternative except to note the absolute lack of "simple caring for" in the Breedloves' lives (122). The novel's own brand of ethnicized difference within a larger transcultural project of heroine construction lies thus in its powerful critique of "the scale of absolute beauty" (122). In the next section of this chapter, I will examine another critique of idealized whiteness from an Asian American perspective that does try to offer an alternative virtue in response to the preponderance of beauty.

BEAUTY AND WHITENESS—OUTSIDE THE PALE: LOIS-ANN YAMANAKA'S *WILD MEAT AND THE BULLY BURGERS*

Like Morrison's Pecola, Yamanaka's adolescent heroine in *Wild Meat and the Bully Burgers* (1996), Lovey Nariyoshi, a "Japanee," (person of Japanese origin raised in Hawaii), is inculcated into the dream for whiteness as she internalizes an American obsession with Shirley Temple. Unlike Pecola, Lovey narrates her own adolescent longings in the first-person point-of-view, and her spectrum of anxiety spans not just insecurities of race, but of nation, class, age, sex, and family. Lovey documents her adolescent anxieties and yearnings in the present tense, a strategy that allows readers to experience a sense of real time passing through the gamut of emotions and thoughts describing her conscious desires, reports of regular everyday youthful skirmishes, and more latent feelings of guilt and shame. Our heroine's identity is thus more whole in this novel than Pecola's in *The Bluest Eye*. In a way, the fact of her own narrating ability saves Lovey from the subjective darkness reserved for Pecola and her madness; Lovey's desires have the pace and space to be more developed, resolved, or simply lived through.

However, our direct glimpse into Lovey's perspective makes her wishes and dreams seem somehow more crudely material than Pecola's. Rather than fixate upon the symbolic blue eyes, Lovey expounds incessantly upon the things she wishes she could have and the person she wishes she could be. Her desires converge upon a loose conceptualization of idealized whiteness, or middle-class suburban normalcy:

> Blond hair. Good. Betty Cooper and Marcia Brady. Barbie and Twiggy. . . . Black hair. Evil. Veronica Lodge. . . . Just better to be haole. Live in Riverdale. Be Vicky or Jenny. Talk straight to the mainland Japanese cousins who say things like "Gee, you talk funny. . . ." Better to have straight blond hair and long Miss America legs and lots of boobs like Ginger Geiger, 'cause, to me, no sense in sending Miss Hawaii to Atlantic City unless she's haole 'cause she never makes the finals, only Miss Congeniality. She got lots of Aloha Spirit that's why. . . . Live in a house with Dixie cup dispensers, bunk beds with ruffled sheets, bendable straws, rose-shaped soap, Lysol, and Pez. . . . I wanna be Lovey Beth Cole. . . . A Japanee with a haole last name. (29)

This last sentence underlines the cultural hegemony deployed by a "white supremacist capitalistic patriarchy."[12] Its ideals are internalized by minority and majority citizens alike in complex and timeless psychological systems and cultural narratives akin to Franz Fanon's description of colonialism and the "manichean allegory."[13] This shared yearning between Pecola and Lovey and the tonal weight of their desires suggests that their developmental fates will be similar. A closer examination into the structural and thematic dynamics of heroine construction in the novels reveals some significant differences in the experiences and subjective potential of these two characters. These differences, which are based on the structural rules of heroine construction with which these novels engage, reveal in turn the extent to which concepts of ethnicity and femininity are relational and narrative concepts.

Unlike Pecola Breedlove, Lovey will learn to question her insecurities with time, as she must deal with the conflict in standards upheld by her working-class parents and the consumerist elitist culture responsible for her persistent sense of inadequacy. Serialized above, Lovey's desires, even while they reveal her feelings of inferiority under a "haole" (white) norm, offer a site of reversal by way of their direct expression in the narrative. The main purpose of the novel's structure lies in the expression, confession, and cleansing of such yearning. Like Morrison, Yamanaka suggests that as long as the narratives of social hierarchies, exclusion, and beauty exist, there can be no true reward, and thus no conventional resolution. As Morrison also critiques intra-racial discrimination and class hierarchies based on black skin-tone, Yamanaka too outlines an established system of cultural signification based on rules and standards, which, among Hawaiians of Asian descent, are relational to the cult of whiteness.[14] Yamanaka explores this alternative system through Lovey's desperate attempts to catalogue and classify the standards of each group and each system to which she would like to belong and by which she would like to be affirmed. The nuances of these cultural and counter-cultural systems are overwhelming, and their depiction in Yamanaka's novel adds an extra sense of futility while our author delves into the misery felt by countless ethnic groups and explores more minority subjectivities than Morrison's *The Bluest Eye*. Although in her early adolescence Lovey feels that being "haole" or growing up and marrying a haole man will solve all her problems, the standards of her peer group when she is a few years older reveals an alternative, locally-conceptualized and significantly relational hierarchy of aesthetic value: "In our school, if part Hawaiian goes with pure Jap, that's the ultimate. Everybody wants a hapa girlfriend or boyfriend. Everybody wants a part Hawaiian person" (217). Jenks, the "hapa" hunk at Lovey's school, a young man voted the "Cosmopolitan May Day Prince," enjoys a similar popularity to the power enjoyed by the light-skinned "high yellow" Maureen Peal (Meringue Pie) in *The Bluest Eye*. Light-skinned or cosmopolitan, these qualities are cast in relation to an idealized whiteness by peer groups who learn that while whiteness may be impossible to attain, some other type of ideal moves into the top place on the "scale of absolute beauty" (Morrison 122).

Yamanaka explores the weight of these ideals and their influence over female subjectivity and the search for identity in an almost hyperreal Hawaiian melange of ethnic possibilities. Identifiers and classifications such as "Japanee," "hapa," "Portugee," and "Filipino" are hurled as insults back and forth as classmates label each other as "Pearl Harba bomba," "Midget," and "Okinawan peanut." A resigned school-teacher scolds the fighting students wearily: "You are all so appall-ing. You are dis-gusting" (15). This intensity of stratification involves even sub-national competition, causing Lovey, a poor Japanee, to feel inferior to upper-middle-class Japanee girls, members of the popular club "Rays of the Rising Dawn." These more fortunate girls, Lovey informs us, "have the same Japan pencils in Japan pencil cases" (190). Testifying to their power in numbers, Lovey ads, "They all smell like Love's Baby Soft. Or like lemons. . . . And all the *same* scent on the *same* day." As Lovey grows older, she idolizes Crystal Kawasaki, an older girl and the girlfriend of Lovey's best friend's brother. Interestingly, Crystal, like Pecola, cannot be "selfed" by the novel. She is a symbol for the novel's thematic exploration of beauty, and for Lovey and Jerry (Lovey's best friend) she represents the comfort, luxury, and superiority of beauty—a type of beauty revered within their ethnic community:

> Hers is the face of a Japanese angel. A princess from the Japanese comics in Hatsuko's Barbershop. A perfect oval face. Pure smooth white. Pink cheeks and red lips. And white, white teeth. All straight and not too tiny like Marcia Brady and not too much like Marie Osmond. (205)

Her beauty is thus unique, a distinct type in a cultural market in which white female youth reigns. Crystal is also a star pupil and first-chair-clarinet of the youth orchestra. A nice girl, she is sadly unknowable in her symbolic state. After getting pregnant for the second time with her boyfriend (and after being sent to Japan to hide the fact that she had an abortion), she kills herself. Crystal's larger-than-life image in this context demonstrates the impact of relationally constructed standards within young peer groups, the members of which struggle to define themselves against dominant cultural ideals. In this label-ridden social climate, Lovey finally begins to find her own voice by learning to side with her family—a family she feels ashamed to be a part of because of its poverty and the working-class status that it holds:

> Lori says she's heard that we buy all our vegetables from the Open Market at the bay-front parking lot because we can't afford the fresh

produce in Sure Save. My father feeds us meat that he catches, we're so poor, and he sells flowers to the Lei Stand for extra cash. Ours is the kind of family who doesn't iron their clothes and doesn't give out candy at Halloween, which is the only time we pretend to be Jehovah's Witnesses. (195)

Unlike Pecola Breedlove and Mona Chang of Gish Jen's *Mona in the Promised Land,* Lovey must define herself against several collective group identities, all of which seem to want to reject her. Pecola and Claudia are some out of several African American girls in their school and social circles. Mona Chang (discussed in the next section) remains the only Chinese girl in her class throughout her adolescence, a fact that allows her to capitalize on unique subjective possibilities. Lovey's daily classroom and social contexts, on the other hand, allow no premium on uniqueness, only specific types.

The differences in the cultural dynamics of these novels critique the spatial imbalances permeating within an American aesthetic sphere that fosters a collective self-envisioning of a mainstream, white, mainland ideal. Class and race-based determinants of American culture and access to white American resources, for example, relegate Chinese culture to the confined space of "ghettoized" labor within an "urban, industrial culture"(Lowe 121–122).[15] While American culture and social-policy performs this spatial imbalance, all ethnic categories, including whiteness, are visualized and conceptualized through an exoticized distance. As in the Chinatowns of mainland American space, Hawaiian culture is a commodity only for white tourists who consume a "culture" that is maintained by economic inequities of which they cannot conceive. Ultimately, whiteness is completely alien to Lovey and her peers who see it as other-worldly and of the mainland, far away from their realities. They must learn to create and then privilege other ethnic types as they perpetuate the same painful social hierarchies within which they are raised as children.

Lovey's experiences demonstrate that adolescent development under these circumstances involves a desperate mediation of peer-pressure and an incessantly changing current of societal expectations. Fortunately, Lovey has a partner in battling such formidable group pressures; her best friend, a boy named Jerry, provides a sort of surrogate boyfriend for Lovey. His relationship with Lovey conveys her heterosocial potential for loyalty, honesty, and compassion within such hostile social breeding-grounds. While their relationship is clearly unromantic, Lovey and Jerry's feelings for each other allow us to envision Lovey's capability for intimacy, a significant feature of contemporary heroine construction that hints, though obliquely, at our heroine's prospects for evoking and enacting meaningful, sustaining relationships in the future. The more of this type of social potential a heroine has, the more readers may gauge her prospects for success in marriage and society later, under cultural standards which privilege romantic social ability. Unlike Pecola, with whom no other person is intimate, Lovey at least has a partner in her social displacement. Their larger peer group, however, responds to Lovey's and Jerry's friendship with censure; the nature of this friendship confuses young adults who have been conditioned to think of relationships in terms of heterosexual romance based upon a foundation of a hierarchical scale of beauty and popularity. "Why—the hag cannot fight her own battles, so one fag gotta fight for one lez-lee?" asks one of Lovey's antagonists (185). Lovey's response to this accusation is equally cruel: "Aw fuck off, Gina . . . you stink rotten little Okinawan. Go collect some pig slops with your uncle them from Uka side, then put um in your grandma's andagi." Insults are a commodity in this marketplace of social shame. Gina ultimately wins this argument by attacking Lovey's family, her class, culture, and sexuality in a sweeping jibe whose details and emotional force, though directed at Lovey, stem from a self-loathing shared by Lovey and her Japanee peers:

> Wise off, you loser numba one. You eva wonder why you no mo' friends, hah, Lovey? You one queer fucka, your whole family, fuckin' ka-naka style everybody sleeping on your living-room floor, eh? No mo' nuff beds and blankets so gotta use army sleeping bags from the Surplus Store, eh? (185)

Such heartbreakingly mean-spirited language clouds the potential for conventional conflict-resolution within the narrative. Lovey's prospects for a successful construction of a self-affirming identity seem dim; the novel offers only a few redemptory, though ambivalently related, moments for our heroine through a softened version of the pained, longing tone serving as Lovey's inner voice.

As we read further, we wonder as to the viability of other virtues and attributes such as creativity, inner strength, and self-confidence in this social milieu. However, in Lovey's world, even creative endeavor and expression come attached with obstacles. Music lessons, for example, cost money that the Nariyoshis cannot afford to spend. When Lovey remedies this lack by joining the school band, she learns a lesson about the realities of a social economy within which a clear, creative expression of her true voice cannot be heard: "That's what it was about band. The sound of the voices from each instrument. I couldn't hear my clarinet rise above the others. . . . A deep voice. Like invisible waves." (57) "Even in the band," Lovey tells us, "they never liked me. They all looked alike and acted alike." Oddly enough, Lovey's mother, the same person who tells her that the family cannot afford the cost of music lessons, is the only other person who appreciates the "invisible waves" of Lovey's voice through the clarinet (57, 59). Lovey also attempts to mediate the material pressure she feels to dress well by learning to sew her own clothes, an act sanctioned by her family in that they accept the cost of sewing lessons. Again, Lovey's peers' responses to her efforts to be self-sufficient accord her with less admiration and respect than she expects: "Rip-off patchwork denim. Phony-ass, fake stuff. Looks Wigwam or worse yet. Home-made" (201).

These sewing lessons occur towards the end of the novel, as Lovey begins to value familial support and her familial identity despite her family's inability to conform to the suburban white ideal Lovey has aspired to reach for most of her life. When Lovey decides to quit sewing class, her father challenges her not to quit but to help him sew some vests from animal hides he has tanned. The gratification Lovey feels while patching together hides of animals that represent memories from her childhood is similar to the happiness she feels in sewing patchworks of old clothes belonging to members of her family. She feels sustained by the pleasure of having a secret bond with her family, a bond that is incomprehensible to her peers and untranslatable in terms of class hierarchies and social economics. "Grandma, Mother, Calhoun, Father, and me at that moment in the patchwork denim bell-bottom hiphuggers whose scraps nobody in the room could name but me," she tells us (204). At this point in the novel, Lovey's homemade hip-huggers symbolize the crafting of an ethnic identity. Her other sewing efforts have failed, but with this garment Lovey successfully creates her own style from the scraps of her family members' old clothes while using a popular and conventional pattern to guide her efforts. Socioeconomic circumstances, not artistic genius, necessitate this tailoring; thus Yamanaka narrates this moment of artistic success with some ambivalence. This episode is bittersweet in that Lovey's awareness of peer-pressure does not disappear with her successful effort at being fashionable.

Yamanaka's narration of Lovey's development in these pages contains a tension between a critique of economic and racial hierarchies and the cultivation of personal potential. In this way, the patchwork jeans serve as a metaphor for Yamanaka's version of female ethnicity in positing a creative, though second-hand articulation of self. Like the fashioning of jeans from a sewing pattern, Lovey's formation of identity involves and depends upon her understanding of conventional mores. However, this moment is Yamanaka's first indication to the reader that Lovey will be able to experience self-efficacy. Her sewing venture with her father and her ability to create a "rip-off" outfit which her peers cannot classify as store-bought or homemade comes only after her persistent efforts to create a relational, positive identity in the midst of hostility and antagonism. Yamanaka demonstrates her heroine's learned strength and social promise in this instance by allowing Lovey to respond to unkindness and social prejudice with confident words that, instead of matching cruelty with anger, diffuse harsh intent with playful words. When a classmate tries to tease Lovey about her new (possibly homemade) outfit by saying "pull up your hiphuggas. Can see your ass-cleavage," Lovey readily quips: "Hey man, I planned it that way" (204).

This phase in Lovey's development marks an important stage of self-actualization for our heroine because she realizes where her real social allegiances must lie if she is to find happiness and fulfillment. In a climactic exchange of words, she argues with her father over having to use a homemade stereo system. After she tells her father that she hates him, Mr. Nariyoshi angrily reports the painful truth of Lovey's external and internal realities: "-Good-for-nothin' nobody. You always make like we something we not, I tell you. When you going to open your eyes and learn, hah? You ain't rich, you ain't haole, and you ain't strong inside. You just one little girl" (260).

While Toni Morrison's novel critiques more harshly than Yamanaka's the racialized class dynamics which may serve as foundation for domestic ideals (such as psychologically nurturing parenting), Yamanaka offers a useful reversal of white middle-class ideals of fatherhood in the figure of Mr. Nariyoshi. Though his words are indisputably harsh and perhaps unjustified, Yamanaka allows him to impart a significant piece of advice to his daughter without having to use a storybook, idealized "haole" language that Lovey expects from a father. In his angry indictment of his daughter's abilities and subjective potential lies a prospect she has previously overlooked: the fact that she "ain't strong inside." Mr. Nariyoshi's words also underscore her difficult social prospects, which are determined by her class and race, and they are uttered with the same scorn and admonition as those uttered by Celie's husband to Celie in Alice Walker's *The Color Purple,* and Janie's grandmother to Janie in Hurston's *Their Eyes Were Watching God.*[16] At this moment, the reader glimpses one road to self-actualization unexplored by our heroine. Simultaneously, a secret about the role of virtue within heroine construction becomes apparent; the degree of self-confidence possessed by a developing female subject determines the mood and tone of her story. The narrative bleakness maintained by the author's critique of cultural hegemony falters under the promise of narrative resolution offered by a virtue Lovey's father tells her she does not posses. While forces of social displacement due to her race, class, and gender may be beyond her control, her father suggests that the development of inner strength is within her grasp.

Lovey's father loses his sight in a hunting accident just days after this argument, and to show him that she has taken his words to heart, Lovey decides to take on a task of inner strength that will demonstrate her resourcefulness, determination, and familial loyalty. She evinces this higher attribute by running away from home to go to her father's birthplace after raising the money for the trip by burning scrap metal. Lovey gathers sand from her father's childhood home and brings it to him in a bag mixed with dirt from the grounds of their current home. A ritualistic gesture symbolizing heaven on earth, Lovey's task proves to her father that she has been listening to the stories he has told of his childhood. The last words of the novel, "I be home," are Lovey's father's, and he utters them to his daughter "across the night" to acknowledge her act of strength and familial allegiance. Reminiscent of Jo March's rash but thoughtful decision to cut her hair to raise money for her mother to visit her injured father, Lovey's action too implies a sacrifice of her former internalized lessons in cultural training and self-loathing. Both actions are beyond the realm of the culturally feminine, but are in keeping with the textual reconfigurations of femininity, which have been evolving in heroine characterization since the birth of the novel. That is, both protagonists demonstrate through their actions that they are more than just "girls," and, perhaps paradoxically, become stronger heroines. A true heroine at last, Lovey proves to her father that she is not just "one little girl," but independent and stronger than he thinks.

Though not necessarily the "happy-ending" Lovey expects from Shirley Temple movies, this ending is more optimistic about Lovey's future than Morrison's *The Bluest Eye*. *The Bluest Eye* and *Wild Meat and the Bully Burgers* commence their stories of heroine development under the weight of similarly foreboding circumstances and similarly impossible desires. Both heroines' stories enact powerful critiques of exclusionary, hierarchical aesthetic standards and cultural ideals and thereby reveal the relational structuring mechanisms within culturally-envisioned categorizations of ethnicity. Such structures equate whiteness with goodness, beauty and purity, and blackness with evil, "Funk," and immorality—with all other racial categories being relationally removed from both extremes along the axis of class. Lovey's character illustrates the stratified construction and differentiation of these ethnic classifications when she tries unsuccessfully to have her hair permed. The home perm results are disastrous, and Lovey's disappointment is narrated in racialized terms: "When we finish, I have an Afro. Not like Shirley Temple but tighter. Like Christie Love. Frizzy and borinki" (52). "Christie Love," the black heroine of an early 1970's television detective series starring Teresa Graves, is a far less admirable pop-culture icon in

Lovey's mind than Shirley Temple. As these novels progress, it seems that both heroines will be trapped by the lack of substance underlying their desires, circumscribed by the sheer impossibility of their yearnings. Instead of blue eyes, Pecola achieves madness, and in this way serves as a parable to the MacTeer sisters and all others who encounter her story. Yamanaka saves Lovey Nariyoshi from madness and despair by resorting to the cultivation of virtue when she plants in Lovey the seeds of an inner strength that will serve as the foundation of her future self-confidence.

Lovey and Pecola, as heroines, teach us about the parameters of narrating stories of female development. In relation to each other, these stories reveal the function of stock female attributes which resonate with the possibilities for happy or sad endings, and for which readers may be looking as they consume their heroines as objects.[17] Lovey's development seems unhealthy until she learns to value her family, the only collective identity to which she can belong without being emotionally scathed. Significantly, her allegiance to her family instead of her peer group demonstrates that she is "strong inside," an ever-present alternative to the endowments of wealth and beauty in stories of female development.[18] Under these circumstances, does Yamanaka's novel veer away from narrative patterns of resolution and romance espoused by traditional or anglo heroine construction? Or does its more optimistic ending represent the novel's allegiance to a "bourgeois individualism and the social order" that marks a devaluation of cultural authenticity?[19]

While it does respond to hegemonic narratives of white middle-class ideals, the novel incorporates significant elements of traditional heroine construction that do not necessarily cohere to a strictly "decolonizing" socioeconomic critique. Lovey's heterosocial connection to Jerry, already outlined above, accords her greater social value. Also, her infatuation for the "hapa," handsome and popular Jenks when she is older culminates in their one long slow dance together, allowing her some redemption as a female subject in the objectifying heterosexual gaze represented by her peers' obsession with beauty, popularity, and romance. This dance, at least, supports the expectations of conventional female narratives in allowing Lovey to dance like Cinderella with a boy who is seemingly beyond her social reach. Of course, she later learns to be critical of Jenks's hypocrisy and learns to privilege her friendship with Jerry over her attraction to Jenks. Regardless, Yamanaka's decision to entertain common adolescent heterosexual romantic fantasies in this way must be seen in terms of a shared, transcultural project of heroine construction. For readers to understand Lovey's character in relation to other heroines functioning in the literary marketplace, they must first understand her potential as a heterosexual romantic object in a pre-marital young-adult context. Just as she must learn to cultivate at least one important virtue (inner strength and confidence) if her development is to be successful and productive, she must engage with the narrative requirement of young-adult romantic drama to be a marketable heroine.

Such relational heroine construction ensures authors that their heroines will find empathy from their readers. My phrasing above performs the skepticism with which I approach the binaries between Western and ethnic, and political and romantic. I am not suggesting that Morrison or Yamanaka consciously differentiate between these categories and thereby infuse their critiques of race, class, and gender with more romantic plot elements. The similarities of heroine construction in these novels evoke reader expectancy for romance that in turn influences the culmination of the developmental narratives in a symbiotic process. As Lee Edwards states of heroism, "it connects tendencies in any given social world to imaginative constructs that suggest hypothetical consequences" (Edwards 16). Thus, despite the initial similarities of tone in these novels, structural features mediate the processes between critique and resolution, desire and gratification, self-expression and collective order. In the end, Lovey's and Pecola's pain is mitigated not by the nourishment provided by any one specific cultural identity but rather the individual choices they make in struggling against very similar social pressures. They perform their ethnicities as two similar individuals making two different choices; blackness and "Japaneeness," though they stem from different contexts, evoke the same emotions in the narratives. Our heroines' stories thus demonstrate the narrative shape of ethnicity as it weaves through structural possibilities. The final section of this chapter will continue to probe into the role of poetic language and structure in defining ethnicity and femininity by focusing on another stock female attribute in heroine construction: wit.

WIT, THE BEAUTIFUL VOICE OF INNER STRENGTH: GISH JEN'S *MONA IN THE PROMISED LAND*

Mona Chang is the favorite daughter, and she knows it. She is practically as smart as her sister, who is studying at "Practically Harvard" (Harvard-Radcliffe), but Mona is more spirited, funnier, and certainly more strong-willed than her sister Callie. In Mona's case, the cultural confusion she faces as a second-generation Chinese American adolescent growing up in the late 1960s in a predominantly Jewish "Scarshill," New York is not as frustrating as her inability to communicate this confusion to her conservative parents. In *Mona in the Promised Land* (1996), our heroine takes matters into her own hands, finding solace in the youth community at the local Jewish temple after converting to Judaism. She good-humoredly allows her peers to call her "Most honorable Miss Changowitz" (Jen 90). Jen characterizes her generally "spriggy" heroine by bemusedly noting Mona's "aplomb" and wit. Amongst her upper-middle-class white peer group, Mona learns first to "make a career" out of being Chinese and later by being a Chinese-Jew (8). In the passage below, one of Mona's friends explains the interrelated nuances of identity-formation, difference, and market value:

> This friend explained how some people resented being valued for their looks, others resented being valued for their money. Wasn't it still better to be beautiful and rich than ugly and poor, though? *You should be just glad,* she said, *that you have something people value.* She said it was like having a special talent, like being good at ice-skating, or opera-singing. (8)

The narrator diffuses a palpable tension here between a typically adolescent desire to be superlative in terms of standardized norms ("beautiful and rich") and the learned appreciation of uniqueness ("special talent"). In answer to the candid confusion represented by Mona's question ("Wasn't it still better to be beautiful"), the friend's response, represented by italicized writing, balks the need to answer this difficult question, offering instead "special" as value.

Like the scale of beauty pervading Pecola and Lovey's youths in Morrison's *The Bluest Eye* and Yamanaka's *Wild Meat and the Bully Burgers,* the scale of "specialness" fluctuates through the course of Mona's adolescence as she shapes her identity to fit her developing beliefs and the standards she comes to value in the greater Scarshill community. While making a career out of being Chinese works when her family first moves into the Jewish neighborhood, as Mona grows older she feels that she must maintain the difference between herself and her parents, her sister, and her friends. After Chinese American, Mona cultivates a Chinese-Jewish-American identity before moving on to a failed attempt to incorporate an African American subjectivity, which she learns is more than shades removed from the more subtle class distinctions between the Jews and the Chinese ("the new Jews"). For Mona these complexities are confusing and often impossible to explain. The novel performs the idea that "difference" is a slippery slope, a potentially abysmal depth to chart once one starts to be aware of both its value in a social market as well as its potential for misunderstanding, division, and prejudice.

In the novel's first chapter, "Mona Gets Flipped," "flipped" refers to her somewhat violent, if humorous, awakening into the complexities of individual and group identity. Mona's first would-be-boyfriend, Sherman Matsumoto, flips her in a defensive Judo move after he is offended by her unwillingness to "switch" to a Japanese identity from a Chinese one, a plan he thinks is necessary for them to be able to get married to each other some distant day in the future. Mona thinks they should just both be American— *"The way you do everything is weird,"* she tells him (21). Mona's introduction to Sherman in homeroom reveals the locally-determined context and parameters of difference. Everyone in her homeroom, including herself, assumes when they see Sherman sitting in class, that he is another Chinese kid. The students all believe that he is Chinese because Mona has already familiarized and preoccupied them with the narrative of Chinese versus American difference, and Mona instinctively feels that her "special" career is now over with Sherman's arrival:

> How much aplomb, however, remains to be seen on said bloomy spring day, as she saunters in late to homeroom, only to experience a personal shock—a new kid in class.
> Chinese. . . . She sits down. She is so cool she reminds herself of Paul Newman. First thing she realizes, though, is that no one looking at her is thinking of Paul Newman. (9)

After their brief experience in puppy-love, and after Mona is flipped, Sherman moves back to Japan. For the next four years, Mona continues to hold on to the idea of Sherman, their premature betrothal in the bushes of her front-yard, and the possibility of his return from Japan when she is older. Some years later Seth Mandell, her boyfriend and future husband, an eccentric though brilliant Jewish boy who lives in a teepee, tells her that Sherman is "not a person, he's an idea. Everyone's first love is an idea" (113). For Mona, experiencing the frustrations of a cultural divide between herself and her parents, and still no stranger to the prejudice and ignorance her Chinese heritage sparks in the minds of many Americans, the idea of Sherman involves a sustaining idea of balance. Their argument over "switching" countries and identities highlights their shared experience as Americans of difference. This shared difference, though spanning two distinct nationalities and cultures, also contains a racial sameness, as explained by the town's lack of understanding and lack of interest in the differences between Japanese and Chinese. In their pervasively white school, and within a predominantly Jewish neighborhood, she and Sherman, similarly different and set-apart in their class, are a match meant to be.

Gish Jen's postmodern yet poignant novel of adolescence is unique in its lightheartedly satirical treatment of ethnic adolescence. It veers away from one of two general patterns in contemporary Asian American heroine construction: the first generally avoids adolescence altogether as a major thematic concern, and the other pattern discusses adolescence in a mostly materialist context with, more often than not, tragic undertones.[20] Maxine Hong Kingston's *The Woman Warrior,* a text that employs similar mechanisms of humor to illustrate bicultural identity, concentrates on no specific developmental stage.[21]As we shall find is the case with Jen's Mona, general patterns in the treatment of Asian American adolescence reveal conscientious and relational narrative practices within a larger project of heroine construction. What does it mean, for example, that while Asian American literary scholar Lisa Lowe critiques the civilizing tendencies of anglo bourgeois fiction by Austen and Dickens used to educate children in the former colonies of the United States and Great Britain, Gish Jen's Vintage Contemporaries edition of *Mona in the Promised Land* is touted on its back cover as "spinning with a wit as dry as a latter-day Jane Austen's"?

Like Frank Chin's *Donald Duk, Mona in the Promised Land* flirts with the conventions of adolescence one might more often find in anglo juvenile fiction within the Judy Blume or Beverly Cleary brand of young adulthood. Blume's heroine in her 1970 young-adult novel *Are You There God? It's Me, Margaret,* wrangles with decisions she must make in choosing a religious faith and social standards that cause girls to be anxious about their bodies and sexual developments. Protagonists in these texts learn psycho-social lessons of identity-construction informed by racialized middle-class norms of heterosexuality, sex role definition, intra-community status, and wealth. *Donald Duk* and *Mona in the Promised Land* focus on adolescence as a space of subjective potential, without a sustained consideration of the material realities of adulthood. Also, both novels employ a hyperbolic language, detailing everyday occurrences in the comedic present tense within the familial and community unit to highlight a larger-than-life point-of-view experienced by the developing "I." Ultimately, this satirical view turns inward to reveal the protagonists' overwhelming sense of alienation from their own families. Both Donald and Mona make amends for their radically New World behavior and ideas by trying to rekindle feelings of support and respect from their parents—the very figures who seem the most absurd in the beginning of both novels. Thematically speaking then, these novels seem only just to skirt more complex issues of American ethnicity, class, and race because their use of humor implies that the more pressing conflict of the narratives lies within the more conventionally adolescent realm of parent-child struggles.

On the other hand, the satirical foundation of *Mona in the Promised Land,* as in *Donald Duk,* holds the protagonists at an ironic distance from themselves. Almost in the same way that Toni Morrison is unable to inhabit Pecola Breedlove in the first person in *The Bluest Eye,* Jen decides to impart first-hand experiences by way of the third-person perspective. Thus, we are meant to read Mona's deepest desires through the distance of comedic empathy. Antagonism is impossible to sustain in this narrative mode. At any given moment, the reader understands that the main character's beliefs are certainly no more enlightened than those characters that threaten or hinder the protagonist's development. Consider, for example, a scene in "The New Chapter" that depicts Mona's decision to convert to Judaism and her mother's responsive unmitigated frustration and consternation. Mona is certain that her mother's anger is informed by "an escalating series of incomprehensible and distinctly menacing developments, such as Mona's buying a down jacket, and wanting not only her own car . . . but her own telephone line" (48). Trying to reason with her mother by way of logic and interpersonal communication, Mona reminds Mrs. Chang of her own words about the importance of being flexible and adaptable in a new country and understanding that the next generation could not be "pure Chinese anymore, the parents had to accept we would be something else." The following excerpt of a mother-daughter argument encapsulates Helen Chang's illogical responses as well as the nearly painfully funny attempts by Mona to be as objective and juridical as possible. This attempt is captured by the narrator's commentary on Mona's internal calculation on what exactly next to say to her mother in this ultimately failed attempt at a healthy parent-child discussion:

> "American, not Jewish." Helen assigns Mona a piece of pork to slice while she herself cleans the fish, and it calms them both down to see what a nice job Mona can still do. . . .

> "Jewish is American," Mona says, "American means being whatever you want, and I happened to pick being Jewish."

> "Since when do children pick this, pick that? You tell me. Children are supposed to listen to their parents. Otherwise, the world becomes crazy. Who knows? Tomorrow you'll come home and tell me you want to be black."

> "How can I turn black? That's a race, not a religion." (Mona says this even though she knows some kids studying to be Bobby Seale. They call each other brother, and eat soul food instead of subs, and wear their hair in the baddest Afros they can manage.)

> "And after that you are going to come home and tell me you want to be a boy instead of a girl. . . after that you are going to come home and tell me you want to be a tree."

"Whoever heard of someone turning into a tree?" Mona tactfully refrains from
bringing up this poet Ovid her English class is reading, never mind that he did-
n't write in English. . . . She goes to sleep thinking that they have had a heart-to
heart communication such as leads to true intergenerational understanding and
tolerance." (49)

This last sentence briskly satirizes a larger project of identity-
differentiation undertaken by second-generation Asian Americans. Although
the need for freedom of individual expression is indisputably the focus of
novels like *Mona in the Promised Land*, the humor laced through its representation gently mocks this desire. The comedy offers several insights into
the problems of bicultural identity-construction while it performs a post-
structuralist dig at the failure of language and communication as well as the
biases of a bourgeois, capitalist obsession with the articulation of an actualized, individual identity. Helen Chang's unwillingness to follow her daughter's progressive logic in the scene above points to an untranslatable quality
between anglo, New World ideals and an immigrant sensibility that adheres
to the no-nonsense rigors of tradition and material survival. For example, as
they argue Helen keeps her eye on the clock and continues to clean fish for
dinner. The narrator inserts a reminder about Helen's material world of domestic duties and work into this comedic scene as the free-indirect discourse
details tasks to be done and repairs to be made. Jen writes: "After the pork,
there is still the fish and also some spinach to do, and then it's time to get
back to the pancake house." The narrator goes on, "The kitchen used to be
the warmest room in the house, but recently they had to turn the radiator
off because of a leaking valve" (49). The discrepancy between Mona and
Helen's version of the American dream is obvious in the lines introducing
the mother-daughter discussion above, lines which set material sustenance
and comfort apart from ideals arguably derived from the mental luxury
these comforts allow. "For if you asked her," Jen writes of Mona's mother,
"she would say that she signed up for her own house and garage, but not for
her children to become big-mouthed separate accounting units" (48). Such
obvious distinctions between generations of ethnic identities and their primary goals is reminiscent of Zora Neale Hurston's discussions of the conflict between Janie's yearning for self-expression and psychological
nurturing and her grandmother's fetishization of big houses and property in
Their Eyes Were Watching God.

Though secondary to questions of identity, the racialized material real-
ties of a late-1960s-American class system do surface in probing ways. A subplot involving Alfred, a black pancake chef and employee of Mona's father,

hilariously underscores the complexities of race, religion, class, and nation, in the often futile attempts at ethnic categorization and a cross-ethnic idealism of pluralistic empathy. Though he warms up to Barbara Gugelstein (Mona's best friend) and her "Jew Daddy" because Barbara offers Alfred shelter in her house when he is evicted, Alfred remains aloof to Mona's attempts to bridge the gap between constructions of race and nation as she tries to lesson the friction between the black prep staff and the Chinese management of the pancake house. In fact, Mona's final attempt to garner respect from her mother hinges upon Alfred's agreement to drop a lawsuit he introduces against the elder Changs for racial discrimination in the workplace. In her and Seth's final meeting with Alfred at Alfred's home, Mona feels the true lived disparities of American blackness and her own relatively more soluble difference from a white, suburban ideal. Alfred hesitatingly "reports" that his friend and self-professed civil rights leader "the Race Man" "got beat just about dead," and to represent the force of this realization on Mona's understanding of racial politics, Jen writes that "Mona's heart blows open" (292).

After touching on this event of racial violence, Jen then softens its weight in the novel by having Alfred immediately and slyly change the subject to discuss the comedic details of the lawsuit. Mona then succeeds in persuading Alfred to drop the suit and rushes home to reconcile with her mother after a self-imposed exile of some weeks. When Mona returns to her home, the material truths assembled in her parents' kitchen assault her even while she experiences the "warm" "enveloping" quality of her house. Suddenly, Mona feels the fact of her own difference from her family as she stares at the proof of her parents' material efforts and striving, which are embodied in the "piles" of goods forming a "veritable jumble," representing "all the years her family has spent shopping the bargain basement" (293). Then, similar to Frank Chin's description in *Donald Duk* of Mr. Duk's creative fusion cooking as representative of his productive philosophy of ethnicity, Jen narrates Mona's awakening into the more positive truths of her bicultural heritage in terms of kitchen styles and food preservation. Mona realizes that she has been developing within a self-imposed binary, one which positions the clean kitchen maintenance of the Gugelstein family, with its systematically organized, "elegant" refrigerator against her family's own storage of "pickley, primordial foods." Mona realizes she might adopt either of the two kitchen schemas in her own future home, it being, after all, only food.

Jen reinforces Mona's revelation here about difference by characterizing Helen Chang's distracted and cold reaction to her daughter coming home. "Who is this?" Helen asks of Mona, as she addresses her daughter wearing an old worn bathrobe and looking much older than when Mona left the house, just weeks ago (294). Mona rants enthusiastically that Alfred will be dropping the suit: "We talked to him!" Helen's response sums up her inability and unwillingness to think of life in the progressive, solution-based mentality of her daughter: "What are you talking about, talked to Alfred?" Then she adds, "And who is this *we?*" (295). This italicized word captures Helen's final disappointment in her daughter's alliance with the Jewish faith and a Jewish boyfriend. Mona's exile from home is in fact prolonged after her parents discover her in bed with Seth Mandel in her sister's dorm room (whether her parents truly see them together or not is left up to the reader's imagination). The years of generational misunderstanding between the elder and younger Changs culminates with the disapproval connoted in Helen's use of "we" in her final question to Mona, making the complexities of race, class, nation, and sex, seem finally most unmanageable in Mona's selection of a boyfriend. However, Seth Mandel figures into most of the novel without being the subject of real conflict between Mona and her parents. As the narrator maintains throughout the course of the novel, Helen Chang's irritation with her children's behavior is unfixed and constantly shifts targets. Thus, one might read Mona's final expulsion from her mother's good graces and approval in terms of the finally untranslatable difference between the views of mother and child that happen to become self-evident in Helen's disapproval of Seth Mandel. Helen goes back into her bedroom, an action, signifying to Mona that she, the daughter, "can be trusted to leave by herself. Finally she's big enough not to be told" (295).

The epilogue takes readers years into the future of Mona and her mother's estrangement, to the day of the wedding between Mona and Seth (who have already had a child together). Though the novel ultimately reunites mother and daughter (and granddaughter) in a tearful embrace, whose poignant, conclusive impact seems outside the scope of the novel's pervasive satire, it offers no true explanation of the real cause of the rift between mother and daughter. The wedding also clouds the possibilities for clear interpretation of the novel's otherwise linear progression. Years have been unaccounted for—post-adolescent years in Mona's life—years that we are meant to tie back to this wedding day and its potential as a reunion site. Jen's nod to the marriage plot here is confusing, to say the least. Our narrator alludes to multiple happy unions. Even those that seem in earlier chapters unlikely to last (as in Alfred's tryst with Barbara's enigmatic cousin Evie) withstand the test of some seven-odd years and result in conclusive pairings, which effect a pleasing, though ironic, comedic resolution at the novel's end:

> Alfred and Evie, the love bugs, Mr. and Mrs. Community Organization. They've marched, they've cooked, they've given up denying that she

married him to assuage her own guilt, or that he's a white-bitch-lover
who shouldn't have needed her to get him through college. They figure
every marriage involves some horse trade; at least theirs worked. (297)

Jen's use of marriage subplots aims at some types of cultural reversals. But
in the meantime, what could it mean that Jen must resort to the heterosexual romantic subplot in the ways she chooses?

"A Most Mannerly Fellow" is the title of the penultimate chapter in
which Seth Mandel turns up to rescue Mona from exile at Harvard University.
Seth reveals that he has in fact been the voice of her long-lost first-love Sherman
Matsumoto over the telephone, haunting Mona all of these years later. Seth's
confession in part signifies his transformation from a cynical and unmannered
though politically progressive young man into a reformed progressive young
man (one who decides finally to go to college). His transformation, we are to
understand, comes about because of his love for Mona and her constant criticism of his lack of interest in social grace. While Jane Austen's famous marriage
plot structures ingratiate themselves into Jen's text in this momentary allusion
to Mr. Darcy's social transformation and in Jen's denouement of multiple wed-
dings, the narrator continues to maintain that comedic and almost critical distance from the emotional weight of these events. "And Seth is supposed to be
that?" Mona asks herself, "Her own true love?" (277) One final question
within Mona's ambivalent mind seems put forth by the novel to the reader:
"This is supposed to be some kind of comedy?" Our heroine seems uncon-
vinced, in fact uncertain, that she should reconcile with Seth and become romantically involved with him again. Yet the tension between Mona's often
self-deprecating and emotionally non-committal world-view and the promise
of romantic fulfillment and general well-being enacted by the novel's tone and
use of comedic structures offers a type of contemporary revision to the problem of marital expectations and heroine construction. While this revision may
not seem radically different from feminist practices of reformed marriage plots,
in *Mona in the Promised Land* these reversals are humorous and ironic re-
articulations of dominant cultural narratives voiced within ethnic contexts.

Jen performs these narrative reversals through the third-person-limited
perspective of a heroine gifted with superior wit, a deliberate alternative to
superior beauty, superior virtue, and superlative imaginative prowess, all of
which are stock attributes of the marketable heroine. Mona and Andy
Kaplan's dialogue in the passage below demonstrates Jen's investment in
Mona's unique sense of humor:

Andy Kaplan gives her a cuff. "Very funny. Where'd you get that wit of
yours from anyway?"

"I'm afraid I'm a self-made mouth," Mona says.

Andy laughs. (90)

Heterosocial energies are in Mona's favor in this scene, as it is obvious to the reader that Mona's wit endears her to Andy even though Andy has entered the scene "hand in hand" with his girlfriend Eloise Ingle (89–90). The words "wit" and "self-made," are particularly revealing in the passage. "Wit," a necessary attribute of several Austenian heroines, carries with it connotations of neoclassical sophistication. In Mona's case, her wit not only indicates that she has an unusual amount of intelligence and creative potential, the use and characterization of her abilities illustrate her middle-class life-style and peer group. Mona, as a character, represents the promise not only of narrative engagements between female writers of yore and their contemporary ethnic predecessors, her self-expression also represents the promise of actualized individual potential ("self-made") within an American capitalist market.

The cultivation of wit in Jen's novel is in fact one of narrative ambivalence for a few reasons. It is, as mentioned above, a transhistorical element of heroine construction as heroines evolve and are cast in relation to each other. However, Jen must also consider an entire tradition of Asian American fiction in creating her heroine, as well the anglo comedic tradition with which she seems most obviously to engage. Mona's wit thus functions almost atavistically, summoning up a narrative potential for success in a market of heterosocial and heterosexual economies and appealing to the reader's most subconscious desires for pleasurable endings by use of a feminine attribute that has a tradition in positive self-fashioning. Because Jen, for most of the novel, eschews adult themes of marriage or vocational development and instead emphasizes adolescence, "wit" then attests more to Mona's heterosocial, not heterosexual success. Her first heterosexual desires, introduced with the entrance of Sherman Matsumoto, are explored within the safe space of pre-pubescence and narrated from a voice of extreme bemusement. Conveniently, Sherman goes on to become "an idea"—almost an obsession. While the object of Mona's romantic affection turns into a humorous fiction and fantasy, the reader can focus instead on Mona's heterosocial development and its quirky trajectory. Her propensity towards humor also wins favor with her mother who considers Mona the favorite over the more conventionally "perfect" Callie. With these comedic gears and their social rewards set in motion, Mona's voice within the novel collects a sort of reactionary steam as our heroine navigates the world of old China, America, the Jewish suburbs, and the space of her own desires.

As we approach the end of the novel, the central conflict, which began as a sort of general cultural confusion, now asserts itself as the pressure

Mona faces to conform to her parents' expectations of the proper Chinese daughter. In this light, we might see Jen's narrative voice (wit, irony, and satire enacted in free-indirect discourse) as a generic performance of the novel's central theme. While Mona struggles to be the free and independent daughter of the Chang household, the pressure of paternal authority forces her to use humor as a rhetorical strategy and defense mechanism. Similarly, Jen's narrative voice mediates the tensions between an objective material reality informed by a context of Asian American immigrant experience and the desire for an individualized authorial identity and its free expression.

In *Imagining the Nation,* David Leiwei Li contextualizes the binary between these two types of Asian American narrative patterns in his chapter on "Immigrant Incarnations" of American cultural narratives. Li views Gish Jen's fiction as representative of a movement away from "ethnic nationalism" towards "the many analogous narratives of national consent" (Li 102). The aim of Jen's literary efforts in cultivating a new narrative voice, Li would argue, is "to create a fiction beyond the negative embodiments of race and ethnicity" (102). Xiao-huang Yin, too, notes the ways in which Jen's "cosmopolitan, transcultural, and easy going" style differs from many examples of Asian American fiction (Yin 243). "Wit" thus embodies this tension between traditional narrative expectations and cultural specificity as Mona ambivalently enters the arena of American adolescent heterosocial potential and performs her version—an ethnicized revision—of a superlative subjectivity worthy of success within a marriage market as well as the publishing marketplace. Jen thus tests the "limits of comedy" from a specific context of Asian American letters as she mixes generic experimentation with immigrant subject matter more often discussed through the lens of material inequity than lighthearted social dramas. [22]

The word "negative" in Li's observations, and the "easy going" quality Yin assigns to Jen's works above are striking as these casual references to mood and emotion within critical discussions of race, ethnicity, and gender gloss over those potentially ambivalent struggles within and against dominant discourse that actually foster the creation of new patterns of expression. Assignations of "positive," "negative," and "easy going" point to our relational reading habits as ethnic texts are evaluated against anglo texts, and vice versa. These categorical perspectives of scholarship should in fact help us better understand and help us to be more sensitive and critically receptive towards the indisputably relational patterns of transcultural narrative production, or those forces which compel writers to cast conventional virtues and values in new personae, as well as those considerations that ensure reformulated poetics. To a great extent, this chapter's arguments have not only challenged the academic assumption that contemporary novels of feminine ethnicity must in some way be "negative" in tone, they have attempted to shed light on the ways in which women writers negotiate the pressures and expectations for happy and unhappy endings for contemporary heroines.

My exploration of adolescence has, in this chapter, charted the terrain of adolescent female characterization to extract those narrative sites which are emblematic of conventional feminine virtues and attributes and which typify more transhistorical and transcultural relationships between female protagonists than are likely to be theorized within feminism and ethnic studies. Adding to my discussions of romance and marriage subplots, the objectification of female characters, and the relational concept of space in ethnic female identity, this last chapter's examination of adolescent narratives concludes my explication of the role of ambivalence and anxiety in configuring and performing concepts of ethnicity. Ethnic writers may attempt to avoid comedic scenarios of female development as they negotiate pressures from an academic marketplace, which prioritizes politics over the personal; on the other hand, they strive to produce heroines whose identities will be affirmed by empathetic readership and commercial success. In the introduction to this chapter, I briefly discussed A. J. Verdelle's *The Good Negress*, a novel that engages with issues of sexual and racial discrimination and experiments with the narration of traumatic memory through the eyes of a confident, cool-headed, capable young woman whose inner monologues uphold the optimism of more conventionally envisioned schemas of feminine development. One is less likely to find scholarship on Verdelle's novel, Gish Jen's *Mona in the Promised Land,* and Lois-Ann Yamanaka's *Wild Meat and the Bully Burgers* than one is likely to find on Morrison's *The Bluest Eye.* Those narratives that more overtly demonstrate the severity of racial, ethnic, and sexual discrimination in American culture are more likely to be discussed in academic scholarship today.

Our scholarship should consider the implications of such obvious critical trends and look to the similarities between older, conventional narratives of female adolescence and more contemporary versions. Doing so provides us with insight into the influence of narrative and structure over the cultivation of our ideals and identities. Perhaps what is most difficult to assess and analyze in our considerations of race, nation, gender, and class, is our subconscious reader investment in the language of movement towards possibility from potential, from isolation to community, from dirty dishwater to pastoral elegance. This chapter's examination of ethnicity, femininity, and the conventional virtues of beauty, inner strength, and wit espoused within heroine construction reveal that these mechanics of creative self-expression are still values that resonate positively in our cultural expectations for young women and our lingering wish that they will be able to rewrite empowering, as well as optimistic, stories for themselves.

Epilogue

My analysis of transcultural heroine construction and significant structural similarities between anglo and ethnic fiction is informed by my reading of Charlotte Brontë's *Villette*. In some sense, everything begins and ends with this 1853 novel—everything, that is, that has to do with subjective potential, women, and novels written in English. Though *Villette* is not as popular and not as widely-studied as Brontë's *Jane Eyre*, this later text offers a template of female subjective development that is perhaps more applicable to our contemporary world. As our most exigent political concerns demand that we use the study of literature to combat social ills like colonialism, racism, sexism, and class-conflict, we can find a model for the effects of these forces in the story of Lucy Snowe, a "woman without a country or a community," whose narrative serves as a poetics of modern alienation (Gilbert and Gubar 405). How can I make this claim when the novel never discusses race or imperialism? As an outcast/outclassed woman in nineteenth-century England, Lucy's story inevitably inscribes the narrative developmental potential for subjects-in-the-making in relation to the expanding networks of exclusionary social-stratification. Within Brontë's teleology, Lucy is the ultimate marginalized social being, and her outsider status in many ways transcends specificities of gender, race, nation, or class. It implicates all of these categories, however, as Lucy struggles for belonging while appraising herself in relation to the people around her and measuring her social worth in accordance to hierarchical levels of social existence. She learns to think of herself as utterly alien to any community. At its core, Lucy's story is one of ceaseless longing engendered by society and its promises, and the novel probes social and cultural investments in particular types of narratives of selfhood. After reporting the tragic events at the novel's end, events that destroy Lucy's final hopes for happiness as a socialized individual, she suddenly terminates her account in order to spare her readers' "sunny imaginations" (Brontë 617). Her conclusion is written in the tone of a revealingly paradoxical, passionate detachment: "Let it be theirs to conceive the delight of joy born again fresh out of great terror, the rapture of rescue from peril, the wondrous reprieve from dread, the fruition of return. Let them picture union and a happy succeeding life" (617). This "happy succeeding life" connotes various forms of subjective promise ranging from economic prosperity, vocational self-fulfillment, matrimonial contentment, and personal affirmation, all of which are dominant themes of the modern novel, which experienced a surge in popularity in the mid-nineteenth century through the influence of industrialism, capitalism, and colonialism.[1]

Aside from these more general subjective forces and themes, *Villette* also exemplifies a type of feminist heroine construction as Lucy's story represents "the cold that always endangers female survival" (Gilbert and Gubar 405). As the above passage indicates, Lucy's narration of events in her life provides a metanarrative on the trajectories for heroine development. I explained in chapter 3 of this project that the formation of Lucy's subjective identity involves her conceptualization of other women's prospects for happiness in relation to her own. Her sense of self thus functions as a result of a fundamental subjective competition that is narrated as the difference between "sunshine" and "cloud," and "Reason" and "Imagination" (Brontë 287, 530, 548). In fact, she uses feminine archetypes to discuss the difference between reason and the imagination as she identifies herself as the child of reason. To Lucy, "Reason" is a "hag," "step-mother," and "devil," while "Imagination" is "soft," "sweet," and "bright"—angelically feminine qualities found in the character of Paulina, the woman with whom Lucy's beloved Graham Bretton falls in love (287). In this way, *Villette* configures the themes and poetics of the heroine construction discussed in this study including the potential for and emphasis on heterosexual romantic success and the evaluative language of female or heroine objectification. Lucy's story also involves two of the other elements of heroine construction examined in this study: the search for place and position in society, and the narrative account of female adolescence. The novel begins with Lucy's recollection of her early adolescent self, and early on, she subtly explores her budding sense of romantic desire for Graham Bretton. When Lucy grows older, her story explores this desire while simultaneously describing her training as a teacher. Her development thus also configures and reconfigures the marriage plot as "Lucy represents all women who must struggle toward an integrated, mature, and independent identity by coming to terms with their need for love, and their dread of being single" (Gilbert and Gubar 406).

I see *Villette* as a thematic and poetic model for relational subjective development. We realize, as we read, that Lucy's unhappiness stems from her lack of self-esteem, which results from the ways in which she defines herself in relation to other women and cultural values of feminine worth. Her story, in fact, performs ambivalent female subjectivity through its uneasy interaction with conventional standards of heroism. Because Lucy doubts her own ability to be a heroine in the conventional sense, her narration is reserved and ambiguous while it cultivates qualities of rationality and detachment. Consider, for example, the subtlety with which she explores her desire for Graham Bretton's love, a love she feels she cannot have because she does not see herself as the type of conventionally desirable woman to whom Graham would be attracted. Lucy begins recollecting her childhood with a description of Graham in the larger context of her first description of the Bretton home. She demonstrates her intimacy with the whole family and the "people" with whom the Brettons are friends:

> People esteemed it a grievous pity that she hadn't conferred her complexion on her son, whose eyes were blue—though, even in boyhood, very piercing—and the colour of his long hair such as friends did not venture to specify, except as the sun shone on it, when they called it golden. (6)

This description, taken out of context, contains an emotional longing that is not quite so apparent when read along with Lucy's description of the Bretton's comfortable home and her relationship with Mrs. Bretton, all of which occur on the first page of the novel. In fact, Lucy consistently describes Graham in these "golden" terms without ever saying directly that she loves him. Yet we are still aware that she does. This dynamic unfolds as Lucy's narrative identity engages with the criteria for conventional heroine construction.

On the whole, Lucy is reluctant to tell us any of her desires in direct terms. Her consistent loneliness underlines her need for love and inclusion as it manifests itself in her tentative descriptions of Graham's and Paulina's love affair and her matter-of-fact narration of her employment at Madame Beck's school. The formal distance of the above passage parallels Lucy's tenuous position in the Bretton household; Mrs. Bretton is only the godmother to Lucy, not the primary caregiver. And yet, Lucy tells her readers nothing about her own home or her own family. We assume, because she is staying with "kinsfolk" that Lucy is an orphan, the Bretton family being the only connection to a nuclear family she has. Her knowledge of what "people esteemed" in the passage above demonstrates a strange intimacy with the family and implies that no matter what other people believe or think of Graham Bretton's complexion or his hair, she perceives differently. Her knowledge of the family is in fact non-communicable and non-demonstrative: it is knowledge that comes from love and longing where there is no hope for true reciprocity or the abatement of need.

The novel is the account of almost a lifetime's length of subjective long-ing for love and affirmation. We experience this need as Lucy expends most of her energies talking about the other people around her, beginning with the Bretton home and then the girls at Madame Beck's school and the residents of Villette. Lucy waits until the second chapter to tell us her name, and even then only to tell us her thoughts about young Paulina. "I, Lucy Snowe, plead guiltless of that curse, an overheated and discursive imagination," she states, attempting even this early to ground her story in the language of the real and the objective. She would rather have us believe that the story is a simple, no-nonsense account of a middle-class English woman finding her way in a Belgian town. But her words are loaded. "When I was a little girl I went to Bretton about twice a year, and *well I liked* the visit" (1). She continues: "I liked peace so well, and sought stimulus so little, that when the latter came I *almost felt it* a disturbance, and *wished rather it had held aloof*" (6; em-phasis mine). What she does not say is that she loves, not likes the Bretton home, and that her sanctity there is altered dramatically by the presence of another more loveable child. Understated and seemingly candid, her words are arranged with a syntactical elegance and rhythm that contains her need for poetic justice. The love Lucy cannot find around her must come from the unobtrusive and gentle weight of her inner knowledge. What she cannot have, she must know. As the first chapters of the novel are about the others around her, Lucy creates an image of herself as a quiet, unremarkable, or-phaned presence in a lively household.

We know what Lucy wants because these are things she does not and cannot say. She cannot say that she wishes that Mrs. Bretton would keep her permanently in her home, and that she wishes Paulina never came, or that she wishes that young Graham would play and talk with her as he does with Paulina. She does not say these things because their utterance would nullify her meager sense of self-efficacy and identity. She cannot say what she wants because to do so would prevent the need for the narrative, the chance for her to explore in written intimacy the people whom she loves while developing, in the reader's mind, the tiniest hope that the story may change and envelope her in the way that she needs it to. This mid-nineteenth-century novel provides us with a poetic template for bourgeois, middle-class anglo femininity as what Lucy wants and needs lies between the lines of the first page of the novel:

> The house and its inmates specially suited me. The large and peaceful rooms, the well-arranged furniture, the clear wide windows, the balcony outside, looking down on a fine antique street, where Sundays and hol-idays seemed always to abide—so quiet was its atmosphere, so clean its pavement—these things pleased me well. (1)

The language rings with materiality as it mentions spacious architecture, cleanliness, comfort, and the luxury of time, which contribute to aesthetic appreciation and taste: "well-arranged furniture" and a "fine antique street." As I discussed in chapter 3, Lucy is searching for a particular place in society, as well as a particular role in the Bretton family, and she learns to create a position for herself by dint of creating whatever relationships she can with Graham, Paulina, and Mrs. Bretton. In the passage above, she includes a reference to herself twice ("me") as she situates her individual appreciation for a house and family she cannot, by legal creeds stipulating ownership and familial relationship, lay claim to. Not having the fortune to enjoy such an existence, Lucy establishes a narrative trajectory for herself that positions her in direct contact with a class of people above her own. She uses her intelligence and training to become a teacher at a school for wealthy girls. Sure of no hope of Graham returning her love, she becomes a confidant to his lover Paulina, and becomes the spinster companion of a now elderly Mrs. Bretton.

Despite these narrative complexities, Lucy's story seems remarkably familiar to us. A young orphaned girl in the home of wealthier people who have a son a few years older than her, a godmother who pampers her "a good deal"—these facts, related to us on the first page of the novel, compel us to think of redemptory possibilities. These possibilities are based on our reading of other stories—our training in the narrative movement towards happiness, towards the fulfillment of dreams, the answers to prayers, and the rewards of diligent labor. We think immediately of Graham's falling in love with Lucy, as Edmund does with Fanny in Austen's *Mansfield Park* (1814) and as David does with Agnes in Dickens's *David Copperfield* (1850). We associate the generosity of benefactors and guardians with the promise of romantic love, as we associate physical plainness with superior intelligence and moral fortitude when we read transatlantic fiction. Thus, Lucy Snowe's story is an exercise in practical fantasy—her story is fueled by the possibility that she may someday experience the material and emotional bliss of the people with whom she surrounds herself. This potential operates at the nexus of reader expectation and authorial enterprise as they engage with the possibilities for heroine development explored in texts published in years past.

But Lucy Snowe is Jane Eyre's other half, her brooding sister who has a darker outlook on life. Lucy's story exemplifies the bleak, lonely trajectory of a woman with no social prospects who internalizes the rational, objective codes of a material reality. The consummate outsider, Lucy's dark temperament serves as a critique of social exclusion, analogous to critiques of ethnocentricism furthered by contemporary ethnic heroines like Pecola Breedlove or Lovey Nariyoshi, who are not beautiful, not confident, and not wealthy like the "sunnier" Paulinas of their stories. Their stories are always told in relation to other girls, other women, and other heroines of other narratives that promise other, better circumstances of happiness and fortune.

What does it mean that we can trace the paradigms of ultimate subjective happiness and ultimate subjective despair back to the same writer? While Jane's story meets the expectations of "Hope," Lucy's answers the dire prophecies of cruel "Reason." In the same way Claudia Tate explores the configuration of personal desire in the less popular, less canonical fiction of writers lauded for their revolutionary politics, one might examine this pair of Brontë texts and conceptualize *Villette*'s role in serving as a canvas for the writer's darker vision for heroines. We might consider the possibility that Jane and Lucy represent, for Brontë, twin trajectories of self and other, a relationship that is poetically demonstrative of our contemporary narratives of colonialism, neocolonialism, and other models of power imbalances in social contexts that pit fortune against failure. Lucy is the woman whom Jane cannot afford to become. While the pairing between Jane and Bertha Mason has prevailed in analyses of Brontë's fiction, I maintain that Jane and Lucy are the real sisters, both masters of their own narratives; Bertha is simply, to use Gayatri Spivak's words, "tangential" (Spivak 272). Postcolonial dynamics, among others, apply to this model established by Brontë's two novels as the relationship between Lucy and Jane embodies "the special quality of loneliness that grows out of the fear of the war between oneself and one's image in the mirror" (Ghosh 204).[2] Such longing involves the self-navigation towards subjective possibility offered in other stories, other alternatives, and in other selves. This dynamic, as my project asserts, underlines heroine construction and drives Lucy's ambivalent narration of the story of her life. We might say that *Villette* represents Brontë's ambivalence towards her earlier, more positive exploration of heroine potential and thus captures another emotive, oppositional response to the narrative question of how best to delineate "what throbs fast and full, though hidden" in the narrative lives of women (Brontë, *Juvenilia* 383).[3]

I see this oppositional relationship between Brontë's twin heroines as emblematic of heroine construction's fundamental reliance on convention and structural templates. As the practice of creating a heroine necessarily involves characterization in relation to fictional and cultural standards of femininity, Brontë's representation of the poles of feminine subjective potential exemplifies narrative's role in perpetuating opposites, differences, and Others. Our narratives offer only so many alternatives. Brontë's fiction captures both the best and worst case scenarios for socially-displaced heroines in the space of six years in the nineteenth century, within an indisputably

anglo context, without mention of race or national "Others." Yet as I explained in chapter 3 of this study, the stories of ethnic female development
in novels like Jade Snow Wong's *Fifth Chinese Daughter* and Jamaica
Kincaid's *Lucy,* inscribe narrative moments and structural elements that are
similar to those within the narrated life of Lucy Snowe in *Villette.* Ethnic
American writers, like Brontë and other anglo writers, conduct the project
of heroine construction with some ambivalence towards the practice of narrating conventional fictional female subjective identity.

Chapters 1 and 2 focused on the ambivalence of writing about ideas of
romance and marriage permeating transcultural women's fiction. This ambivalence manifests itself in ways similar to the forces of ambivalence in
Villette, and writers like the Eaton sisters and Jessie Fauset mediate the tension between literary convention and the need for individuated written
voices even as they provide social commentary on the specificities of African
and Asian American cultural politics. These intricacies of cultural politics,
however, cohere around significant structural relationships with anglo, traditional literary conventions such as the role of romance, the language of
heroine objectification, the search for place and position, and the exploration of adolescent subjective potential. As I have shown, "ethnicity" in
these women's texts is narratively defined, and is a concept and quality that
changes as writers twist plots, experiment with characterization, engage
with social commentary and expand conventional class-critiques.

Finally, in chapter 4, I examined contemporary ethnic adolescent narratives in order to respond to ethnic-studies scholarly trends that equate cultural authenticity and political progressiveness with the more "negative" or
subjectively bleak tonal elements of ethnic fiction. This chapter culminated
with an examination of Gish Jen's fiction as an ethnicized articulation of wit,
or prowess in comedic irony, established by writers like Jane Austen in the
mode of the courtship novel. Jen's *Mona in the Promised Land* challenges
the idea that ethnic novels about women are, and must be, negative in scope
to articulate authentically and effectively a cultural politics that challenges
dominant cultural ideals and standards. As my arguments have maintained,
critical binaries like anglo and ethnic, political and romantic, and positive
and negative can obscure our vision of the structural exchange occurring
transculturally within heroine construction. To view anglo fiction as lighthearted or positive in scope and ethnic fiction as a more serious narrative
corrective blinds us not only towards the meaning of our preoccupation
with such schemas, it also prevents us from experiencing the richness of individual subjective experience. If reading *Villette* teaches us anything about
the relationship between anglo and ethnic fiction, it tells us that an ultimate

scenario for negativity can be found in this mid-nineteenth-century British novel, embodied in its cynical heroine's poignant acknowledgment that she "cannot lull the blast" of the realizations of her worst fears.

Notes

NOTES TO INTRODUCTION

1. Please see my section on terminology and language for my explanation of the ways in which I use the labels "anglo" and "ethnic."
2. In his essay "Come All Ye Asian American Writers of the Real and Fake," Frank Chin also attempts a characterization of Asian American poetics as he castigates those Asian American writers who use allegedly Western Christian narrative modes like autobiography and confession.
3. In his analysis of the imperial spatial politics of Austen's *Mansfield Park*, Edward Said, in line with the theoretical description of colonialist fiction outlined by JanMohamed, points out that the "spatial moral order" configured by the fiction of canonical writers like Austen and Dickens relegates British colonial spaces around the world to "outlying spaces of deviation and uncertainty." He explains that the texts scholarship today labels as imperialistic "stress the continuing existence" of England and "never advocate giving up the colonies, but take the long-range view that since they fall within the orbit of British dominance, that dominance is a sort of norm, and thus conserved along with the colonies" (*Culture and Imperialism* 74, 79).
4. By "transcultural" I refer to both transatlantic and transnational structural similarities in the characterization of female protagonists in English language fiction. As I will focus on both Asian American and African American female subjectivity in relation to canonical anglo heroines from nineteenth-century American and British fiction, the term "transcultural" allows me to discuss similarities between African and Asian American texts while furthering an open conceptualization of "ethnicity" and examining the narrative or textual relationships between ideas of race, nation, and class.
5. Postcolonial theory has become increasingly more pertinent to discussions of national identity and the United States, both from a colonial and neo-colonial (racial discrimination, immigration acts) perspective. Even relatively early postcolonial texts like *The Empire Writes Back* remind us that the cultural and economic stronghold enjoyed by the United States in the twentieth century comes after centuries worth of a conscious production of an American cultural identity that was conceived as in tune with, but necessarily different, from a British sensibility.

6. See Kingston's recorded interview with Bill Moyers, formatted in 1994.
7. Chin's fiction and scholarly work is committed to the preservation of Chinese masculinity, which is threatened by what he sees as an American publishing market fixated upon spurious, exoticized representations of Asian American women and their stories. See his essay on "The Real and Fake" in *The Big Aiiieeeee!*
8. I allude most specifically to the texts by duCille and Lowe already discussed. Several scholars, including Claudia Tate, have expressed concern over the academic privileging of the political in the literary analysis of minority fiction.
9. See Ling's *Narrating Nationalisms: Ideology and Form in Asian American Literature* (1998), pp.139-145 and "Preface" for enumerated ways in which Asian American literary scholarship, influenced by American politics in the 1970's, has concentrated on "literature's social or political function," the result of which is a "prioritizing of 'contemporary' over 'traditional' writings." Other examples of recent scholarship on Asian American literature that challenge and contextualize this critical emphasis on cultural politics include Yunte Huang's *Transpacific Displacement: Ethnography, Translation, and Intertextual Travel in Twentieth-Century American Literature* (2002), and David Leiwei Li's *Imagining the Nation: Asian American Literature and Cultural Consent* (1998).
10. By "culture-specific," I refer to culture as a discursive concept often conceptualized in criticism as a subject-position typified by collective understandings of race or nation.
11. See bell hooks's "Third World Diva Girls" in *Yearning* for a reading of the mechanics of class influencing pronouncements of "model minority" status.

NOTES TO CHAPTER ONE

1. I allude to several important feminist studies ranging from Helen Papashvily's *All the Happy Endings,* Lee Edwards's *Psyche as Hero,* Janice Radway's *Reading the Romance* to examples of ethnic studies feminism like Claudia Tate's *Domestic Allegories of Political Desire,* Hazel Carby's *Reconstructing Womanhood,* and Ann duCille's *The Coupling Convention.* These works attempt to ground love and marriage in political struggles against sexism and racism. Radway's text, like Suzanne Juhasz's *Reading From the Heart,* dares to probe more deeply into the significance of shared feminine schemas of romance and the consumption of romance narratives.
2. See Jinqui Ling's *Narrating Nationalisms: Ideology and Form in Asian American Literature.* Critiquing the contemporary academic emphasis on political narratives, Ling distinguishes between Asian American works published before 1950 (denoting these as "traditional") and those "contemporary" works published after this date.
3. For most of this chapter I will refer to both sisters by their Asian pseudonyms (Sui Sin Far for Edith Eaton and Onoto Watannna for Winnifred Eaton).
4. Amy Ling in "Winnifred Eaton: Ethnic Chameleon and Popular Success," S. E. Solberg in "Sui Sin Far/Edith Eaton," Annette White-Parks in her biography

of Sui Sin Far, and Dominika Ferens in *Edith and Winnifred Eaton* have all discussed and speculated about the advantages of having a Japanese identity over a Chinese identity in late nineteenth-century America and its system of cultural prejudice which, for that historic moment, favored Japanese immigrants.

5. Annette White-Parks states in *Sui Sin Far/Edith Maude Eaton* that Onoto Watanna "was putting out novels from major publishing houses at the rate of almost one a year, the most successful of which . . . became a bestseller" (118).

6. See Jane Tompkins's *Sensational Designs* for a thorough discussion and contextualization of sentimentality and domesticity in women's early to mid-nineteenth-century fiction.

7. Orito's characterization resists the long-standing American stereotype of Asian male impotency discussed by Frank Chin, Jeffery Paul Chan, Lawson Fusao Inada, and Shawn Wong, the editors of *The Big Aiiieeeee!*

8. See Dominika Ferens's "Tangled Kites: Sui Sin Far's Negotiations with Race and Readership" for her account of the popularity of Japanese culture and artifacts at the turn of the twentieth century.

9. Eve Oishi hints at reasons for the "critical silence" and "ambivalence" evoked today by Watanna's fiction, including the formulaic elements of romantic fiction and the problematic politics of describing "beguiling geishas" who captivate white American men (xix, xxii).

10. Ferens has also noted the "unprecedented" methods Watanna employs in developing her interracial love triangle (*Edith and Winnifred Eaton* 159). She observes that though Orito's suicide maintains the nineteenth-century idea that "any union between a man of color and a white woman is unnatural and punishable by death," his characterization as a "male hero, to whom several white women are attracted" is unique for this time period.

11. See a discussion of heroine evolution in domestic fiction in "A New Heroine-and Hero," in Helen Papashvily's *All the Happy Endings* and in Nina Baym's *Woman's Fiction*.

12. Dominika Ferens notes that serial publications quadrupled during the latter part of the nineteenth century in her article "Tangled Kites." She cites Theodore Patterson's *Magazines in the Twentieth Century* (1956) as her source for this information.

13. See Ann duCille's *The Coupling Convention*, Deborah McDowell's introduction to the Schomburg edition of *Four Girls at Cottage City*, and Claudia Tate's chapter on *Megda* in her *Psychoanalysis and Black Novels*.

14. In this light, Ferens's methodology is similar to African Americanist Claudia Tate's critical strategy in *Psychoanalysis and Black Novels*.

15. The gift of a jade pendant is significant for several specific reasons in Chinese culture. When I say "culturally encoded," I mean to refer to these reasons as well as the sense of "Western" romance Sui Sin Far constructs in this story. For a similar gift exchange in a mother/daughter context, see Amy Tan's novel *The Joy Luck Club* and the chapter entitled "Best Quality."

16. See Helena Mitchie's *Sororophobia* for an in-depth analysis of the structural dynamics of character differentiation between women. Her work factors into

my analysis of heroine construction and heroine objectification in chapter 2 of this book.

17. Several scholars including Amy Ling, Annette White-Parks, Carol Roh-Spaulding and Xiao-huang Yin have all reported that Sui Sin Far was working on a novel sometime before her death.

18. Anglo heroines like Alcott's Jo March and E.D.E.N. Southworth's Capitola Black perform different techniques of gender-bending, which are indicative of nineteenth-century feminist reconfigurations of heroine construction. (See note 6.) See also Mary Kelley's *Private Woman, Public Stage* for a general theory on women's negotiation of gender roles.

19. See Dominika Ferens's contextualization of the early period of Sui Sin Far's career, a period during which she wrote more conventional material (*Edith and Winnifred* 51).

NOTES TO CHAPTER TWO

1. In *The Proper Lady and the Woman Writer* (1984), Mary Poovey asserts that anxieties about social etiquette in marriage markets inform much of nineteenth-century anglo women's fiction as they critique women's lack of opportunities to ensure financial security independently in a time of increasing industrialization. Jane Austen's fiction, according to Poovey, is fueled by conflicted feelings of self-assertion and obedience to social mores regulating women's public conduct in society. Additional studies on female bildungsromane discuss the Western Christian mores of female propriety emphasized in early English novels like *Clarissa* or *Moll Flanders* while pointing to eighteenth-century society's preoccupation with the potential for social mobility and prosperity. See Nancy Miller's *The Heroine's Text* and Abel et al.'s *The Voyage In*. Studies of nineteenth-century responses to British colonialism in India also point to the symbolic role and construction of feminine virtue as emblematic of national identity. See "The Nation and its Women" by Partha Chatterjee.

2. For more information and a better understanding of popular formulas for nineteenth-century heroine construction see "Other Novelists of the Fifties," in Nina Baym's *Woman's Fiction*.

3. See chapter 1 and the section on Watanna's autobiography for another discussion of the parallel between ideas of marriage and publishing success.

4. See Gilbert and Gubar's *The Madwoman in the Attic* and the chapter on *Jane Eyre* that is entitled "Plain Jane's Progress."

5. See also Burnett's *A Little Princess*.

6. See Elizabeth Epperly's scholarship on the L.M. Montgomery's *Anne of Green Gables* series for juvenile girls. Epperly describes the power of romanticism in shaping the female orphan protagonist's negotiation of self and home.

7. For a reading of *The House of Mirth* in relation to Wharton's interaction with realism and modernism, see Amy Kaplan's *The Social Construction of American Realism*.

8. William Wells Brown's 1853 novel *Clotel* presents the quintessential figure of the "tragic mulatto."

9. In "Three Women's Texts," Spivak points out that "incidental imperialism" occurs in those texts like Mary Shelley's *Frankenstein* which most seem to want to challenge a dominating anglo Western universality (Spivak 273). Texts like *Jane Eyre* and contemporary responses like *Wide Sargasso Sea* are unable to do away with spatial schemas which marginally incorporate characters like Bertha Mason or Christine (the Haitian maid) who demonstrate by their relational positioning and characterization in the novels that "the Other cannot be selfed" (Spivak 277). See also Edward Said's *Culture and Imperialism,* for his discussion on spatial politics in *David Copperfield* and *Mansfield Park*.

10. For the sake of simplicity, I will refer to Kelley-Hawkins as "Kelley" many times in this section.

11. See Helen Papashvily's *All the Happy Endings,* specifically her chapter on E.D.E.N. Southworth's characterization of Capitola Black who was seen as ushering in an era of a "new heroine."

12. Note Sui Sin Far's reference to Tennyson as a figurehead of "American" poetry in "Mrs. Spring Fragrance." Mrs. Spring admires and assigns a Westernized "American" quality to Tennyson's poetry. Her error in thinking that Tennyson is American, as opposed to British, highlights an eagerness on her part to advance herself in terms of relational (yet erroneous) markers. As I indicated in chapter 1, some vague though non-specific performance of anglo culture makes Mrs. Spring more "Western," which means more "American."

13. See John Streamas's "The Invention of Normality in Japanese American Internment Narratives" in *Ethnicity and the American Short Story* (ed. Julie Brown) for a nuanced discussion of the "political protest" lying at the heart of Yamamoto's use of a child narrator in this story (130-138).

14. Joy Kogawa's *Obasan* and Kerri Sakamoto's *The Electrical Field,* both novels about Japanese internment during World War II, are two examples of this narrative concentration on the inner world of memories. Julie Shigekuni's *A Bridge Between Us* also explores the turmoil of a young woman who unwittingly remembers being molested by her grandfather.

NOTES TO CHAPTER THREE

1. This idea informs several readings of nineteenth- and early twentieth-century women's literature. Spatial seclusion offers evidence of social constriction and exclusion as the language of claustrophobia ("Shut Up in Prose," for example in Gilbert and Gubar's text) connects the two ideas. Charlotte Perkins Gilman's "The Yellow Wall Paper" also provides another paradigmatic example of claustrophobic madness.

2. I derive my concept of agoraphobia from Gillian Brown's intriguing use of the term in *Domestic Individualism.*

3. See Baym; and Mary Kelley.

4. Read Sandra Gilbert's essay "The American Sexual Poetics of Walt Whitman and Emily Dickinson" (in *Reconstructing American Literary History*) for a discussion of Dickinson's conscious crafting of a poetic voice and unique identity in light of her "anxiety" of market forces.

5. Edward Said discusses the colonialist implications of "the spatial order" of Austen's novel in *Culture and Imperialism*.

6. Commenting on the narrative's marketability, Xiao-huang Yin notes that Wong's autobiography was selected for the "Book of the Month Club" as well as the "Christian Herald Family Book Club" (135).

7. In *Asian American Literature*, Elaine Kim explains that Jade Snow Wong's original manuscript was much longer, and that "English teachers" and "publishing house editors" were involved in cutting and rearranging the text (Kim 71). Their involvement raises interesting questions about the politics of representation. Because Kim is not able to provide specific information on which portions of the original manuscript were cut out, I feel that the fact of these edits does not weaken my observations here. Instead, I see Wong's participation in a collaborative editing process as further proof of her need to achieve cultural blending.

8. There are far too many examples of this narrative tradition (which I term as "the governess syndrome" in the next section), but obviously *Jane Eyre* comes to mind. Also consider the examples in texts as generically varied and historically separated as *Lady Audley's Secret, The Turn of the Screw, The Buccaneers, The Bread Givers,* and *The Good Negress.* The latter three discuss the class-distinction accorded to poor women who make respectable living by dispensing education.

9. See the end of Lorna Ellis's *Appearing to Diminish* for a discussion of this "tragic paradigm" and its significance in proffering a new, but cynical model of female development as heroines like Maggie Tulliver and Edna Pontilier choose not to accommodate their personal ideals and desires to accommodate dominant mores of female behavior. Their decisions, of course, lead to their literal deaths by drowning, and figurative deaths as unfulfilled female subjects. The use of this paradigm culminates in the late nineteenth century, when women writers veer away from the discussions of female protagonists who successfully fashion actualized selves in relation to dominant mores.

10. I use Barbadian and "Bajan" interchangeably to refer to Selina's cultural community.

11. See the last chapter and its endnotes for a reference to Helena Michie's *Sororophobia.*

12. The introduction of Suzanne Juhasz's *Reading From the Heart* provides a useful and pertinent discussion of the appeal of enclosed and nurturing spaces.

NOTES TO CHAPTER FOUR

1. Li's text, though it was published before the release of the Disney film *Mulan*, provides a context for understanding the creation and consumption of Disney's Asian heroine.

2. See Peter Cohen's article published online (dated August 21, 2001), which summaries Disney's use of "Zoog Disney" as an interactive medium to target "tweens."

3. See the official "Gilmore Girls" web page on the Warner Brothers website.

4. Although earlier African American texts like *Brown Girl, Brownstones, Their Eyes Were Watching God,* and *Plum Bun* chronicle typical adolescent moments and epiphanies for their heroines, the texts are more concerned with development into full adulthood and discuss marital prospects in some detail. Few, if any, African American texts before Toni Morrison's *The Bluest Eye,* limit narrative events to one to three years within the pre-adult/pre-marital space of adolescent life and thereby leave questions of adult sexuality open. Within Asian American fiction, texts discussing adolescence occur even less frequently until the 1970s and 1980s. It is not until the early 1990s that novels like *A Bridge Between Us* and *Monkey Bridge* present adolescent narrators and allow for more in-depth analysis of this developmental stage. Still fewer novels like *Donald Duk* and *Mona in the Promised Land* focus on general adolescent themes like peer pressure and identity-formation. Chapter 2 of this project references studies in the female bildungsroman and ethnic bildungsromane like Abel's *The Voyage In,* Ellis's *Appearing to Diminish,* and Feng's *The Female Bildungsroman.*

5. While the conventions of genre and the differences of audiences consuming juvenile fiction as opposed to adult "literary" ethnic fiction naturally determine different subject matters, my point is that Asian American fiction seems more obviously invested in avoiding themes that could be interpreted as lighthearted.

6. See the following websites for information on the genre of "Chick Lit," a form introduced to readers after the commercial success enjoyed by Helen Fielding's 1998 *Bridget Jones's Diary*: abcnews.go.com/sections/wnt/Entertainment/chicklit030830.html, www.mdlib.org/divisions/raig/chick, www.chiklit.com. This genre encompasses several ethnic texts, including the work of Hispanic, Asian, and African American women writers.

7. Lowe's *Immigrant Acts* and duCille's *The Coupling Convention* also address the changing structure of the coming-of-age-novel in relation to "decolonizing" challenges to what they see as Western or "European American" ideals. They do not discuss adolescence in depth and are instead concerned with explicating ethnic alternatives to marital subplots found within anglo novels.

8. For an introduction to the interdisciplinary aspects of the study of adolescence and narratives of adolescence, see *Delinquents and Debutantes,* ed. Sherrie Inness.

9. Interpretative practices within scholarship on girl culture, adolescence, and adolescent narratives tend to align themselves with one of two general critical stances. Girls and girl heroines are either victims of cultures forces, which, in adolescence, begin to configure them as sexual objects, or they are engaged in a more complex and subtle process of empowered identity signification within patriarchal culture. See Angela Hubler, "Beyond the Image: Adolescent Girls,

Reading, and Social Reality," Sherrie Inness's "Anti-Barbies," Mary Trachel's "Horse Stories and Romance Fiction" and Andrews's and Whorlow's "Girl Power and the Post-Modern Fan" for just some examples of the dissension within scholarship on adolescence and popular culture.

10. I derive this idea of sameness and difference from Helena Michie's *Sororophobia,* which contextualizes female identity in these terms, although it does not discuss adolescence specifically.

11. Few white American heroines and fewer ethnic heroines produced for adult mainstream consumption before 1970 are truly adolescent and remain adolescent for the course of an entire novel. One noteworthy example of a novel of adolescence from this time period is Louise Meriwether's *Daddy Was a Number Runner,* which can be read as a retelling of Betty Smith's *A Tree Grows in Brooklyn.*

12. I take this phrase and concept directly from bell hooks's *Yearning.*

13. Abdul JanMohamed's application of this theory in his analysis of literature ("Colonialist Literature") provides a convenient guide to understanding more latent structural forces of cultural hegemony operating in esteemed and beloved cultural narratives.

14. By "signification" I refer to Henry Louis Gates's theory of individual and collective performances of identity, which require mediating the tensions between ideas of sameness and difference. See *The Signifying Monkey.*

15. Lisa Lowe also discusses these spatial imbalances in terms of the differences between "Chinatown novels" and anglo fiction, as Asian American materialist poetics critique the exclusionary processes of American citizenship.

16. See the introduction of chapter 2 for a citation of these speeches.

17. Suzanne Juhasz's *Reading From the Heart* discusses a process of female reading consumption, appealing heroines, and their relation to a system of nurturing created by a text, heroine, and reader.

18. There are several instances of these revisionary aesthetics in nineteenth-and early twentieth-century anglo fiction, including the following popular texts: *Pride and Prejudice, Jane Eyre, Villette, Vanity Fair,* and *Little Women.* In Abel et al.'s *The Voyage In,* Marianne Hirsch's "Spiritual Bildung: The Beautiful Soul as Paradigm," contextualizes nineteenth-century heroines' reliance on inner strength and inner lives in terms of a "pre-Oedipal phase outlined in psychoanalytic writing" (27). While this "spiritual bildung" resists the social realities of patriarchy and constrictive social mores, Hirsch points out that in several nineteenth-century texts, this female attribute is characterized in ambivalent terms because "inner life" also implies "passive." Though Hirsch does not discuss resistance to aesthetic standards in her essay, I refer to her critique of gender constraints limiting the development of nineteenth-century heroines here to allude generally to existing criticism on women and identity-formation in the midst of social pressure and social alienation.

19. Although I take this phrase from Lisa Lowe (Immigrant Acts 99) who uses these words to discuss Austen's *Pride and Prejudice,* I allude to theoretical

distinctions between anglo and ethnic texts explicated in her work along with Pin-chia Feng's and Ann duCille's studies of race, gender, and class. Frank Chin too makes blatant claims about the difference between Western subjectivity and "real" Asian and Asian American self-expression in "Come All Ye." I should also add a rejoinder to clarify once again that unlike Lowe, duCille does not deny the role of romance and resolution in African American texts, but *The Coupling Convention* does take the stance that these works use these textual elements to a greater political degree than do anglo texts, a critical move that demonstrates some important relationships between scholarly enterprise and political expectations in feminism and ethnic studies. In her introduction, duCille writes: "Making unconventional use of conventional literary forms, early black writers appropriated for their own emancipatory purposes both the genre of the novel and the structural of the marriage plot" (3). While valid, duCille's argument confers uniqueness onto African American women's literary experiments with genre, which then implies that anglo women's texts do not use marriage politically. Feng attempts similar distinctions when she asserts that writers like Toni Morrison and Maxine Hong Kingston "transform a traditionally personal and privatized genre into a political one and provide a postmodern interpretation of the axiom 'the personal is political'" (Feng 36).

20. Notable examples include Patti Kim's *A Cab Called Reliable* and Lan Cao's *Monkey Bridge*.
21. Its use of an adult narrator remembering her childhood in flashbacks is now a common feature of Asian American subjectivity. Two significant novels that use adult women who recollect their childhoods in fragmented narratives are Joy Kogawa's *Obasan* and Kerri Sakamoto's *The Electrical Field*.
22. I take "limits of comedy" from Lee Edwards's *Psyche as Hero,* in which she argues that the conventions of literary comedy (represented by Austen's novels) actually circumscribe female subjective potential and that these conventions are in fact influenced by patriarchal mores of female compliancy.

NOTES TO EPILOGUE

1. Any number of postcolonial critiques will describe this lineage of the modern novel. For an introduction to these ideas, see Benedict Anderson's 1983 *Imagined Communities: Reflections on the Origin and Spread of Nationalism.*
2. I take these words from Amitav Ghosh's 1988 novel, *The Shadowlines,* which is conceived partly as a mirror response to Conrad's fiction. It highlights the story of a young unnamed male protagonist who longs to be a part of some enchanted British story, much like Dickens's Pip yearns for a place in Miss Havisham's strange, but upper-class, world.
3. These words are cited in a note to the text of Charlotte Brontë's *Juvenilia* (ed. Frances Beer) and are taken from an 1850 letter to W.S. Williams. Interestingly, Brontë writes these words as a way of explaining her dislike of Jane Austen's fiction.

Bibliography

SELECTED BIBLIOGRAPHY OF SECONDARY CRITICISM

Abel, Elizabeth, Marianne Hirsch, and Elizabeth Langland, eds. *The Voyage In: Fictions of Female Development.* Hanover: University Press of New England, 1983.

Anderson, Benedict. *Imagined Communities: Reflections on the Origin and Spread of Nationalism.* London: Verso, 1983.

Ashcroft, Bill, Gareth Griffiths, and Helen Tiffin. *The Empire Writes Back: Theory and Practice in Post-Colonial Literatures.* New York: Routledge, 1989.

Bachelard, Gaston. *The Poetics of Space.* Trans. Maria Jolas. New York: Orion Press, 1964.

Baym, Nina. *Woman's Fiction: A Guide to Novels by and About Women in America, 1820–1870.* Ithaca: Cornell University Press, 1978.

Bhabha, Homi K., ed. *Nation and Narration.* London: Routledge, 1990.

Brooks, Peter. *Reading for Plot: Design and Intention in Narrative.* 1984. Cambridge: Harvard University Press, 1992.

Brown, Gillian. *Domestic Individualism: Imagining Self in Nineteenth-Century America.* Berkeley: University of California Press, 1990.

Carby, Hazel V. *Reconstructing Womanhood: the Emergence of the Afro-American Woman Novelist:* New York: Oxford University Press, 1987.

Chatterjee, Partha. "The Nation and Its Women." *A Subaltern Studies Reader, 1986–1995.* Ed. Ranajit Guha. Minneapolis: University of Minnesota Press, 1997.

Cheung, King-kok. *Articulate Silences: Hisaye Yamamoto, Maxine Hong Kingston, Joy Kogawa.* Ithaca: Cornell University Press, 1993.

Chin, Frank. "Come All Ye Asian American Writers of the Real and Fake." *The Big Aiiieeeee! An Anthology Of Chinese American and Japanese American Fiction.* Eds. Jeffery Paul Chan et al. 1975. New York: Meridian, 1991. 1–93.

Chu, Patricia P. *Assimilating Asians: Gendered Strategies of Authorship in Asian America.* Durham: Duke University Press, 2000.

Cohen, Peter. Summary on "Zoog Disney." Internet. 21 Aug. 2001.

Denniston, Dorothy Hamer. *The Fiction of Paule Marshall: Reconstructions of History, Culture, and Gender.* Knoxville: University of Tennessee Press, 1995.

duCille, Ann. *The Coupling Convention: Sex, Text, and Tradition in Black Women's Fiction.* New York: Oxford University Press, 1993.

Edwards, Lee R. *Psyche as Hero: Female Heroism and Fictional Form.* Middletown: Wesleyan University Press, 1984.

Ellis, Lorna. *Appearing to Diminish: Female Development and the British Bildungsroman, 1750–1850.* Lewisburg: Bucknell University Press, 1999.

Ellison, Ralph. "The World and the Jug." *Shadow and Act.* New York: Random House, 1964.

Epperly, Elizabeth. *The Fragrance of Sweet Grass: L.M. Montgomery's Heroines and the Pursuit of Romance.* Toronto: University of Toronto Press, 1992.

Feng, Pin-chia. *The Female Bildungsroman by Toni Morrison and Maxine Hong Kingston: A Postmodern Reading.* New York: Peter Lang, 1998.

Ferens, Dominika. *Edith and Winnifred Eaton: Chinatown Missions and Japanese Romances.* Urbana: University of Illinois Press, 2002.

———. "Tangled Kites: Sui Sin Far's Negotiations with Race and Readership." *Amerasia Journal* 25.2 (1999): 116–144.

Gates, Henry Louis, Jr. *The Signifying Monkey: A Theory of African American Literary Criticism.* New York: Oxford University Press, 1988.

Ghymn, Esther Mikyung. *Images of Asian American Women by Asian American Writers.* New York: Peter Lang, 1995.

Gilbert, Sandra M. "The American Sexual Poetics of Walt Whitman and Emily Dickinson." *Reconstructing American Literary History.* Ed. Sacvan Bercovitch. Cambridge: Harvard University Press, 1986.

Gilbert, Sandra M., and Susan Gubar. *The Madwoman in the Attic: The Woman Writer and the Nineteenth-Century Literary Imagination.* New Haven: Yale University Press, 1979.

"Gilmore Girls." Internet. www.thewb.com

hooks, Bell. *Yearning: Race, Gender, and Cultural Politics.* Boston: South End Press, 1990.

Huang, Yunte. *Transpacific Displacement: Ethnography, Translation, and Intertextual Travel in Twentieth-Century American Literature.* Berkeley: University of California Press, 2002.

Hubler, Angela. "Beyond the Image: Adolescent Girls, Reading, and Social Reality." *NWSA Journal* 12.1: 84–99.

———. "Can Anne Shirley Help Revive Ophelia?" *Delinquents and Debutantes.* Ed. Sherrie Inness. New York: New York University Press, 1998.

Inness, Sherrie A. "Anti-Barbies": The American Girls Collection and Political Ideologies. *Delinquents and Debutantes.* Ed . Sherrie Inness. New York: New York University Press, 1998.

JanMohamed, Abdul R. "The Economy of Manichean Allegory: The Function of Racial Difference in Colonialist Literature." *Race, Writing, and Difference.* Ed. Henry Louis Gates, Jr. Chicago: University of Chicago Press, 1986. 78–107.

Juhasz, Suzanne. *Reading From the Heart: Women, Literature, and the Search for True Love.* New York: Viking, 1994.

Kaplan, Amy. *The Social Construction of American Realism.* Chicago: University of Chicago Press, 1992.

Kelley, Mary. *Private Woman, Public Stage: Literary Domesticity in Nineteenth-Century America.* New York: Oxford University Press, 1984.

Kim, Elaine H. *Asian American Literature: An Introduction to the Writings and Their Social Context.* Philadelphia: Temple University Press, 1982.

Kingston, Maxine Hong. *"Stories of Maxine Hong Kingston": Interview with Bill Moyers.* Prod. Leslie Clark. Films for the Humanities. Videocassette. Public Affairs Television, 1994.

Li, David Leiwei. *Imagining the Nation: Asian American Literature and Cultural Consent.* Stanford: Stanford University Press, 1998.

Ling, Amy. *Between Worlds: Women Writers of Chinese Ancestry.* New York: Pergamon Press, 1990.

———. "Winnifred Eaton: Ethnic Chameleon and Popular Success." *MELUS: The Journal of the Society for the Study of Multi-Ethnic Literature of the United States* 11.3 (1984): 5–15.

Ling, Jinqui. *Narrating Nationalisms: Ideology and Form in Asian American Literature.* New York: Oxford University Press, 1998.

Lowe, Lisa. *Immigrant Acts.* Durham: Duke University Press, 1996.

Marshall, Paule. Address. Spelman College, Atlanta. 1 Nov. 2001.

McDowell, Deborah E. *"The Changing Same": Black Women's Literature, Criticism, and Theory.* Bloomington: Indiana University Press, 1995.

———. Introduction. *Four Girls at Cottage City.* By Emma D. Kelley-Hawkins. New York: Oxford University Press, 1988.

Michie, Helena. *Sororophobia: Differences Among Women in Literature and Culture.* New York: Oxford University Press, 1992.

Miller, Nancy K. *The Heroine's Text: Readings in the French and English Novel, 1722–1782.* New York: Columbia University Press, 1980.

Oishi, Eve. Introduction. *Miss Numè of Japan.* By Onoto Watanna. Baltimore: Johns Hopkins University Press, 1999. xi–xxxiii.

Papashvily, Helen W. *All the Happy Endings: A Study of the Domestic Novel in America.* New York: Harper and Brothers, 1956.

Pipher, Mary. *Reviving Ophelia: Saving the Selves of Adolescent Girls.* New York: Putnam, 1994.

Poovey, Mary. *The Proper Lady and the Woman Writer: Ideology as Style in the Works of Mary Wollstonecraft, Mary Shelley, and Jane Austen.* Chicago: University of Chicago Press, 1984.

Radway, Janice. *Reading the Romance: Women, Patriarchy, and Popular Literature.* Chapel Hill: University of North Carolina Press, 1984.

Roh-Spaulding, Carol. "Wavering Images: Mixed-Race Identity in the Stories of Edith Eaton/Sui Sin Far." In *Ethnicity and the American Short Story.* Ed. Julie Brown. New York: Garland Publishing, 1997.

Said, Edward. W. *Culture and Imperialism.* 1993. New York: Vintage-Random, 1994.

Showalter, Elaine. *A Literature of Their Own: British Women Novelists From Brontë to Lessing.* Princeton: Princeton University Press, 1977.

Solberg, S. E. "Sui Sin Far/Edith Eaton: First Chinese-American Fictionist." *MELUS* 8 (Spring 1981): 27–29.

Sollors, Werner. "A Critique of Pure Pluralism." *Reconstructing American Literary History.* Ed. Sacvan Bercovitch. Cambridge: Harvard University Press, 1986.

———. "Nine Suggestions for Historians of American Ethnic Literature." *MELUS* 11.1 (1984): 95–96.

———, ed. *Theories of Ethnicity: A Classical Reader*. New York: New York University Press, 1996.

Spivak, Gayatri C. "Three Women's Texts and a Critique of Imperialism." *Race, Writing, and Difference*. Ed. Henry Louis Gates, Jr. Chicago: University of Chicago Press, 1986. 262–280.

Streamas, John. "The Invention of Normality in Japanese American Internment Narratives." In *Ethnicity and the American Short Story*. Ed. Julie Brown. New York: Garland Publishing, 1997.

Tate, Claudia. *Domestic Allegories of Political Desire: The Black Heroine's Text at the Turn of the Century*. New York: Oxford University Press, 1992.

———. *Psychoanalysis and Black Novels: Desire and the Protocols of Race*. New York: Oxford University Press, 1998.

Tompkins, Jane. *Sensational Designs: The Cultural Work of American Fiction, 1790–1860*. New York: Oxford University Press, 1985.

Tuan, Yi-Fu. *Space and Place: The Perspective of Experience*. Minneapolis: University of Minnesota Press, 1977.

Trachsel, Mary. "Horse Stories and Romance Fiction: Variants or Alternative Texts of Female Identity? *Reader: Essays in Reader-Oriented Theory, Criticism, and Pedagogy*. 38–39 (Fall/Spring 1997–98): 20–41.

Ty, Eleanor. "Struggling With the Powerful (M)other: Identity and Sexuality in Kogawa's Obasan and Kincaid's Lucy." *International Fiction Review* 20.2 (1993): 120–126.

Verdelle, A. J. "The Good Negress." Lecture/Discussion in Dr. Rudolph Byrd's Seminar On the Novel in African American Literary Tradition. Emory University, Atlanta. 16 Apr. 1999.

Walker, Alice. "In Search of Our Mothers' Gardens." 1972. *Within the Circle: An Anthology of African American Literary Criticism From the Harlem Renaissance to the Present*. Ed. Angelyn Mitchell. Durham: Duke University Press, 1994. 401–409.

Wall, Cheryl A. *Changing Our Own Words: Essays on Criticism, Theory, and Writing by Black Women*. New Brunswick: Rutgers University Press, 1989.

Washington, Mary Helen. Afterword. *Brown Girl, Brownstones*. By Paule Marshall. New York: The Feminist Press, 1981. 311–324.

White, Barbara A. *Growing Up Female: Adolescent Girlhood in American Fiction*. Westport: Greenwood Press, 1985.

White-Parks, Annette. *Sui Sin Far/Edith Maude Eaton: A Literary Biography*. Urbana: University of Illinois Press, 1995.

Whorlow, Rosie, and Maggie Andrews. "Girl Power and the Post-Modern Fan." *All the World and Her Husband: Women in Twentieth-Century Consumer Culture*. Eds. Maggie Andrews and Mary M. Talbot. London: Cassell, 2000.

Wong, Sau-ling Cynthia. "Ethnicizing Gender: An Explication of Sexuality as Sign in Chinese Immigrant Literature." *Reading the Literatures of Asian America*. Eds. Shirley Geok-lin Lim and Amy Ling. Philadelphia: Temple University Press, 1992.

Woolf, Virginia. *A Room of One's Own*. London: Hogarth Press, 1929.

Yin, Xiao-huang. *Chinese American Literature since the 1850s*. Urbana: University of Illinois Press, 2000.

Yogi, Stan. "Rebels and Heroines: Subversive Narratives in the Stories of Wakako Yamauchi and Hisaye Yamamoto." *Reading the Literatures of Asian America*. Eds. Shirley Geok-lin and Amy Ling. Philadelphia: Temple University Press, 1992.

SELECTED BIBLIOGRAPHY OF PRIMARY WORKS

Alcott, Louisa May. *Little Women*. 1868–1869. New York: Grosset and Dunlap, 1983.

Austen, Jane. *The Complete Novels*. New York: Grammercy Books, 1981.

Austen, Jane, and Charlotte Brontë. *The Juvenilia*. Ed. Frances Beer. New York: Penguin, 1986.

Blume, Judy. *Are You There God? It's Me, Margaret*. 1970. New York: Laurel Leaf, 1974.

Braddon, Mary Elizabeth. *Lady Audley's Secret*. 1862. London: Penguin, 1998.

Brontë, Charlotte. *Jane Eyre*. 1847. New York: Penguin Classics, 1986.

———. *Villette*. 1853. Oxford: Oxford University Press, 1998.

Burnett, Frances Hodgson. *The Secret Garden*. 1911. New York: Harper Collins, 1987.

Byatt, A.S. *Possession: A Romance*. 1990. New York: Vintage-Random, 1991.

Chin, Frank. *Donald Duk*. Minneapolis: Coffee House Press, 1991.

Dickens, Charles. *David Copperfield*. 1849–1850. Ware: Wordsworth, 1992.

———. *Great Expectations*. 1860–1861. New York: Bantam, 1986.

Dreiser, Theodore. *Sister Carrie*. 1900. New York: Bantam, 1982.

Ellison, Ralph. *Invisible Man*. 1952. New York: Vintage-Random 1990.

Far, Sui Sin (Edith Eaton). *Mrs. Spring Fragrance and Other Writings*. Eds. Amy Ling and Annette White-Parks. Urbana: University of Illinois Press, 1995.

Fauset, Jessie R. *Plum Bun*. 1928. London: Pandora Press, 1985.

Ghosh, Amitav. *The Shadow Lines*. 1988. Delhi: Oxford University Press, 1995.

Gilman, Charlotte Perkins. "The Yellow Wall Paper." 1892. *The Norton Anthology of American Literature*. 5th ed. 2: 657–669. New York: Norton, 1998.

Hardy, Thomas. *Far From the Madding Crowd*. 1874. London: Folio Society, 1985.

Hurston, Zora Neale. *Their Eyes Were Watching God*. 1937. New York: Harper and Row, 1990.

Imagining America: Stories From the Promised Land. Eds. Amy Ling and Wesley Brown. New York: Persea Books, 1991.

James, Henry. *The Awkward Age*. 1899. New York: Alfred A. Knopf, 1993.

———. *The Turn of the Screw*. 1898. New York: Norton, 1966.

———. *Washington Square*. 1880. New York: Penguin, 1986.

Jen, Gish. *Mona in the Promised Land*. 1996. New York: Vintage-Random, 1997.

Johnson, James Weldon. *The Autobiography of an Ex-Colored Man*. 1912. New York: Dover, 1995.

Kelley-Hawkins, Emma Dunham. *Four Girls at Cottage City*. 1898. New York: Oxford University Press, 1988.

Kim, Patti. *A Cab Called Reliable*. New York: St. Martin's Press, 1997.

Kincaid, Jamaica. *Lucy*. New York: Plume, 1991.

Kingston, Maxine Hong. *The Woman Warrior*. 1976. New York: Vintage, 1989.

Kogawa, Joy. *Obasan.* 1981. New York: Anchor-Random, 1994.

Marshall, Paule. *Brown Girl, Brownstones.* 1959. New York: Feminist Press, 1981.

Martin, Ann M. *Baby-Sitter's Club Summer Vacation: Super Special, 2.* New York: Scholastic, 1990.

McCullers, Carson. *The Heart is a Lonely Hunter.* 1940. New York: Bantam, 1953.

———. *The Member of the Wedding.* 1946. New York: Bantam, 1958.

Montgomery, L.M. *The Annotated Anne of Green Gables.* Eds. Wendy E. Barry et al. New York: Oxford University Press, 1997.

Morrison, Toni. *The Bluest Eye.* 1970. New York: Plume, 1994.

Sakamoto, Kerri. *The Electrical Field.* New York: Norton, 1999.

Shigekuni, Julie. *A Bridge Between Us.* New York: Anchor, 1995.

Tan, Amy. *The Joy Luck Club.* New York: G. P. Putnam's Sons, 1989.

Verdelle, A. J. *The Good Negress.* New York: Harper Perennial, 1996.

Walker, Alice. *The Color Purple.* New York: Pocket-Simon and Schuster, 1985.

Watanna, Onoto (Winnifred Eaton). *The Heart of Hyacinth.* New York: Harper and Brothers, 1903.

———. *Me, A Book of Remembrance.* New York: The Century Co., 1915.

———. *Miss Numè of Japan.* 1899. Baltimore: Johns Hopkins University Press, 1999.

Wharton, Edith. *The Buccaneers.* 1938. New York: Viking, 1993.

———. *The House of Mirth.* 1905. New York: Bantam Books, 1986.

Wong, Jade Snow. *Fifth Chinese Daughter.* 1950. Seattle: University of Washington Press, 1997.

Yamamoto, Hisaye. *Seventeen Syllables and Other Stories.* 1988. New Brunswick: Rutgers University Press, 1998.

Yamanaka, Lois-Ann. *Wild Meat and the Bully Burgers.* New York: Farrar, Straus, and Giroux, 1996.

Yezierska, Anzia. *Bread Givers.* 1925. New York: Persea Books, 1999.

Index

A

Abel, Elizabeth (et al.) xiii, 136, 140
adolescence xviii, xxiv, xxvi, 84, (femininity
    and mass media) 94–95, (and
    ethnicity) 97–98) (and fiction)
    99–101, 104, 106, 113–115,
    121, 123, 126, 139–140
African American literature (literary criti-
    cism) xii–xiii, xvi, xviii, xxi, 7,
    11, 23–24, 30–31, 38, 77, 95,
    135, 139, 141
agoraphobia xxv–xvi, 58–60, 70, 85, 137
Alcott, Louisa May 39–40, 42–44, 50
ambivalence xvii, 2, 4, 11–16, 20–21, 29,
    58, 82, 90, 95, 99, 108, 121,
    123, 130–131, 135
anglo fiction xiii, xvi–xvii, xxi, xxiv,
    xxvi–xxii, 28, 31, 32, 38, 60,
    74, 131, 140
artist heroine 67 , 76
Asian American literature (literary criticism)
    xii, xvi, xxi, 2, 95, 115, 134
Austen, Jane xii–xiii, 6, 16, 28, 33–34, 26,
    49, 60, 67, 115, 120–121, 129,
    131, 136, 138, 140–141
autobiography xii, xx–xxi, 29, 65, 67, 133,
    136, 138, 147 (see also *Me: A
    Book of Remembrance,* and
    Fifth Chinese Daughter)*

B

Bachelard, Gaston (*The Poetics of Space*) 58,
    70, 76–77, 79, 83–84
beauty (and heroines) xviii, xxii, xxiv–xxvi,
    7–9, 12, 25, 31, 34–36, 43–44,
    48, 50–51, 52, 54, 81, 98–105,
    107, 110–113, 120, 123

Bhabha, Homi 15
bildungsroman 47, 66–67, 77, 90–92,
    95–96, 136, 139
Bluest Eye, The xxvi, 98, 100–103, 104,
    110, 113, 115, 123, 139
Brontë, Charlotte 32, 36, 68–69, 72, 74–75,
    125, 126, 130, 131, 141
Brooks, Peter xvii
Brown, Gillian 137
Brown Girl, Brownstones xxv, 58, 76–92,
    139
Byatt, A.S. 59

C

Cheung, King-kok xix
Chin, Frank 62, 67, 133, 135, 141
Chu, Patricia 3, 23
class xxi–xxii, 7, 31, 32, 38, 41–49, 68,
    75–79, 84, 86–91, 101–104,
    108–109, 113, 116, 125,
    128–129, 131, 134, 138,
cross-dressing (as narrative sign) 21–23, 30,
    44
claustrophobia xxv, 57–60, 62, 78, 85, 137
cultural authenticity 93, 111, 131
cultural politics xix, xxiv–xxvii, 3, 11, 16,
    32, 55, 131, 134

D

Denniston, Dorothy 77, 80
Dickinson, Emily 59, 138
Disney 93–94, 139
domestic fiction xv, 4, 7, 10, 22, 25, 36, 38,
    44, 58, 135
Donald Duk xv, 61–62, 115, 118, 139, 147
duCille, Ann (*The Coupling Convention*) xii,
    xvi–xvii, 23, 38, 134, 141

E

Edwards, Lee 49, 67, 112, 134
Ellis, Lorna 33, 55, 69, 91, 138–139
Ellison, Ralph xiv, 84
essentialism xiv, 30
ethnicity xiv, xvi, xxi–xxiv, xxvi, xxviii, 1–4, 7, 9, 13, 15, 17, 22–24, 28, 30–32, 38, 41, 45, 57, 60, 67, 74, 88, 95–97, 99, 104, 108, 110, 112, 115, 118–123, 131, 133, 137
ethnic studies (and feminism) xix, xxiii, (general trends in scholarship) 1–4, 24, 38, 93, 95, 97, 99, 123, 131, 134, 141

F

Fa Mu Lan 21–22, (film version of story) 93
Far, Sui Sin (Edith Eaton) xxv, 1–4, 10, 13–24, 28, 30, 134, 135, 136,
Fauset, Jessie xvi, xxii, 45–50, 131
Feng, Pin-chia xv, xix, 77, 96, 102, 141
Ferens, Dominika 2, 14, 19, 27, 29, 135
Fifth Chinese Daughter xxv, 58, 60–68, 90, 131
Four Girls at Cottage City xxv, 32, 38–45, 55, 135

G

Gates, Henry Louis 140
gender xii, xxv, 4, (as textual sign) 22–23, 31, (and class) 44, 49, (and space) 57–58, 75–76, 78, 80, 85, (and contemporary culture/narratives) 95–96, (gender-bending) 136
genre 2–3, 7–8, 14–15, 19–20, 25, 29–30, 139, 141
Ghymn, Esther Mikyung 51
Gilbert, Sandra and Susan Gubar (*The Madwoman in the Attic*) 57, 125–126
Good Negress, The xxvi, 96–97, 123, 138
governesses 68–70, 74–76, 138

H

Hardy, Thomas 32, 34, 36
Hawkins-Kelley, Emma D. xi, 7, 39, 43, 137
Heart of Hyacinth, The 3, 24–28

heroines xi, xviii, xx–xxii, xxiv–xxvii, (turn-of-the century generic conventions) 3–4, 7–9, 25, 30 (and Sui Sin Far) 16, 19, 22, (and objectification) 31–37, (and turn-of-the-century African American literature) (39–44), (anglo heroines) 47, 55, 133, 136) early Asian American women's fiction) (51–56), (as governesses) (68–76), (and contemporary literature) 93–98, (and failed self-actualization) 138
"High-Heeled Shoes, The" 53
hooks, bell 134, 140
House of Mirth, The xxi, xxv, 9, 33, 36, 38, 48, 54–55, 75, 80, 136
Huang, Yunte xiv, 134
humor 45, 115–117,121–122
Hurston, Zora Neale xiii-xiv, 109, 117, 139

I

immigration xiii, xxi, 14, 21, 60, 68, 75, 80, 133
"Inferior Woman, The" 17–18, 20, 29, 30
inner strength (and heroines) xvii, xxvi, 36, 96–99, 107, 109, 110–112, 123, 140
Inness, Sherrie 94, 139

J

James, Henry 36, 59
Jane Eyre xviii, xxi-xxii, 11, 34–35, 51, 68–69, 97, 125, 136, 137, 138, 140
JanMohamed, Abdul xix, 133
Jen, Gish xi, xxvi, 96, 113, 115, 117–118, 120–122
Johnson, James Weldon xx, xxi, 30
Juhasz, Suzanne xiii, xiv, xxiii, 134, 138, 140
juvenile fiction xxvi, 33, 36, 95, 97, 115, 139

K

Kaplan, Amy 37, 136
Kim, Elaine 138
Kincaid, Jamaica 69, 70, 75
Kingston, Maxine Hong xiii-xiv, 22–23, 67, 141

L

"Legend of Miss Sasagawara, The" 51–54
Li, David Leiwei 60–61, 93, 122, 134
Ling, Amy 2, 4, 14, 29–30, 134, 136
Ling, Jinqui xvi, 134
Little Women xxv, 11, 38–39, 41–43,
    54–55, 140
Lowe, Lisa (*Immigrant Acts*) xii, xvii, xxiii,
    38, 106, 115, 134, 140, 141
Lucy xiii, xxv, 68–75

M

Mansfield Park 28, 60, 129, 133, 137
marriage market xxiv, 1, 8–10, 16, 18, 22,
    33–34, 45, 56, 99, 122
marriage plot xxiv–xxv, 19, 22, 31, 36, 45,
    55, 59, 67, 76, 90, 92, 119–120,
    126, 141
Marshall, Paule xiii, 77–84, 86–90
mass media xxv, xxvi, (visual media and ob-
    jectification) 31, (contemporary
    narratives) 94–95, 97, (see also
    "Disney")
McCullers, Carson 100
McDowell, Deborah 41–42, 46, 50
Me: A Book of Remembrance 3, 9, 11–13
Michie, Helena xiii, xx, 32, 138, 145
Miss Numè of Japan 2–9, 21, 45, 50
Mona in the Promised Land xi, xxvi, 98,
    106, 112–124
Montgomery, L.M. 96–97
Morrison, Toni 96, 98, 100–102, 104–105,
    112, 116, 141
Mrs. Spring Fragrance and Other Stories
    13–24

O

Obasan 95, 137, 141
objectification (and heroines) xvii, xxiv-xv,
    30–38, 41–43, 45–46, 48, 50,
    51–52, 54, 56, 58, 75, 123, 126,
    131, 136
Oishi, Eve 3, 7, 11–12, 135,

P

Papashvily, Helen 7, 134–135, 137
Pipher, Mary 98
Plum Bun xxii, xxv, 11, 32, 45–51, 54–55,
    75–76, 79, 85, 139

poetics xi, xii, xiv-xviii, xxiii, xxv-xvi, 11,
    51, 54–56, 76, 90, 101, 122,
    125–126, 133, 140
politics (academic privileging of) xv–xvi, 99,
    123 (see also "cultural politics")
postcolonialism xxiii, 70
Pride and Prejudice xi–xii, 33, 140
publishing market xxii, xxvi, 5, 8–9, 13,
    15–16, 33, 42, 122, 134
psychoanalysis xvii–xviii

R

race (v. ethnicity) xiv, (descriptions of nine-
    teenth-century African American
    heroines) 7, (biracial identity) 16,
    (race and class) 32, 38, 41–49,
    70, 75–76, 78, (narrating race)
    86, (race and nation) 88, 90,
    118, 119, 133, 134, 141, (race
    and religion) 116, (negative im-
    plications in narrative) 122
Roh-Spaulding, Carol 15–16, 136
romance xii, xvii, xxiv, (academic bias
    against) 1–3, (differences in
    writing of Eaton sisters) 13, 24,
    (and fantasy) 22, (and mar-
    ketability) 50, 65–66, (and ado-
    lescent narratives) 95, 99, (and
    cultural authenticity) 111

S

Said, Edward 38, 133, 138
Secret Garden, The 35
sentimentalism xi, 24, 28, 37, 39, 41, 45
Seventeen Syllables 53
Sister Carrie xxii, 12, 60
slave narratives 65
"Smuggling of Tie-Co, The" 21–22, 29
social displacement xiii, xxv, 55, 69, 75–76,
    102, 107, 110
Sollors, Werner xiv
sororophobia (see also "Michie, Helena")
    xiii, 32, 45, 138, 145
space (and heroine construction) xvii,
    xxv–xxvi, 57–91, 123
Spivak, Gayatri xviii, xix, xxi, 38, 75, 130,
    137

T

Tate, Claudia xv, 23, 32, 42–43, 130–134

"Tian Shan's Kindred Spirit" 21–22, 30
transcultural xii, xvi–xvii, xviii, xxi, (as a
      term) xxiii–xxiv, (templates of
      heroine construction) xxvi, 2,
      17, 27, 30, 32–33, 40, 56,
      58–60, 67–68, 99, 102, 111,
      122–123, 125, 131, 133
Tuan, Yi-Fu (*Space and Place*) 58, 70, 78
Ty, Eleanor 72

V

Villette xxi–xxii, xv, 68–70, 72, 74–75,
      125–132

W

Walker, Alice xiii–xiv, 109
Washington, Mary Helen 91
Watanna, Onoto (Winnifred Eaton) xxv,
      1–8, 11–15, 22, 24–25, 26–29,
      45, 50, 135

Wharton, Edith 36–37, 50
White, Barbara 96, 118
White-Parks, Annette 2, 20, 134, 134–136
Wild Meat and the Bully Burgers xvi, 98,
      103–112, 113, 123
wit (and heroines) xxiii, xxvi, 44, 98,
      112–113, 115, 120–123, 131
Wong, Jade Snow 61–66
Wong, Sau-ling Cynthia 22–23
Woolf, Virginia 58–59, 67

Y

Yamamoto, Hisaye 32, 51–56
Yamanaka, Lois-Ann 96, 104–105,
      108–109, 111–112
Yin, Xiao-huang 2, 16, 61–62, 122, 136,
      138
Yogi, Stan 54
"Yoneko's Earthquake" 53

For Product Safety Concerns and Information please contact our EU
representative GPSR@taylorandfrancis.com
Taylor & Francis Verlag GmbH, Kaufingerstraße 24, 80331 München, Germany